O. Henry

at the Holidays

O. Henry

at the Holidays

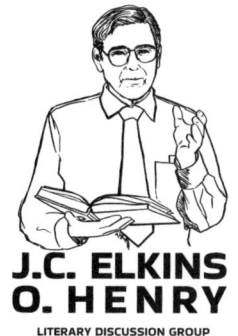

J.C. ELKINS
O. HENRY
LITERARY DISCUSSION GROUP

ISBNs: 979-8-9891874-0-9 (hardcover)
979-8-9891874-1-6 (paperback)
979-8-9891874-2-3 (ebook)

Front cover art/photo courtesy of Hardie
Cover and book design by Mike Corrao, Mayfly Design

Library of Congress Catalog Number: 2023918241
First Printing: 2023
Printed in the United States

For

J.C. Elkins
for starting it all

Jim McKee
for being there
since the beginning

&

Gary Hallock
(July 7, 1951 – April 25, 2023)
for being such an
important part of it

Contents

Finding O. Henry

At the apex of O. Henry's popularity (in the decade following his death) there appeared a volume titled *The Boy Scouts Book of Stories* (1920), edited by Franklin K. Mathiews (1872-1950), the Chief Scout Librarian of The Boy Scouts of America. As Mathiews said in his introduction, "there are stories about boy scouts, school stories, stories of the sea and 'wild west' stories, detective and mystery stories; most of all, though, a goodly number of humorous stories." Amongst the eighteen stories included in the collection were stories by Arthur Conan Doyle ("The Red-Headed League"), Mark Twain ("The Jumping Frog"), Robert Louis Stevenson ("Story of The Bandbox") and O. Henry ("The Ransom of Red Chief").

The Boy Scouts Book of Stories was one of numerous volumes edited by Mathiews that aspired to provide quality, wholesome entertainment for boys. Mathiews had joined the nascent Boy Scouts of America in 1912, and his initial efforts focused on developing the new *Boys' Life* magazine and helping the Boy Scouts of America (BSA) organize and standardize their practices for the rapidly growing entity (by 1914 there were 107,000 boys in the organization).

BSA leadership would soon become concerned with a series of books published by the Edward Stratemeyer Syndicate (the original home of Nancy Drew, the Hardy Boys, the Bobbsey

Twins and Tom Swift). The Stratemeyer Syndicate published a series of books with the Boy Scouts explicitly mentioned in the titles.

St. George Henry Rathborne, an extremely prolific author of juvenile fiction, who confirmed directly to Mathiews's inquiries that he wrote for the Stratemeyer Syndicate, published several titles featuring the Boy Scouts: *Boy Scout Adventures; or, Lost in the Everglades* (1912), The Boy Scout Series (under the pseudonym Herbert Carter): *The Boy Scout's First Campfire* (1913), *The Boy Scouts On The Blue Ridge* (1913), *The Boy Scouts On Sturgeon Island* (1914), et al.; (under the pseudonym Major Archibald Lee Fletcher) *Boy Scouts In The Northern Wilds* (1913), *Boy Scouts In Alaska* (1913), *Boy Scouts In The Coal Caverns* (1913) et al. O. Henry alludes to Rathborne in his 1905 short story "Tommy's Burglar."

> At ten o'clock P. M. Felicia, the maid, left by the basement door with the policeman to get a raspberry phosphate around the corner. She detested the policeman and objected earnestly to the arrangement. She pointed out, not unreasonably, that she might have been allowed to fall asleep over one of St. George Rathbone's novels on the third floor, but she was overruled. Raspberries and cops were not created for nothing.

There were innumerable Boy Scout books by other authors: The Boy Scouts Of The Air (series) by Gordon Stuart (pseudonym of Harry Lincoln Sayler) starting with *The Boy Scouts Of The Air At Eagle Camp* (1912); *The War Zone Of The Kaiser or Boy Scouts Of The North Sea* by Captain V.T. Sherman (1913) and the "Boy Scouts" series by Colonel George Durston (twenty four volumes; the Colonel George Durston moniker was a pseudonym owned by the Saalfield Publishing Company and was ghostwritten by Frederic van Rensselaer Dey, J.W. Duffield, William A. Wolf, and Georgia Roberts Durston, amongst others).

Corry Kanzenberg, Curator of Collections and Exhibitions for the National Scouting Museum, in a 2012 article "The Boy Scouts of America and Literature for Youth 1910-1935" deftly summarized the BSA's objections to the sensational scouting tales:

> The leadership of the organization was critical of these books, which did not embody the ideas of their brand nor the spirit of Scouting that they wished to promote. In *Boy Scouts on The Great Divide* (Fletcher, A.L., 1913) for example, Scouts on a campout use revolvers to thwart off a band of adult foes. Additionally, Scouts of the unauthorized novels, especially G. Harvey Ralphson's, disliked the outdoors and held little respect for nature in general, indiscriminately killing bald eagles, bears and other game, typically with guns. Overall, the books were undesirable for their reckless and lowbrow portrayal of Scouts.

The BSA would push back forcefully against such perceived defamation. In 1914, Franklin K. Mathiews wrote an article for *The Outlook* with the provocative title "Blowing Out the Boy's Brains." Mathiews outlines his basic argument:

> Because these cheap books do not develop criminals or lead boys, except very occasionally, to seek the Wild West, parents who buy such books think they do their boys no harm. The fact is, however, the harm done is simply incalculable. I wish I could label each one of these books: "Explosives! Guaranteed to Blow Your Boy's Brains Out." One of the most valuable assets a boy has is his imagination. In proportion as this is nurtured a boy develops initiative and resourcefulness. The greatest possible service that education can render is to train the boy to grasp and master new situations as they constantly

present themselves to him; and what helps more to make such adjustment than a lively imagination? Story books of the right sort stimulate and conserve this noble faculty, while those of the viler and cheaper sort, by overstimulation, debauch and vitiate, as brain and body are debauched and destroyed by strong drink.

The article was widely circulated (reprinted in several magazines and newspapers) and was influential in framing the argument for the nobility of the types of "good" books the BSA hoped to promote. As a result of Mathiews's extensive traveling and proselytizing (Mathiews had been a pastor at Baptist churches) on the subject, in 1915 Mathiews was instrumental in creating the Safety First Juvenile Book Week, which by 1919 had morphed into Children's Book Week (held in November each year, just in time for the holiday gift buying season).

One cannot know for sure what O. Henry would have made of the debate, but as a young boy he voraciously devoured the dime novels that were ubiquitous in his youth. On the other hand, in response to the intended compliment that he was an American Guy de Maupassant, O. Henry protested, "I never wrote a filthy word in my life, and I don't like being compared to a filthy writer."

At this point you might be wondering: interesting perhaps, but what *really* does any of this have to do with O. Henry?

It must have occurred to Franklin K. Mathiews, thinking of O. Henry's inclusion in *The Boy Scouts Book of Stories*, that O. Henry was just the sort of purveyor of wholesome (meritorious) stories that aligned perfectly with the stated values of the BSA.

Mathiews followed *The Boy Scouts Book of Stories* up with *The Ransom of Red Chief and Other O. Henry Stories For Boys* (1921). The volume features twenty-four stories which, as

Mathiews writes in the introduction, "In this selection you will find stories of the wild and woolly west. Cow-punchers, Indians, desperados . . . good men and bad men aplenty, crowd one another on and off the page. As you read, one moment you will be thrilled and the very next, if you don't watch out, you will find yourself laughing so loudly you'll have to tell 'what's the joke.'"

I became aware in the Spring of 2012 that there was an O. Henry reading group that met at the O. Henry Museum monthly. I began attending *Lunchtime Lit*, hosted by docent J.C. Elkins.

When J.C. Elkins retired at the end of 2014, the group met in January 2015 and decided to continue as the *J.C. Elkins O. Henry Literary Discussion Group*. Gary Hallock and Jim McKee had been attending the *Lunchtime Lit* readings since their inception in 2010, but when I made it known I'd like to curate the group, they let me get on with it. We have met every month for eight-plus years now (during the pandemic we met via Zoom), and it has been one of the most rewarding experiences of my life.

J.C. Elkins used to read the entire story every month and do a limited explanation of allusions in the story and discuss a handful of vocabulary words. I wanted to do a deeper dive each month, focusing on all the historical people O. Henry mentions, discuss all the literary allusions and wonderful word play, and examine the vocabulary in greater depth. Intuitively, I realized, if I did that, I needed to let others in the group, more often than not, be the readers, so it was not me running my mouth non-stop. I think it was a wise decision on my part. It seemed to quickly build up camaraderie amongst the group. We have had some terrific special guest readers over the years, and we have visited other museums and hosted readings at sites of interest all over central Texas. It has sometimes been a bit of work to make it come together successfully but it has always been tremendous fun.

The first time Brush Square Museums Foundation (BSMF) President Clay Leben suggested the idea of a collection of O. Henry stories tied to the holidays, I thought, "ooh, that's a good idea!" I was juggling a lot of projects at the time, and the idea kind of faded to the back of my mind, to (possibly) be resurrected sometime in the future.

Many months later, when Clay again suggested the idea, it struck a chord with me, and I was determined to be a part of making the idea come to fruition.

I knew I had several top-notch Christmas stories suitable for a holiday-themed collection, quality Thanksgiving and Independence Days stories to choose from, but could I easily come up with an appropriate O. Henry story tied to each of the other holidays?

Making my preliminary list, I started at Christmas, worked back to Thanksgiving, then skipped haphazardly from holiday to holiday trying to come up with the story best suited for each holiday.

The very last story I chose for this collection was for the first holiday, New Year's Day. I was stuck on this one for quite a while. One early idea was to go with "The Day We Celebrate" under the logic that it could be argued both as a Christmas story and an Independence Day story, and since I had good alternatives for both holidays, I could slip it into the New Year's Day slot as it was a holiday story and it is, per the story's title, definitely a day we "celebrate." Eventually, I decided to go with "A Service of Love." The poignant story of the early days of marriage of artists Joe Larrabee and Delia Caruthers does not allude to New Year's

Day, but, as New Year's Day has all the potential and promise of the new year to come, so does the marriage of the newlyweds have all the potential and promise of their life together to come. Also, there was a connection to another story (and holiday) that I was partial to (but more on that later). Still, I did waver on my selection, for quite a while. I was worried the connection I made in my mind was a tenuous one. I wanted to get this collection off to a good start and have O. Henry speak to the meaning and spirit of New Year's as eloquently as he does for a couple of other holidays elsewhere in this collection.

Eventually I recalled "New Year's Eve," included by Mary Sunlocks Harrell in her 1939 collection *O. Henry Encore*, a collection of stories and sketches from O. Henry's brief stint as a writer for the Houston *Daily Post*.

The first sentence of "New Year's Eve": "We that would properly welcome the new year should view it with the eye of an optimist, and sing its praises with the coated tongue of a penitent."

This was precisely what I was looking for, and I almost decided to have it take the New Year's Day story slot, but eventually decided it is (as stated in *O. Henry Encore*) a sketch and not a full-fledged story. But I was definitely going to include it; so, as a "bonus," it precedes "A Service of Love."

O. Henry was a popular writer, not a social reformer, and was a product of his times. It is in that light and context we must keep in mind when contemplating his depictions of minorities in his stories. O. Henry had a basic decency and sympathetic concern for the downtrodden and disenfranchised, but he was not above usage of an (infrequent) slur (and in one story one gross abuse). But O. Henry saw and portrayed nobility in all persons, regardless of race and creed. Such is the case of Uncle Bushrod in "The Guardian of the Accolade." O. Henry's description of the Weymouth family servant: "Of the color of the mahogany bank furniture . . . thus dark was he externally . . . white as the uninked pages of the bank ledgers was his soul."

It may sound artless to us a century plus later, but it is certainly in keeping with Dr. King's expressed sentiment: "I have a dream that my four little children will one day live in a nation where they will not be judged by the color of their skin but by the content of their character."

"The Guardian of The Accolade" is often ascribed to having first been published in *The Cosmopolitan* for May, 1903. But in Paul Clarkson's indispensable O. Henry reference "A Bibliography of William Sydney Porter (O. Henry)" Clarkson relates that the story originally premiered in (the short lived) *Brandur Magazine* for October 11, 1902. In both *Brandur Magazine* and *The Cosmopolitan* the story was first published as "The Guardian of the Scutcheon." By either name it is an engaging story and I am happy to include it as our Martin Luther King, Jr. Day entrant.

Love and romance (often leavened with humor) are prevalent in many of O. Henry's stories. Three, however, leapt out as possible inclusions in this volume for the Valentine's Day story. "Roses, Ruses and Romance," "The Plutonian Fire" and "Cupid à la Carte" are all meritorious and would have served suitably, but "Cupid à la Carte" seemed just a bit more fleshed out, some degree more humorous and brimming with romantic tension, a vital element necessary to any good love story.

The first, obvious candidate for our Presidents' Day story was "A Snapshot at the President," an 1894 story that first appeared in *The Rolling Stone*. It's a whimsical tale of a Texas reporter's visit to Washington D.C. and his interaction with President Grover Cleveland. The story's length merits reference as a short story, but I always find myself thinking of it more as a (humorous) sketch. For the longest time, I thought the Presidents' Day story in this volume was going to be "The Rose of

Dixie." It's a fine story, and obliquely references the historical person (by my unofficial estimation) most frequently referenced in the complete works of O. Henry (read the story for the answer). Thinking back on the history of Presidents' Day (and its derivation from Washington's Day) got me thinking of "A Philistine in Bohemia" and the artful introduction wherein Washington (or rather his statue) watches over Union Square (literally) and New York City (metaphorically) and ultimately I decided to go with "A Philistine in Bohemia."

William Sydney Porter was working as a reporter for the Houston *Daily Post* in 1895 when he got a summons to stand trial in Austin for embezzlement from the First National Bank in Austin where Porter had been previously employed. Porter took a train, headed to Austin, but upon changing trains to continue his journey, he instead took a train headed east, and would wind up in New Orleans. Porter's stay in New Orleans was brief (mere weeks by some accounts, a few to several months in others), before making his way to Honduras, which had no extradition treaty with the United States. Though his stay in New Orleans was brief, Porter really absorbed the atmosphere of the city and would go on to write a handful of delightful stories based there: "Whistling Dick's Christmas Stocking," "The Shamrock and The Palm," "Phoebe," "A Matter of Mean Elevation," "Helping the Other Fellow," "The Renaissance of Charleroi," "Cherchez la Femme" and "Blind Man's Holiday." Enjoyable stories all, the last three were given consideration for inclusion as this volume's Mardi Gras story. For quite a while it was between "The Renaissance of Charleroi" and "Cherchez la Femme," with the latter eventually getting the upper head in my mind. The story has such a wonderful atmosphere. I enjoyed "Blind Man's Holiday," but it was a longish story, much of it featuring a narrator waxing philosophical. I had adapted the story for our *O. Henry Players* group (our theatrical offshoot of the *J.C. Elkins O. Henry Literary Discussion Group*) and was proud of being able to figure out a way to make it dramatic and yet remain extremely faithful to the original story. Unfortunately, the Covid pandemic derailed our plans to present a dramatization of the story and (as of this writing) we have yet to present it to an audience. Before making the final decision of going with "Cherchez la Femme," I pulled out my dramatization of "Blind Man's Holiday" and re-read it. Then I skimmed over the original story. The early part of the story was compelling enough to keep the reader's attention until the plot fully "kicked in," there was a clear connection to Mardi Gras in the story, and "holiday" was right there in the title; "Blind's Man Holiday" it was to be.

O. Henry had memorable Irish American protagonists headlining his stories "Tobin's Palm" (Daniel Tobin), "The Greater Coney" (Dennis Carnahan) and "The Shamrock and The Palm"(James Clancy). Any of these stories would make for a great story to fill the St. Patrick's Day slot. In "The Greater Coney" Dennis Carnahan reconciles with his girlfriend Norah Flynn at the seaside amusement park after having harsh words. I particularly enjoyed Norah's responses to Dennis's queries about her enjoyment of park attractions (by which he knew she had been by the old pavilion by the waves where they had declared their love the summer past and not enjoying Coney Island as she claimed). "The Greater Coney" is a charming, if slight, story. "Tobin's Palm" has long been a favorite of mine. Daniel Tobin's implacable faith in being able to find his lost sweetheart Katie Mahorner regardless of circumstances makes for a winsome tale. I spent many, many months writing a script adaptation of "Tobin's Palm" in 2012 and 2013 and found it rather difficult to finish, but the struggle of completing it and my ultimate satisfaction with the finished script made me appreciate "Tobin's Palm" even more (the script and the original short story). "Tobin's Palm" also has a fascinating backstory. Recent Harvard graduate and new junior *McClure's* reader Witter Bynner had been reading story submissions for months without finding anything he could recommend when he came across "Tobin's Palm." He heartily recommended it to his superior, Viola Roseboro'. When Bynner found out that his esteemed superior had sent the story back to O. Henry with a rejection slip, Bynner went directly to publisher S.S. McClure and practically demanded they accept "Tobin's Palm." Bynner's enthusiasm won over McClure, who authorized Bynner to write and ask O. Henry to resubmit the story. Bynner, who remembered the return address on the manuscript submission, went directly to O. Henry's apartment lest the story have time to be submitted (and accepted) elsewhere. Bynner and O. Henry became friends and couple of years later (1904) when McClure, Phillips & Co. attempted to get O. Henry to write a novel (outside of Rudyard Kipling, short story collections were not selling well) and O. Henry demurred (he did not have the discipline or demeanor to remain focused on a single story for the months it would take to write a novel), it was Bynner who had the idea of taking O. Henry's existing disparate short stories set in Central America and tweak them ever so slightly and refashion them into a single, novel-length narrative. Bynner worked with O. Henry to help him meld the various stories into a cohesive whole, and even came up with the title, *Cabbages and Kings*, based on a reference to Lewis Carroll's *Through the Looking Glass* poem "The Walrus and the Carpenter."

So, I almost went with "Tobin's Palm," but, in the end, I decided to go with "The Shamrock and The Palm" and James Clancy, the "American with an Irish diathesis and cosmopolitan proclivities." The Shamrock in the story's title and its iconic association to St. Patrick's Day and the opportunity to feature the (rarer) original version that appeared in *Ainslee's* for March 1903 (as opposed to the *Cabbages and Kings* version that is easily found in print or online) won out. "The Shamrock and the Palm" is an entertaining, humorous revenge tale; a reminder that revenge is a dish best served cold. Or is it hot? Like a certain Irishman, I'm apt to mix those two up.

For our Easter story, three stories came to mind for consideration, "The Day Resurgent," "The Easter of the Soul" and "The Red Roses of Tonia." "The Day Resurgent" is centered on the domestic life of the McCree family. At Easter, the family breadwinner, gruff Danny McCree, contemplates the meaning of Easter (and his blind father's strange remark about a hippopotamus). The story has some wonderful passages and nicely conveys the familial love of a boisterous but loving Irish family. "The Easter of the Soul" also reflects on the domestic life of an Irish family, following "Irish loafer" Mr. Jimmy "Tiger" McQuirk as he makes his rounds against the backdrop of winter (finally) giving way to Spring at Easter. O. Henry, a handful of times, re-wrote stories ("The Miracle of Lava Canyon" as "An Afternoon Miracle," "Struggle of the Outliers" as "Girl," "The Point of the Story" as "No Story," etc.) giving a more polished more fully fleshed out version of a theme or plot he had earlier attempted as the experience of writing had given him a more mature, surer hand. Though "The Day Resurgent" and "The Easter of The Soul" are independent of each other in plot and theme, they are of a very similar type, and it would not be a stretch to misidentify either as a re-write or reworking of the other as O. Henry had done (multiple times) before. The tell that this is not the case is the polished phraseology and apt turns of phrase(s) indicative of O. Henry at his most assured being present in both stories.

"The Red Roses of Tonia" explores the lengths to which two Texans will go in order secure Tonia Weaver, their common love interest, a new Easter hat when the train bringing her hat is unexpectedly delayed. The story is full of drama and adventure (and a love triangle), all desirous ingredients for a compelling romance. Every time I have read the story, I have gotten a kick out of Tonia assuring her mother that she will have a new hat, in time tomorrow, after her mother tries to comfort her when it seems Tonia is destined to do without. Tonia put the right words in her rival suitors' ears, and she knows one of them will come through for her.

There was only one story that merited serious consideration for our Cinco de Mayo entry. "He Also Serves" is O. Henry's only story set primarily in Mexico. The allure of "He Also Serves" was neatly encapsulated in a promotional blurb that appeared in the September 26, 1908 issue of *Collier's* for the upcoming October 31, 1908 issue in which "He Also Serves" first appeared:

> "He Also Serves" is the tale of a heathen god, dead and turned to stone, who comes to life as his beloved approaches. The scene is laid in a ruined temple on a far off island, and has an undertone of romance and dead religions—and yet is told in Bowery cocktail slang. It gives the effect of a funeral march played on a banjo. It is just one more of O. Henry's perfect stories, wherein he strikes the bull's-eye while he is looking the other way and shooting over his left shoulder.

Of late, I find when I contemplate "He Also Serves" my mind invariably goes to two memories tied to, but ultimately independent of, the story itself.

In August 2016, we had 4th-6th graders (Badgerdog Summer Book Crush participants) as our special guest readers of "Joe and Billy," a long-lost O. Henry story about a boy and his pure-bred Merino ram. "Joe and Billy" was published for the first time in 2004 by Southwest Classics Press with an introduction by noted O. Henry expert Jenny Lind Porter (Porter was the niece of O. Henry). The book was illustrated by Jenny Lind Porter's lifelong friend Kay Sims Campbell. Our group got into contact with Mrs. Campbell and had an extremely memorable day trip in September 2016 to Paint Rock, Texas to visit Campbell Ranch, home of a famed collection of Indian pictographs. Our visit occurred during the Autumnal Equinox (first day of fall) a time when Sunlight interacts with the pictographs (known as a "solar marker"). Reading "He Also Serves" at Campbell Ranch was the perfect marriage of venue and story selection.

The other memory was a simple one, our group's beloved (the late) Gary Hallock a couple of times confused "He Also Serves" as being the primary source for "Lo!" the Indian-themed musical O. Henry authored with Franklin P. Adams. Gary and I had wide-ranging conversations about all things O. Henry that began with me reminding Gary that "He Also Serves" and "Lo!" were separate and independent of each other.

For our Mother's Day entry, we have "The Reformation of Calliope," the story of Calliope Catesby, a drunk Texan (the "Terror of Quicksand") who goes on periodic alcohol inspired shooting rampages. Wait, what? At first blush, the story does not seem to bear any connection to Mother's Day whatsoever. But when the old woman enters the story, and you see how her presence affects both her son and Buck Patterson, the City Marshall tasked with disarming Calliope, the mist begins to clear, and the importance of a Mother's Love makes itself manifest.

Next up is our Flag Day story, "The Flag Paramount." Hold up, there has been some sort of mistake. I have included "The Flag Paramount" as our Memorial Day entry. Surely, I have erred. Even though "The Flag Paramount" would work exceptionally well for Flag Day, I have chosen it as our Memorial Day entry as it so beautifully memorializes the heroic (if half-witted) Admiral Don Felipe Carrera.

So, in fact, our actual Flag Day story is "The Fourth in Salvador," a story set on the Fourth of July . . . wait, should this not be our Independence Day story? It certainly fits that bill, but it was chosen for the Flag Day story for the beautiful sentiment expressed in the story's concluding paragraph.

For the longest time, I was intending for our Father's Day entry to be "The Emancipation of Billy," the poignant story of a Southern lawyer trying to step out of the considerable shadow of his father, the state's former Governor, but late in the decision-making process I began to consider "The Church with An Overshot Wheel."

In October of 2022 our group read the story (over Zoom) and were joined by special guest Suzanne Harle of Green Planet Films, the driving force behind the restoration of the 1920 Vitagraph silent film production of "The Church with an Overshot Wheel." Suzanne showed us the restored film with the wonderful new score by Donald Sosin, the prolific and acclaimed silent film composer. The short film is quite faithful to the original short story. "The Church with an Overshot Wheel" is a beautifully told story of faith, in some ways atypical of O. Henry, who was not overtly (or generally) religious (at least in his writing). O. Henry and his first wife Athol were quite involved in the Central Presbyterian Church (Austin, Texas) during their courtship and marriage. It might be inferred that O. Henry's interest was attracted by the church's social rituals and functions rather than any religious edification.

Today, O. Henry is best known for "The Gift of the Magi" and "The Ransom of Red Chief." But when "A Municipal Report" appeared in *Hampton's* for November 1909, it was quickly venerated as O. Henry's masterpiece. In it, O. Henry takes up

Frank Norris's challenge to "write a compelling story about Chicago, or Buffalo or (let us say) Nashville." The story's main protagonist Uncle Caesar, the former slave with the disposition of a royal, is a wonderfully drawn character, but some of the racial stereotypes and descriptions present in "A Municipal Report" were probably key factors in the story gradually losing esteem over time. Though understandable, it is a shame, for the story has much to recommend it. This story, and a handful of others in this collection were (judiciously, I hope) abridged or edited to eliminate references many today would find distasteful.

"The Flag Paramount" and (especially) "The Fourth in Salvador" would have made wonderful entrants for our Independence Day story but we have already utilized them elsewhere, so for our Independence Day story we turn to "The Day We Celebrate," a story that is not sure whether it wants to be an Independence Day story or a Christmas story.

Speaking of Christmas stories, next up is "Vanity and Some Sables." Whoops, I lost my place. I see that next up is our Labor Day story. In "Vanity and Some Sables" we pay tribute to the industriousness of "Kid" Brady (at least after he retired from the Stovepipe Gang and found more legitimate lines of work) and his ilk. In the spring of 2022, when I was researching the (then recently restored) 1950's anthology television series *The O. Henry Playhouse*, I came across a December 1939 mention of "Vanity and Some Sables" kicking off NBC Red's holiday programming slate on *Hollywood Playhouse*.

> Jim Ameche and Gale Page bring to the microphone this adaptation of O. Henry's masterpiece. This is the story of Kid Brady, member of the Stove-pipe gang, of his sweetheart Molly McKeever, and Father Joe, the parish priest who watches over the religious destinies of Hell's Kitchen.

When Kid and Molly marry, he adds to his marriage vows one other . . . to forego his former life of petty crime. However, on their first Christmas together the web of circumstantial evidence threatens Kid with a bird's eye view of life through prison bars.

—Findlay *Republican Courier,* December 20, 1939

I would love to hear this radio adaptation. Seems the adaptation adds a marital component, a new character (Father Joe) and moves the story to Christmastime, but if you give it much thought, it is easy to see how seamlessly "Vanity and Some Sables" works as a Christmas story (despite O. Henry's original story making no such mention). Having the occasion of the Kid's gift of sables be a Christmas gift to Molly raises the emotional stakes considerably. Imagine her disappointment when she learns her Christmas gift was obtained by theft! Easy to imagine the redemptive tone of the resolution when Kid is found to have purchased the sables on the up and up (fitting nicely into the true spirit of Christmas). It really is a clever conceit.

Speaking of clever conceits, "The Ransom of Red Chief" is our choice for Columbus Day. The central premise of the story (kidnappers being frazzled by their abductee to the extent they must pay the parents to take the boy back) is such a strong one that it is no surprise that the story is so iconic and (along with "The Gift of the Magi") probably the best known (and one of the most esteemed) of all O. Henry's stories. "The Ransom of Red Chief" and a connection to Columbus Day is tenuous, but as Columbus interacted with the Native Americans upon his voyage of discovery to the Americas, so too a pair of small-time petty criminals did in Summit, Alabama in the first decade of the 20th century, thanks to the fertile imagination of O. Henry.

"The Ransom of Red Chief" is the only O. Henry story to

premiere in the prestigious *The Saturday Evening Post*, appearing in the July 6, 1907 issue. The story and its central conceit have been adapted many, many times in innumerable television shows and films. Where O. Henry got the original inspiration for "The Ransom of Red Chief" has never been definitively determined, but O. Henry did cite inspiration for another story of his involving kidnapping, "Hostages of Momus," as being derived from Chapter Two of Mark Twain's "The Adventures of Huckleberry Finn" where Tom Sawyer's "gang" discuss kidnapping as a sideline.

Halloween motifs and themes populate "The Marionettes" (spooky atmosphere; the story first appeared in *Black Cat* for April 1902); "The Enchanted Kiss" (Samuel Tansey's rendezvous with Ramon Torres and Torres' backstory regarding chili-con-carne is eminently eerie); "The Ghost That Came To Old Angles" (a delightful ghost story, one of three unpublished O. Henry stories first issued in 2021 in *O. Henry 101 Stories* edited by Ben Yagoda); and "The Head-Hunter" (skeletons and skulls). Any one of these four stories would have served nicely as our Halloween entrant. Ultimately, I decided on "The Head-Hunter."

After the success of The *O. Henry Players'* first production, "A Double-Dyed Deceiver," I thought "The Head-Hunter" would make for a fun follow-up. I called up Gary Hallock one evening in the Summer of 2018 to propose we attempt to "take a stab" at the story. Gary spent twenty minutes or so "letting me down gently." I was quite crushed. Gary had been so instrumental to the success of "A Double-Dyed Deceiver" and I had already made up my mind not to proceed if I could not secure Gary's participation. Gary did say we could talk again the next day, but I left our initial conversation so deflated. When I called the next day, I was not attempting to change his mind (we had already adjudicated the matter) and was pleasantly surprised to have Gary declare from the start that we were definitely tackling "The Head-Hunter." I was not going to question this good turn of fortune, but I did want to know what brought about this change of plans. *He had read the story!*

When we spoke the previous evening, Gary was only partially familiar with the story. After our conversation he went and read the story, and quickly his enthusiasm and sense of the possibilities present in the story for adaptation matched mine. Early on Gary admonished me for presenting it as a Halloween story (it was to premiere on October 31st on the back patio of the O. Henry Museum) but the whole atmosphere of the story seemed apropos to a Halloween presentation.

Right as I began scripting my adaptation, Gary threw me a curve ball. He had seen some theater production featuring a character stepping in and out of the story (and on and off stage) telling a story from the past and featuring another actor as a younger version of the character. It made my adaptation much more challenging, but ultimately much more satisfying, so I was (in retrospect) grateful to be nudged in that direction. Ultimately, our production was a disaster. It rained cats and dogs the evening of our (outdoor) production, there was cast infighting and we had too little rehearsal time for what ended up being an overly ambitious production. I would love to attempt to stage it again someday. It really is an entertaining bit of frivolity.

When it came time to consider which story would be our Veterans Day entry, my mind went instantly to "The Moment of Victory." The story features twenty-nine-year-old war veteran Ben Granger relating the heroic deeds fellow veteran Willie Robbins undertakes and asks us early on to consider what makes heroic veterans do what they do. O. Henry, in the telling of the story, postulates that it likely has, in large part, a cause as old as time, and the story rings true in its depiction of human nature and interpersonal relationships (between the sexes).

Before we get to our Thanksgiving Day story, we first are treated to our second, holiday-themed sketch, aptly titled "Thanksgiving Remarks." At first blush, it seems a mere (entertaining) ramble as O. Henry waxes poetical on the history (loosely) and meaning (facetiously) of the holiday.

But unlike the entirely anthological sketch "New Year's Eve and How It Came to Houston" that opens our collection, "Thanksgiving Remarks" concludes with a narrative poem and unless O. Henry is engaging in indulgence, something else is at work here. Is O. Henry referencing another literary work? He is, and he gives the game away, stating it is based on Longfellow's "beautiful poem." From that, it does not take much research to uncover that O. Henry is referencing "The Courtship of Miles Standish," an 1858 narrative poem by American poet Henry Wadsworth Longfellow about the early days of Plymouth Colony. O. Henry's homage (or is it parody?) in the concluding poem about the maiden Priscilla (according to Longfellow's December 29, 1857 journal entry, "Priscilla" was the working title that, by March 1, 1858, was renamed "The Courtship of Miles Standish") really raises the interest in this sketch and simultaneously turned me on to Longfellow's "beautiful poem" which is quite meritorious in and of itself.

O. Henry wrote two delightful Thanksgiving Day stories, "The Purple Dress" and "Two Thanksgiving Day Gentlemen." "The Purple Dress," the story of Maida (the girl with the big brown eyes) and her (seemingly dashed) efforts to make a good impression at the Bee-Hive Store's company holiday dinner. I have always enjoyed this story and appreciated the dash of Cinderella O. Henry sprinkled in to concoct this delightful tale. But there was not any real debate about which of the two stories to include as our Thanksgiving Day entrant. The opening paragraphs of "Two Thanksgiving Day Gentlemen" eloquently speaks to the importance (and iconography) of Thanksgiving as well (or better) as any other flourishes of a writer's pen ever spoke to the merits of any holiday by any other author at any other time.

Next up is our third and final sketch written by William Sydney Porter whilst employed by the Houston *Daily Post* from 1895-1896. It is a nice appetizer to get us in the Christmas spirit before we reach the big day. O. Henry wrote several meritorious Christmas stories, all worthy of inclusion: "Compliments of The Season," "A Chaparral Christmas Gift," "Whistling Dick's Christmas Stocking," "Christmas by Injunction," "Bulger's Friend" and "The Gift of the Magi."

Initially, I thought to choose any of the stories other than the one I ultimately went with. "The Gift of the Magi" is the story O. Henry is best remembered for, and perhaps this was an opportunity to expose the reader to a lesser-known story.

"Compliments of the Season" starts off with the guise of a postmodern Christmas story. The first sentence sets the tone: "There are no more Christmas stories to write." Shortly thereafter we are warned: "Children are pestilential little animals with which we have to cope under a bewildering variety of conditions." But once the plot kicks in, we are ultimately treated to a heartwarming story of a homeless man who is rewarded for doing right by the spoiled daughter (of a wealthy family) who has lost her beloved rag doll.

"A Chaparral Christmas Gift" starts with an interesting premise. A rival for the affection of the beautiful daughter of "old man" McMullen (of the Sundown Sheep Ranch), decides to eliminate his rival for the young lady's affection by killing him at Christmastime. O. Henry wrote the story whilst in prison and read the story for fellow inmates Al Jennings and Billy Raidler. It brought Raidler to tears. "Damn you, Porter, I never did it in my life before, I didn't know what a tear looked like," he said wiping away tears. Jennings was equally affected and both he and Raidler were shocked that O. Henry did not immediately place the story with publishers as he did with a dozen or so stories whilst he was in prison. The story eventually appeared in *Ainslee's* for December 1903.

"Whistling Dick's Christmas Stocking" is the charming story of a homeless man's assistance rendered to an aristocratic young lady under duress being rewarded at Christmastime in New Orleans. In *Time To Write: How William Sidney Porter Became O. Henry* Jenny Lind Porter neatly encapsulates the story's charms: "anyone who knows New Orleans will recognize the verisimilitude of O. Henry's descriptions, his perfect command of the colors, sounds and fragrances which define its charms." In preparation for our reading group's December 2016 reading of "Whistling's Dick's Christmas Stocking," I was able to acquire from The University of Virginia a copy of "Whistling Sam's Christmas Stocking," an unpublished, (rough draft of a story) early version of "Whistling Dick's Christmas Story." I was tickled by a reference in "Whistling Sam" to a character named Bad Dreams Mike (did he suffer from bad dreams, or did he give others bad dreams?) and lamented that the ambiguously defined character did not find his way into "Whistling Dick's Christmas Stocking."

"Christmas By Injunction" is the entertaining story of a gold prospector who decides to throw a Christmas party for all the kids in town in a town that has no kids. Our reading group tackled the story in December 2015 and I remember it fondly for capping *J.C. Elkins O. Henry Literary Discussion Group's* first year on such a positive note.

"Bulger's Friend" is (yet another) story of a societal outcast at Christmas. The story speaks nicely to the true spirit of Christmas and tells the redemption of Bulger, "the town's odd 'character,' a shiftless, eccentric old man" at Christmas (the time of redemption).

Ultimately though, I had to go with "The Gift of the Magi," it is too iconic, and even if everyone knows it in the abstract, it is always worth re-reading, as it is a beautiful tale in its brevity, simplicity and wonderfully realized delivery. The story first appeared in the N.Y. *Sunday World* for December 10, 1905 and the story was so late that O. Henry had to tell the paper's illustrator the scene to draw for the illustration to accompany the story so he would have time to furnish a drawing for the story O. Henry had yet to write. The story was originally titled "Gifts of the Magi" and could be seen as a reference to gold, frankincense, and myrrh whereas with the slightly altered title "The Gift of the Magi," as the story is now known, O. Henry was able to allude to the connotation of the "gift" the magi truly possessed (wisdom).

The other reason I decided to include "The Gift of the Magi" was I felt (to use an O. Henryism) I was "squaring the circle." "A Service of Love" was first published in January 1905 and "The Gift of the Magi" in December 1905, when O. Henry was arguably at the pinnacle of his talent (1904 and 1905 were O. Henry's most productive years, after which his output would drop precipitously). "A Service of Love" and "The Gift of the Magi" are, despite their distinct individual nature(s), in the broadest terms, the same story—married couples each sacrificing for their spouse. It seemed a nice synergy and a good way to tie this collection nicely together.

I always imagined that "The Gift of the Magi" would be the final story our group would read and discuss. From the onset of the *J.C. Elkins O. Henry Literary Discussion Group* in 2015 I imagined that whether we ran three, four or five years I would end our final year with "The Ransom of Red Chief" in November and "The Gift of the Magi" in December. However, Gary Hallock became aware that the KUT (Austin's National Public Radio station) Book Club was presenting "The Gift of the Magi" for December 2019 and wanted us to see about our group participating in their meeting and the result of our discussions was that we presented the story in tandem, a one-off experience we have not since duplicated. KUT announced at the December 2019 reading that they were taking a sabbatical and would resume in the Spring of the following year. The Covid 19 pandemic hit in March 2020 and KUT Book Club has not had a reading since. I facetiously joke that we killed the KUT Book Club. On a serious note, it has made me so appreciative that our group have been able to meet monthly from 2015 through 2023 (eight and a half years) with no immediate end in sight and no interruption along the way (we met via Zoom for 14 months starting in April 2020 during the Pandemic).

I would like to thank you dear reader for staying with me as I rambled on in this introduction. *The Ransom of Red Chief and Other O. Henry Stories for Boys* was instrumental to this book's conception (even allowing for Clay's proffering the "direct" idea for the volume) and I felt the need to provide some context (and back story), and I thank you for thus indulging me. I realize I spent considerable time talking about stories NOT in this collection (at greater length at times than about stories that DO appear) but I simply wished to make you aware that there are a good number of O. Henry stories that you would do well to familiarize yourself with, for your own enjoyment. O. Henry's stories speak for themselves so eloquently I did not feel the need to over analyze those included in this volume.

I hope that one day, dear reader, you will have read enough O. Henry stories that you can comfortably come up with your own list of O. Henry stories for boys (and girls) and are easily able to assemble your own collection of O. Henry stories for the holidays. Perhaps you will consult this volume from time to time to meditate on the meaning of the holidays, and (of equal importance) to enjoy a wonderful bunch of stories!

—Michael Wenzel
Summer 2023

HOUSTON GREETS THE NEW YEAR.

January 1, 1900

From the front page of the Houston *Daily Post*. William Sydney Porter
(O. Henry) wrote for the Houston *Daily Post* 1895-1896.

Houston *Daily Post* accessed via newspaperarchive.com

New Year's Eve and How It Came to Houston

Sketched at Random as the Old Year Passed

We that would properly welcome the new year should view it with the eye of an optimist, and sing its praises with the coated tongue of a penitent.

We should dismiss from our hearts the cold precept that history repeats itself, and strive to believe that the deficiencies of the day will be supplied by the morrow. Since fancy whispers to us that at the stroke of midnight the old order will change, yielding to the new, let us put aside, if possible, all knowledge to the contrary and revel in the fairy tale told by the merry bells.

Man's arbitrary part of the time into hours, days and years causes no perceptible jolt beneath the noiseless pneumatic tire of the cycle of years. No mortal tack can puncture that wheel. Old Father Time is a "scorcher," and he rides without lamp or warning bell. The years that are as mile-stones to us are as gravel spurned beneath him. But to us, of few days and an occasional night off, they serve as warnings to note the hour upon the face of a mighty clock upon which the hands move silently and are never turned back.

The New Year is feminine. There is no question but that the world has become badly mixed as to the gender of time. And again, the New Year is no cherubic debutante with eyes full of prophetic joys, but a grim and ancient spinster who flutters coyly into our presence with a giddy giggle, rejuvenated for the occasion. We have made obeisance to those same charms time out of mind; we have whispered soft nothings into those same ears many moons ago; we have lightly brushed those painted and powdered cheeks in time gone by when they glowed with the damask bloom of youth. But let us hug once more the dear delusion. Let us say that she is fair and fresh as the rising morn, and make unto ourselves a season of mirth and heedless joy.

The fiddles strike up and the hautboys sigh. Your hand, sweet, coy New Year—take care of that rheumatic knee—come, let us foot it as the gladsome bells proclaim your debut—number 1896.

The last day of the year is generally spent in laying in as big a stock as possible of things suitable for use the next day for swearing-off purposes.

It is so much easier to resolve to do without anything when we have just had too much of it.

How easy it is on New Year's day, just after dinner, when we are full of good resolutions and turkey, to kneel down and solemnly affirm that we will never touch food again. The man who on the morning of the glad New Year stands trembling with fear on the center table, while snakes and lizards merrily play hide and seek on the floor, finds no difficulty in forswearing the sparkling bowl. The dark brown, copper-riveted taste which accompanies what is known to the medical profession as the New Year tongue, is a great incentive to reform.

The beautiful siren-like, Christmas-present cigar that is so fair to gaze upon, when lit turns like a viper and stings us into abjuring my Lady Nicotine forever.

When we attempt to sit upon the early scarlet runner, hand-embroidered rocking-chair cushion presented to us by our maiden aunt and slide out upon the floor upon our spinal vertebrae, we feel inclined to kneel in our own blood with a dagger between our teeth and swear by heaven never to sit down again.

When we go upon the streets wearing the neckties presented to us by our wife, and the loiterer upon the corner sayeth, "Ha, Ha," and the newsboy inquireth, "What is it?" is it any wonder that we curse the necktie habit as an enemy of man, and on New Year's morning swear to abjure it forever?

When we say farewell, and with clenched teeth wend our way into the shirt made for us by the fair hands of our partner in sorrow, and find the collar tighter than the last one worn by the late lamented Harry Hayward, and the tail thereof more biased than a populist editorial, and the bosom in billowy waves that heave upon our manly chest like a polonaise on a Black cook on Emancipation Day, and the sleeves dragging the floor as we walk about, saying, "It's so nice, my dear—just what I wanted," what wonder that we register an oath with the Lord of Abraham and Jacob as the glad New Year bells peal out, nevermore to wear again a garment made by that portion of the earth's inhabitants that sits on the floor to put on its shoes, and regards the male torso as a waste basket for remnant AA sheeting and misfit Butterick patterns?

There are so many things we take a delight in forswearing on New Year's Day.

While strolling aimlessly about the streets of Houston on the last evening of 1895, little sights and sounds obtrude themselves and reveal the spirit of the time, as little pulse beats indicate the general tone of the human system.

It is nearly 6 o'clock, and there is a lively crowd moving upon the sidewalks.

Here comes a lovely little shopgirl, as neat and trim as a fashion plate. Her big hat plumes wave, and her little boot heels beat a merry tictac upon the pavement. Debonaire and full of life and fun, she moves, cheery and happy, on her way to supper. Her bright eyes flash sidelong glances at the jeweler's windows as she passes. Some day she hopes to see upon her white finger one of those sparkling diamonds. Her lips curve in a meaning smile. She is thinking of the handsome, finely-dressed man who comes so often to her counter in the big store, ostensibly to buy her wares. How grand he is, and what eloquent eyes and a lovely mustache he has! She does not know his name; but, well, she knows that he cares a little for the goods she sells. How soft his voice as he asks the price of this and that, and with what romantic feeling he says that we will surely have rain if the clouds gather sufficiently! She wonders where he is now. She trips around a corner and meets him face to face. She gives a little scream, and then her face hardens and a cold glitter comes into her eye.

On his arm is a huge market basket, from which protrudes the cold, despairing legs of a turkey, from which the soul has fled. Two yards of celery trail behind him; turnip greens, cauliflower and the alleged yellow yam nestle against his arm. On his brow is confusion; in his face are hung the scarlet banners of a guilty conscience; in his romantic eyes she reads the tell-tale story of a benedict; by the hand he leads a cold-nosed but indisputable little boy.

She elevates her charming head to a supercilious angle, snaps out to herself the one word "married!" and is gone.

He jerks the limp, sad corpse of the turkey to the other side, snatches the cold-nosed little boy about five feet through the air and vows that never again will he go to market during the joyous year of 1896.

It is New Year's eve.

A citizen is restlessly pacing the floor of his sitting room. There is evidently some crisis near, for his brow is contracted, and his hands are nervously clasped and unclasped behind his back. He is waiting expectantly for something. Suddenly the door opens and his family physician enters smiling and congratulatory. The citizen turns upon him a look full of inquiry.

"All is well," says the physician. "Three fine boys, and everybody getting along first rate."

"Three?" says the citizen in a tone of horror, "Three!" He kneels on the floor and in fervent accents exclaims:

"Tomorrow will be the New Year, and I hereby solemnly swear that—"

Breaking in upon his resolutions comes the merry chime of the New Year bells.

The people come and the people go.

In the stores, looking over remnants of Christmas goods, are to be found that class of people who received presents on Christmas Day without giving any, and are now striving to make late and lame amends by returning the compliment on New Year's Day. The New Year's present is a delusion and contains about as much warmth and soul as a eulogy on the South by the New York *Sun*.

Two ladies are at a bargain counter, maintaining an animated conversation in low but dangerous tones.

"She sent me," says one of them, "a little old nickel-plated card receiver on Christmas Day, and I know she bought it at a racket store. Goodness knows, I never would have thought of sending her anything, but now I've got to return it, of course—the old deceitful thing and I don't know what to get for her. Let's see—oh yes; I have it now. You know they say she used to be a chambermaid in a St. Louis hotel before she was married; I'll just send her this little silver pin with a broom on it. Wonder if she's bright enough to understand?"

"I hope so, I'm sure," says the other lady. "That reminds me that George gave me a nice new opera cloak for a Christmas present, and I just forgot all about him. What are those horn collar-buttons worth?"

"Fifteen cents a dozen," says the salesman.

"Let me see" says the lady meditatively—"Yes, I will; George has been so good to me. Give me three of those buttons, please."

———————————

Viva el rey; el rey está muerto!

The Spanish phrase looks better than the hackneyed French, and it is correct, having been carefully revised by one of the most reliable tamale dealers on Travis Street. The old year is passing; let us stand in with the new. In happy Houston homes light feet are dancing away the hours 'neath holly and mistletoe, but outside stalk those who inherit want and care and misery, to whom the coming season brings nothing of hope or joy.

Two young men are wending their way up Preston Street. One is holding the other by the arm and guiding his steps. The sidewalk seems to run in laps and curves, twisting itself into hills and hollows and labyrinthine mazes. One of the young men thinks he is dying.

The other one is not sure about it, but he hopes he is not mistaken. They are both good friends of the old year, and they hate to see it leave so badly that they have sewed their sorrow up in a sack and tried to drown it.

"Goo' bye, old frien'," says the dying one. "Go 'way and leave me to die here on thish boundless prairie. Sands of life's runnin' out like everyshing. Zat las' dish chick'n salad's done its work. Never see fazzer'n muzzer any more."

"Bob," says the other one, "you're 'fern'l idiot. Never shay die. Zis town Houston can't be more'n ten miles away. We're right on Harvey Wilshon's race track now goin' round'n round. Whazzer mazzer wiz livin' for country'n so forth?"

"Can't do it, old boy; 'stremities gettin' coldsh now. Light's fadin' out of eyes'n worldsh fadin' from view. Can't shay 'er prayer, old boy, 'fore vital spark expires! Can'tcher say lay'm down to sleep, Jim?"

"Don't be a fool, Bob; come on, lesh find city Houston 'n git a drink."

"Jim, I' dead man. Been wicked 'n told liesh, 'n played poker. Zhere ain't no hope for handshome, unscrup'loush shociety man like me. Been giddy butterfly 'n broke senty-five lovin' crea-turesh hearts—jus' listen Jim, I hear angelsh shingin' an' playin' harpsh, 'n I c'n see beau'ful lights 'n heavensh wiz all kind col-ors flashin' from golden gates. Jim, don't you hear angel throng shingin' shongs 'n see lights shinin' in New Jerushalem?"

"Bob, you d'graded lun'tic, don't you know what that ish? That's Salvation Army singin', 'n Ed Kiam's 'lectric sign you shee. Now I know where we're at. Zere's five saloonsh on nex' block."

"Jim, you've shaved m' life. Lesh make one more effort 'fore I die, 'n tell barkeep' put plenty ice in it."

Midnight draws on apace, and while some welcome with revelry the advent of the New Year, others stray in the land of dreams, and allow it to approach unheralded.

Ladies over 30 years of age take on a grim look about the jaw, and bend with a deadly glitter in their eyes over the article in the Sunday paper that treats of "How to avoid wrinkles," and sadly shake their heads when they read that Madame Bonjour, the famous French beauty, kept young and lovely until after 110 years of age by using Bunker's Bunco Balm.

The New Year brings to them sad prospects of another gray hair, or a crow's foot around the eye.

To the little folks the season is but a prolongation of Christmas, and they welcome the turning over of the new leaf without a misgiving.

Would that we all might trace a record upon it as fair as that their chubby hands will scrawl.

Happy New Year to all.

New Year's Day

January 1st

A cartoon of Mr. Jennings drawn by O. Henry after their celebration
of New Year's Eve, 1907.

Jennings, A. (1921). Through the shadows with O. Henry. The H.K. Fly
Company. [FPL-15-A1-008 (detail)]. O. Henry (William Sydney Porter)
Resources Collection (AR.L.015). Austin History Center, Austin Public Library.

A Service of Love

When one loves one's Art no service seems too hard.

That is our premise. This story shall draw a conclusion from it, and show at the same time that the premise is incorrect. That will be a new thing in logic, and a feat in story-telling somewhat older than the great wall of China.

Joe Larrabee came out of the post-oak flats of the Middle West pulsing with a genius for pictorial art. At six he drew a picture of the town pump with a prominent citizen passing it hastily. This effort was framed and hung in the drug store window by the side of the ear of corn with an uneven number of rows. At twenty he left for New York with a flowing necktie and a capital tied up somewhat closer.

Delia Caruthers did things in six octaves so promisingly in a pine-tree village in the South that her relatives chipped in enough in her chip hat for her to go "North" and "finish." They could not see her f—, but that is our story.

Joe and Delia met in an atelier where a number of art and music students had gathered to discuss chiaroscuro, Wagner, music, Rembrandt's works, pictures, Waldteufel, wall paper, Chopin and Oolong.

Joe and Delia became enamored one of the other, or each of the other, as you please, and in a short time were married—for (see above), when one loves one's Art no service seems too hard.

11

Mr. and Mrs. Larrabee began housekeeping in a flat. It was a lonesome flat—something like the A sharp way down at the left-hand end of the keyboard. And they were happy; for they had their Art, and they had each other. And my advice to the rich young man would be—sell all thou hast, and give it to the poor—janitor for the privilege of living in a flat with your Art and your Delia.

Flat-dwellers shall indorse my dictum that theirs is the only true happiness. If a home is happy it cannot fit too close—let the dresser collapse and become a billiard table; let the mantel turn to a rowing machine, the escritoire to a spare bedchamber, the washstand to an upright piano; let the four walls come together, if they will, so you and your Delia are between. But if home be the other kind, let it be wide and long—enter you at the Golden Gate, hang your hat on Hatteras, your cape on Cape Horn and go out by the Labrador.

Joe was painting in the class of the great Magister—you know his fame. His fees are high; his lessons are light—his high-lights have brought him renown. Delia was studying under Rosenstock—you know his repute as a disturber of the piano keys.

They were mighty happy as long as their money lasted. So is every—but I will not be cynical. Their aims were very clear and defined. Joe was to become capable very soon of turning out pictures that old gentlemen with thin side-whiskers and thick pocketbooks would sandbag one another in his studio for the privilege of buying. Delia was to become familiar and then contemptuous with Music, so that when she saw the orchestra seats and boxes unsold she could have sore throat and lobster in a private dining-room and refuse to go on the stage.

But the best, in my opinion, was the home life in the little flat—the ardent, voluble chats after the day's study; the cozy dinners and fresh, light breakfasts; the interchange of ambitions—ambitions interwoven each with the other's or else inconsiderable—the mutual help and inspiration; and—overlook my artlessness—stuffed olives and cheese sandwiches at 11 p.m.

But after a while Art flagged. It sometimes does, even if some switchman doesn't flag it. Everything going out and nothing coming in, as the vulgarians say. Money was lacking to pay Mr. Magister and Herr Rosenstock their prices. When one loves one's Art no service seems too hard. So, Delia said she must give music lessons to keep the chafing dish bubbling.

For two or three days she went out canvassing for pupils. One evening she came home elated.

"Joe, dear," she said, gleefully, "I've a pupil. And, oh, the loveliest people! General—General A. B. Pinkney's daughter—on Seventy-first street. Such a splendid house, Joe—you ought to see the front door! Byzantine I think you would call it. And inside! Oh, Joe, I never saw anything like it before.

"My pupil is his daughter Clementina. I dearly love her already. She's a delicate thing—dresses always in white; and the sweetest, simplest manners! Only eighteen years old. I'm to give three lessons a week; and, just think, Joe! $5 a lesson. I don't mind it a bit; for when I get two or three more pupils I can resume my lessons with Herr Rosenstock. Now, smooth out that wrinkle between your brows, dear, and let's have a nice supper."

"That's all right for you, Dele," said Joe, attacking a can of peas with a carving knife and a hatchet, "but how about me? Do you think I'm going to let you hustle for wages while I philander in the regions of high art? Not by the bones of Benvenuto Cellini! I guess I can sell papers or lay cobblestones, and bring in a dollar or two."

Delia came and hung about his neck.

"Joe, dear, you are silly. You must keep on at your studies. It is not as if I had quit my music and gone to work at something else. While I teach I learn. I am always with my music. And we can live as happily as millionaires on $15 a week. You mustn't think of leaving Mr. Magister."

"All right," said Joe, reaching for the blue scalloped vegetable dish. "But I hate for you to be giving lessons. It isn't Art. But you're a trump and a dear to do it."

"When one loves one's Art no service seems too hard," said Delia.

"Magister praised the sky in that sketch I made in the park," said Joe. "And Tinkle gave me permission to hang two of them in his window. I may sell one if the right kind of a moneyed idiot sees them."

"I'm sure you will," said Delia, sweetly. "And now let's be thankful for Gen. Pinkney and this veal roast."

During all of the next week the Larrabees had an early breakfast. Joe was enthusiastic about some morning-effect sketches he was doing in Central Park, and Delia packed him off breakfasted, coddled, praised and kissed at 7 o'clock. Art is an engaging mistress. It was most times 7 o'clock when he returned in the evening.

At the end of the week Delia, sweetly proud but languid, triumphantly tossed three five-dollar bills on the 8×10 (inches) center table of the 8×10 (feet) flat parlor.

"Sometimes," she said, a little wearily, "Clementina tries me. I'm afraid she doesn't practice enough, and I have to tell her the same things so often. And then she always dresses entirely in white, and that does get monotonous. But Gen. Pinkney is the dearest old man! I wish you could know him, Joe. He comes in sometimes when I am with Clementina at the piano—he is a widower, you know—and stands there pulling his white goatee. 'And how are the semiquavers and the demisemiquavers progressing?' he always asks.

"I wish you could see the wainscoting in that drawing-room, Joe! And those Astrakhan rug portières. And Clementina has such a funny little cough. I hope she is stronger than she looks. Oh, I really am getting attached to her, she is so gentle and high bred. Gen. Pinkney's brother was once Minister to Bolivia."

And then Joe, with the air of a Monte Cristo, drew forth a ten, a five, a two and a one—all legal tender notes—and laid them beside Delia's earnings.

"Sold that watercolor of the obelisk to a man from Peoria," he announced overwhelmingly.

"Don't joke with me," said Delia, "not from Peoria!"

"All the way. I wish you could see him, Dele. Fat man with a woolen muffler and a quill toothpick. He saw the sketch in Tinkle's window and thought it was a windmill at first. He was game, though, and bought it anyhow. He ordered another—an oil sketch of the Lackawanna freight depot—to take back with him. Music lessons! Oh, I guess Art is still in it."

"I'm so glad you've kept on," said Delia, heartily. "You're bound to win, dear. Thirty-three dollars! We never had so much to spend before. We'll have oysters to-night."

"And filet mignon with champignons," said Joe. "Where is the olive fork?"

On the next Saturday evening Joe reached home first. He spread his $18 on the parlor table and washed what seemed to be a great deal of dark paint from his hands.

Half an hour later Delia arrived, her right hand tied up in a shapeless bundle of wraps and bandages.

"How is this?" asked Joe after the usual greetings. Delia laughed, but not very joyously.

"Clementina," she explained, "insisted upon a Welsh rabbit after her lesson. She is such a queer girl. Welsh rabbits at 5 in the afternoon. The General was there. You should have seen him run for the chafing dish, Joe, just as if there wasn't a servant in the house. I know Clementina isn't in good health; she is so nervous. In serving the rabbit she spilled a great lot of it, boiling hot, over my hand and wrist. It hurt awfully, Joe. And the dear girl was so sorry! But Gen. Pinkney!—Joe, that old man nearly went distracted. He rushed downstairs and sent somebody— they said the furnace man or somebody in the basement—out to a drug store for some oil and things to bind it up with. It doesn't hurt so much now."

"What's this?" asked Joe, taking the hand tenderly and pulling at some white strands beneath the bandages. "It's something soft," said Delia, "that had oil on it. Oh, Joe, did you sell another sketch?" She had seen the money on the table.

"Did I?" said Joe; "just ask the man from Peoria. He got his depot to-day, and he isn't sure but he thinks he wants another parkscape and a view on the Hudson. What time this afternoon did you burn your hand, Dele?"

"Five o'clock, I think," said Dele, plaintively. "The iron—I mean the rabbit came off the fire about that time. You ought to have seen Gen. Pinkney, Joe, when—"

"Sit down here a moment, Dele," said Joe. He drew her to the couch, sat beside her and put his arm across her shoulders.

"What have you been doing for the last two weeks, Dele?" he asked.

She braved it for a moment or two with an eye full of love and stubbornness, and murmured a phrase or two vaguely of Gen. Pinkney; but at length down went her head and out came the truth and tears.

"I couldn't get any pupils," she confessed. "And I couldn't bear to have you give up your lessons; and I got a place ironing shirts in that big Twenty-fourth street laundry. And I think I did very well to make up both General Pinkney and Clementina, don't you, Joe? And when a girl in the laundry set down a hot iron on my hand this afternoon I was all the way home making up that story about the Welsh rabbit. You're not angry, are you, Joe? And if I hadn't got the work you mightn't have sold your sketches to that man from Peoria."

"He wasn't from Peoria," said Joe, slowly.

"Well, it doesn't matter where he was from. How clever you are, Joe—and—kiss me, Joe—and what made you ever suspect that I wasn't giving music lessons to Clementina?"

"I didn't," said Joe, "until to-night. And I wouldn't have then, only I sent up this cotton waste and oil from the engine-room this afternoon for a girl upstairs who had her hand burned with a smoothing-iron. I've been firing the engine in that laundry for the last two weeks."

"And then you didn't—"

"My purchaser from Peoria," said Joe, "and Gen. Pinkney are both creations of the same art—but you wouldn't call it either painting or music."

And then they both laughed, and Joe began:

"When one loves one's Art no service seems—"

But Delia stopped him with her hand on his lips. "No," she said—"just 'When one loves.'"

Martin Luther King, Jr. Day

Third Monday in January

Martin Luther King, Jr. (born Michael King Jr.;
January 15, 1929 – April 4, 1968)

"I Have a Dream" speech given during
the March on Washington for Jobs and Freedom

August 28, 1963

The Guardian of
the Accolade

Not the least important of the force of the Weymouth Bank was Uncle Bushrod. Sixty years had Uncle Bushrod—sixty years of faithful service to the house of Weymouth as chattel, servitor and friend. Of the color of the mahogany bank furniture was Uncle Bushrod—thus dark was he externally; white as the un-inked pages of the bank ledgers was his soul. Eminently pleasing to Uncle Bushrod would the comparison have been; for to him the only institution in existence worth considering was the Weymouth Bank, of which he was something between porter and generalissimo-in-charge.

Weymouth lay, dreamy and umbrageous, among the low foothills along the brow of a Southern valley. Three banks there were in Weymouthville. Two were hopeless, misguided enterprises, lacking the presence and prestige of a Weymouth to give them glory. The third was The Bank, managed by the Weymouths—and Uncle Bushrod. In the old Weymouth homestead—the red brick, white-porticoed mansion, the first to your right as you crossed Elder Creek, coming into town—lived Mr. Robert Weymouth (the president of the bank), his widowed daughter, Mrs. Vesey—called "Miss Letty" by every one—and her two children, Nan and Guy. There, also in a cottage on the grounds, resided Uncle Bushrod and Aunt Malindy, his wife. Mr. William Weymouth (the cashier of the bank) lived in a modern, fine house on the principal avenue.

Mr. Robert was a large, stout man, sixty-two years of age, with a smooth, plump face, long iron-gray hair and fiery blue eyes. He was high-tempered, kind, and generous, with a youthful smile and a formidable, stern voice that did not always mean what it sounded like. Mr. William was a milder man, correct in deportment and absorbed in business. The Weymouths formed The Family of Weymouthville, and were looked up to, as was their right of heritage.

Uncle Bushrod was the bank's trusted porter, messenger, vassal, and guardian. He carried a key to the vault, just as Mr. Robert and Mr. William did. Sometimes there was ten, fifteen, or twenty thousand dollars in sacked silver stacked on the vault floor. It was safe with Uncle Bushrod. He was a Weymouth in heart, honesty, and pride.

Of late Uncle Bushrod had not been without worry. It was on account of Marse Robert. For nearly a year Mr. Robert had been known to indulge in too much drink. Not enough, understand, to become tipsy, but the habit was getting a hold upon him, and every one was beginning to notice it. Half a dozen times a day he would leave the bank and step around to the Merchants and Planters' Hotel to take a drink. Mr. Robert's usual keen judgment and business capacity became a little impaired. Mr. William, a Weymouth, but not so rich in experience, tried to dam the inevitable backflow of the tide, but with incomplete success. The deposits in the Weymouth Bank dropped from six figures to five. Past-due paper began to accumulate, owing to injudicious loans. No one cared to address Mr. Robert on the subject of temperance. Many of his friends said that the cause of it had been the death of his wife some two years before. Others hesitated on account of Mr. Robert's quick temper, which was extremely apt to resent personal interference of such a nature. Miss Letty and the children noticed the change and grieved about it. Uncle Bushrod also worried, but he was one of those who would not have dared to remonstrate, although he and Marse Robert had been raised almost as companions. But there was a heavier shock coming to Uncle Bushrod than that caused by the bank president's toddies and juleps.

Mr. Robert had a passion for fishing, which he usually indulged whenever the season and business permitted. One day, when reports had been coming in relating to the bass and perch, he announced his intention of making a two or three days' visit to the lakes. He was going down, he said, to Reedy Lake with Judge Archinard, an old friend.

Now, Uncle Bushrod was treasurer of the Sons and Daughters of the Burning Bush. Every association he belonged to made him treasurer without hesitation. He stood AA1 in colored circles. He was understood among them to be Mr. Bushrod Weymouth, of the Weymouth Bank.

The night following the day on which Mr. Robert mentioned his intended fishing-trip the old man woke up and rose from his bed at twelve o'clock, declaring he must go down to the bank and fetch the pass-book of the Sons and Daughters, which he had forgotten to bring home. The bookkeeper had balanced it for him that day, put the cancelled checks in it, and snapped two elastic bands around it. He put but one band around other pass-books.

Aunt Malindy objected to the mission at so late an hour, denouncing it as foolish and unnecessary, but Uncle Bushrod was not to be deflected from duty.

"I done told Sister Adaline Hoskins," he said, "to come by here for dat book to-morrer mawnin' at sebin o'clock, for to kyar' it to de meetin' of de bo'd of 'rangements, and dat book gwine to be here when she come."

So, Uncle Bushrod put on his old brown suit, got his thick

hickory stick, and meandered through the almost deserted streets of Weymouthville. He entered the bank, unlocking the side door, and found the pass-book where he had left it, in the little back room used for consultations, where he always hung his coat. Looking about casually, he saw that everything was as he had left it, and was about to start for home when he was brought to a standstill by the sudden rattle of a key in the front door. Some one came quickly in, closed the door softly, and entered the counting-room through the door in the iron railing.

That division of the bank's space was connected with the back room by a narrow passageway, now in deep darkness.

Uncle Bushrod, firmly gripping his hickory stick, tiptoed gently up this passage until he could see the midnight intruder into the sacred precincts of the Weymouth Bank. One dim gas-jet burned there, but even in its nebulous light he perceived at once that the prowler was the bank's president.

Wondering, fearful, undecided what to do, Uncle Bushrod stood motionless in the gloomy strip of hallway, and waited developments.

The vault, with its big iron door, was opposite him. Inside that was the safe, holding the papers of value, the gold and currency of the bank. On the floor of the vault was, perhaps, eighteen thousand dollars in silver.

The president took his key from his pocket, opened the vault and went inside, nearly closing the door behind him. Uncle Bushrod saw, through the narrow aperture, the flicker of a candle. In a minute or two—it seemed an hour to the watcher—Mr. Robert came out, bringing with him a large hand-satchel, handling it in a careful but hurried manner, as if fearful that he might be observed. With one hand he closed and locked the vault door.

With a reluctant theory forming itself beneath his hair, Uncle Bushrod waited and watched, shaking in his concealing shadow.

Mr. Robert set the satchel softly upon a desk, and turned his coat collar up about his neck and ears. He was dressed in a rough suit of gray, as if for travelling. He glanced with frowning intentness at the big office clock above the burning gas-jet, and then looked lingeringly about the bank—lingeringly and fondly, Uncle Bushrod thought, as one who bids farewell to dear and familiar scenes.

Now he caught up his burden again and moved promptly and softly out of the bank by the way he had come locking the front door behind him.

For a minute or longer Uncle Bushrod was as stone in his tracks. Had that midnight rifler of safes and vaults been any other on earth than the man he was, the old retainer would have rushed upon him and struck to save the Weymouth property. But now the watcher's soul was tortured by the poignant dread of something worse than mere robbery. He was seized by an accusing terror that said the Weymouth name and the Weymouth honor were about to be lost. Marse Robert robbing the bank! What else could it mean? The hour of the night, the stealthy visit to the vault, the satchel brought forth full and with expedition and silence, the prowler's rough dress, his solicitous reading of the clock, and noiseless departure—what else could it mean?

And then to the turmoil of Uncle Bushrod's thoughts came the corroborating recollection of preceding events—Mr. Robert's increasing intemperance and consequent many moods of royal high spirits and stern tempers; the casual talk he had heard in the bank of the decrease in business and difficulty in collecting loans. What else could it all mean but that Mr. Robert Weymouth was an absconder—was about to fly with the bank's remaining funds, leaving Mr. William, Miss Letty, little Nan, Guy, and Uncle Bushrod to bear the disgrace?

During one minute Uncle Bushrod considered these things, and then he awoke to sudden determination and action.

"Lawd! Lawd!" he moaned aloud, as he hobbled hastily toward the side door. "Sech a come-off after all dese here years of big doin's and fine doin's. Scan'lous sights upon de yearth when de Weymouth fambly done turn out robbers and 'bezzlers! Time for Uncle Bushrod to clean out somebody's chicken-coop and eben matters up. Oh, Lawd! Marse Robert, you ain't gwine do dat. 'N Miss Letty an 'dem chillun so proud and talkin' 'Weymouth, Weymouth,' all de time! I'm gwine to stop you ef I can. 'Spec you shoot Uncle Bushrod's head off ef he fool wid you, but I'm gwine stop you ef I can."

Uncle Bushrod, aided by his hickory stick, impeded by his rheumatism, hurried down the street toward the railroad station, where the two lines touching Weymouthville met. As he had expected and feared, he saw there Mr. Robert, standing in the shadow of the building, waiting for the train. He held the satchel in his hand.

When Uncle Bushrod came within twenty yards of the bank president, standing like a huge, gray ghost by the station wall, sudden perturbation seized him. The rashness and audacity of the thing he had come to do struck him fully. He would have been happy could he have turned and fled from the possibilities of the famous Weymouth wrath. But again he saw, in his fancy, the white reproachful face of Miss Letty, and the distressed looks of Nan and Guy, should he fail in his duty and they question him as to his stewardship.

Braced by the thought, he approached in a straight line, clearing his throat and pounding with his stick so that he might be early recognized. Thus he might avoid the likely danger of too suddenly surprising the sometimes hasty Mr. Robert.

"Is that you, Bushrod?" called the clamant, clear voice of the gray ghost.

"Yes, suh, Marse Robert."

"What the devil are you doing out at this time of night?"

For the first time in his life, Uncle Bushrod told Marse Robert a falsehood. He could not repress it. He would have to circumlocute a little. His nerve was not equal to a direct attack.

"I done been down, suh, to see ol' Aunt M'ria Patterson. She taken sick in de night, and I kyar'ed her a bottle of M'lindy's medercine. Yes, suh."

"Humph!" said Robert. "You better get home out of the night air. It's damp. You'll hardly be worth killing to-morrow on account of your rheumatism. Think it'll be a clear day, Bushrod?"

"I 'low it will, suh. De sun sot red las' night."

Mr. Robert lit a cigar in the shadow, and the smoke looked like his gray ghost expanding and escaping into the night air. Somehow, Uncle Bushrod could barely force his reluctant tongue to the dreadful subject. He stood, awkward, shambling, with his feet upon the gravel and fumbling with his stick. But then, afar off—three miles away, at the Jimtown switch—he heard the faint whistle of the coming train, the one that was to transport the Weymouth name into the regions of dishonor and shame. All fear left him. He took off his hat and faced the chief of the clan he served, the great, royal, kind, lofty, terrible Weymouth—he bearded him there at the brink of the awful thing that was about to happen.

"Marse Robert," he began, his voice quivering a little with the stress of his feelings, "you 'member de day dey-all rode de tunnament at Oak Lawn? De day, suh, dat you win in de ridin', and you crown Miss Lucy de queen?"

"Tournament?" said Mr. Robert, taking his cigar from his mouth. "Yes, I remember very well the—but what the deuce are you talking about tournaments here at midnight for? Go 'long home, Bushrod. I believe you're sleep-walking."

Drawn by E. W. Kemble.

" HE WAS UNDERSTOOD
AMONG THEM TO BE
MR. BUSHROD WEY-
MOUTH, OF THE WEY-
MOUTH BANK."

Uncle Bushrod
The Cosmopolitan
May 1903
Drawn by E.W. Kemble (January 18, 1861 – September 19, 1933)

"Miss Lucy tetch you on de shoulder," continued the old man, never heeding, "wid a s'ord, and say: 'I mek you a knight, Suh Robert—rise up, pure and fearless and widout reproach.' Dat what Miss Lucy say. Dat's been a long time ago, but me nor you ain't forgot it. And den dar's another time we ain't forgot—de time when Miss Lucy lay on her las' bed. She sent for Uncle Bush-rod, and she say: 'Uncle Bushrod, when I die, I want you to take good care of Mr. Robert. Seem like'—so Miss Lucy say—'he lis-ten to you mo' dan to anybody else. He apt to be mighty fractious sometimes, and maybe he cuss you when you try to 'suade him but he need somebody what understand him to be 'round wid him. He am like a little child sometimes'—so Miss Lucy say, wid her eyes shinin' in her po', thin face—'but he always been'—dem was her words—'my knight, pure and fearless and widout reproach.'"

Mr. Robert began to mask, as was his habit, a tendency to soft-heartedness with a spurious anger.

"You—you old windbag!" he growled through a cloud of swirling cigar smoke. "I believe you are crazy. I told you to go home, Bushrod. Miss Lucy said that, did she? Well, we haven't kept the scutcheon very clear. Two years ago last week, wasn't it, Bushrod, when she died? Confound it! Are you going to stand there all night gabbing like a coffee-colored gander?"

The train whistled again. Now it was at the water tank, a mile away.

"Marse Robert," said Uncle Bushrod, laying his hand on the satchel that the banker held. "For Gawd's sake, don' take dis wid you. I knows what's in it. I knows where you got it in de bank. Don' kyar' it wid you. Dey's big trouble in dat valise for Miss Lucy and Miss Lucy's child's chillun. Hit's bound to destroy de name of Weymouth and bow down dem dat own it wid shame and triberlation. Marse Robert, you can kill ole Bushrod ef you will, but don't take away dis 'er' valise. If I ever crosses over de

Jordan, what I gwine to say to Miss Lucy when she ax me: 'Uncle Bushrod, wharfo' didn' you take good care of Mr. Robert?'"

Mr. Robert Weymouth threw away his cigar and shook free one arm with that peculiar gesture that always preceded his outbursts of irascibility. Uncle Bushrod bowed his head to the expected storm, but he did not flinch. If the house of Weymouth was to fall, he would fall with it. The banker spoke, and Uncle Bushrod blinked with surprise. The storm was there, but it was suppressed to the quietness of a summer breeze.

"Bushrod," said Mr. Robert, in a lower voice than he usually employed, "you have overstepped all bounds. You have presumed upon the leniency with which you have been treated to meddle unpardonably. So you know what is in this satchel! Your long and faithful service is some excuse, but—go home, Bushrod—not another word!"

But Bushrod grasped the satchel with a firmer hand. The headlight of the train was now lightening the shadows about the station. The roar was increasing, and folks were stirring about at the track side.

"Marse Robert, gimme dis 'er' valise. I got a right, suh, to talk to you dis 'er' way. I slaved for you and 'tended to you from a child up. I went th'ough de war as yo' body-servant tell we whipped de Yankees and sent 'em back to de No'th. I was at yo' weddin', and I was n' fur away when yo' Miss Letty was bawn. And Miss Letty's chillun, dey watches to-day for Uncle Bushrod when he come home ever' evenin'. I been a Weymouth, all 'cept in color and entitlements. Both of us is old, Marse Robert. 'Tain't goin' to be long till we gwine to see Miss Lucy and has to give an account of our doin's. De ole Bushrod won't be 'spected to say much mo' dan he done all he could by de fambly dat owned him. But de Weymouths, dey must say dey been livin' pure and fearless and widout reproach. Gimme dis valise, Marse

30

Robert—I'm gwine to hab it. I'm gwine to take it back to the bank and lock it up in de vault. I'm gwine to do Miss Lucy's biddin'. Turn 'er loose, Marse Robert."

The train was standing at the station. Some men were pushing trucks along the side. Two or three sleepy passengers got off and wandered away into the night. The conductor stepped to the gravel, swung his lantern and called: "Hello, Frank!" at some one invisible. The bell clanged, the brakes hissed, the conductor drawled: "All aboard!"

Mr. Robert released his hold on the satchel. Uncle Bushrod hugged it to his breast with both arms, as a lover clasps his first beloved.

"Take it back with you, Bushrod," said Mr. Robert, thrusting his hands into his pockets. "And let the subject drop—now mind! You've said quite enough. I'm going to take the train. Tell Mr. William I will be back on Saturday. Good night."

The banker climbed the steps of the moving train and disappeared in a coach. Uncle Bushrod stood motionless, still embracing the precious satchel. His eyes were closed and his lips were moving in thanks to the Master above for the salvation of the Weymouth honor. He knew Mr. Robert would return when he said he would. The Weymouths never lied. Nor now, thank the Lord! could it be said that they embezzled the money in banks.

Then awake to the necessity for further guardianship of Weymouth trust funds, the old man started for the bank with the redeemed satchel.

Three hours from Weymouthville, in the gray dawn, Mr. Robert alighted from the train at a lonely flag-station. Dimly he could see the figure of a man waiting on the platform, and the shape of a spring-wagon, team and driver. Half a dozen lengthy bamboo fishing-poles projected from the wagon's rear.

"You're here, Bob," said Judge Archinard, Mr. Robert's old friend and schoolmate. "It's going to be a royal day for fishing. I thought you said—why, didn't you bring along the stuff?"

The president of the Weymouth Bank took off his hat and rumpled his gray locks.

"Well, Ben, to tell you the truth, there's an infernally presumptuous old meddler belonging in my family that broke up the arrangement. He came down to the depot and vetoed the whole proceeding. He means all right, and—well, I reckon he is right. Somehow, he had found out what I had along—though I hid it in the bank vault and sneaked it out at midnight. I reckon he has noticed that I've been indulging a little more than a gentleman should, and he laid for me with some reaching arguments.

"I'm going to quit drinking," Mr. Robert concluded. "I've come to the conclusion that a man can't keep it up and be quite what he'd like to be—'pure and fearless and without reproach'— that's the way old Bushrod quoted it."

"Well, I'll have to admit," said the judge, thoughtfully, as they climbed into the wagon, "that the old fussbudget's argument can't conscientiously be overruled."

"Still," said Mr. Robert, with a ghost of a sigh, "there was two quarts of the finest old silk-velvet Bourbon in that satchel you ever wet your lips with."

Valentine's Day

February 14th

THE STORY OF HIS LIFE.

The Story of his Life

Drawn by Charles Dana Gibson
(September 14, 1867 – December 23, 1944)

Courtesy of Alamy

Cupid à la Carte

"The dispositions of woman," said Jeff Peters, after various opinions on the subject had been advanced, "run, regular, to diversions. What a woman wants is what you're out of. She wants more of a thing when it's scarce. She likes to have souvenirs of things that never happened. She likes to be reminded of things she never heard of. A one-sided view of objects is disjointing to the female composition.

" 'Tis a misfortune of mine, begotten by nature and travel," continued Jeff, looking thoughtfully between his elevated feet at the grocery stove, "to look deeper into some subjects than most people do. I've breathed gasoline smoke talking to street crowds in nearly every town in the United States. I've held 'em spellbound with music, oratory, sleight of hand, and prevarications, while I've sold 'em jewelry, medicine, soap, hair tonic, and junk of other nominations. And during my travels, as a matter of recreation and expiation, I've taken cognisance some of women. It takes a man a lifetime to find out about one particular woman; but if he puts in, say, ten years, industrious and curious, he can acquire the general rudiments of the sex. One lesson I picked up was when I was working the West with a line of Brazilian diamonds and a patent fire kindler just after my trip from Savannah down through the cotton belt with Dalby's Anti-explosive Lamp Oil Powder. 'Twas when the Oklahoma country was in first bloom. Guthrie was rising in the middle of it like a lump of self-raising dough. It was a boom town of the regular kind—you stood in line to get a chance to wash your face; if you ate over ten minutes you had a lodging bill added on; if you slept on a plank at night they charged it to you as board the next morning.

"By nature and doctrines I am addicted to the habit of discovering choice places wherein to feed. So I looked around and found a proposition that exactly cut the mustard. I found a restaurant tent just opened up by an outfit that had drifted in on the tail of the boom. They had knocked together a box house, where they lived and did the cooking, and served the meals in a tent pitched against the side. That tent was joyful with placards on it calculated to redeem the world-worn pilgrim from the sinfulness of boarding houses and pick-me-up hotels. 'Try Mother's Home-Made Biscuits,' 'What's the Matter with Our Apple Dumplings and Hard Sauce?' 'Hot Cakes and Maple Syrup Like You Ate When a Boy,' 'Our Fried Chicken Never Was Heard to Crow'—there was literature doomed to please the digestions of man! I said to myself that mother's wandering boy should munch there that night. And so it came to pass. And there is where I contracted my case of Mame Dugan.

"Old Man Dugan was six feet by one of Indiana loafer, and he spent his time sitting on his shoulder blades in a rocking-chair in the shanty memorializing the great corn-crop failure of '96. Ma Dugan did the cooking, and Mame waited on the table.

"As soon as I saw Mame I knew there was a mistake in the census reports. There wasn't but one girl in the United States. When you come to specifications it isn't easy. She was about the size of an angel, and she had eyes, and ways about her. When you come to the kind of a girl she was, you'll find a belt of 'em reaching from the Brooklyn Bridge west as far as the court-house in Council Bluffs, Ia. They earn their own living in stores, restaurants, factories, and offices. They're chummy and honest and free and tender and sassy, and they look life straight in the eye. They've met man face to face, and discovered that he's a poor creature. They've dropped to it that the reports in the Seaside Library about his being a fairy prince lack confirmation.

"Mame was that sort. She was full of life and fun, and breezy; she passed the repartee with the boarders quick as a wink; you'd have smothered laughing. I am disinclined to make excavations into the insides of a personal affection. I am glued to the theory that the diversions and discrepancies of the indisposition known as love should be as private a sentiment as a toothbrush. 'Tis my opinion that the biographies of the heart should be confined with the historical romances of the liver to the advertising pages of the magazines. So, you'll excuse the lack of an itemised bill of my feelings toward Mame.

"Pretty soon I got a regular habit of dropping into the tent to eat at irregular times when there wasn't so many around. Mame would sail in with a smile, in a black dress and white apron, and say: 'Hello, Jeff—why don't you come at meal-time? Want to see how much trouble you can be, of course. Friedchickenbeefsteakporkchopshamandeggspotpie'—and so on. She called me Jeff, but there was no significations attached. Designations was all she meant. The front names of any of us she used as they came to hand. I'd eat about two meals before I left, and string 'em out like a society spread where they changed plates and wives, and josh one another festively between bites. Mame stood for it, pleasant, for it wasn't up to her to take any canvas off the tent by declining dollars just because they were whipped in after meal times.

"It wasn't long until there was another fellow named Ed Collier got the between-meals affliction, and him and me put in bridges between breakfast and dinner, and dinner and supper, that made a three-ringed circus of that tent, and Mame's turn as waiter a continuous performance. That Collier man was saturated with designs and contrivings. He was in well-boring or insurance or claim-jumping, or something—I've forgotten which. He was a man well lubricated with gentility, and his words were such as recommended you to his point of view. So, Collier and me infested the grub tent with care and activity. Mame was level full of impartiality. 'Twas like a casino hand the way she dealt out her favors—one to Collier and one to me and one to the board, and not a card up her sleeve.

"Me and Collier naturally got acquainted, and gravitated together some on the outside. Divested of his stratagems, he seemed to be a pleasant chap, full of an amiable sort of hostility.

"'I notice you have an affinity for grubbing in the banquet hall after the guests have fled,' says I to him one day, to draw his conclusions.

"'Well, yes,' says Collier, reflecting; 'the tumult of a crowded board seems to harass my sensitive nerves.'

"'It exasperates mine some, too,' says I. 'Nice little girl, don't you think?'

"'I see,' says Collier, laughing. 'Well, now that you mention it, I have noticed that she doesn't seem to displease the optic nerve.'

"'She's a joy to mine,' says I, 'and I'm going after her. Notice is hereby served.'

"'I'll be as candid as you,' admits Collier, 'and if the drug stores don't run out of pepsin I'll give you a run for your money that'll leave you a dyspeptic at the wind-up.'

"So Collier and me begins the race; the grub department lays in new supplies; Mame waits on us, jolly and kind and agreeable, and it looks like an even break, with Cupid and the cook working overtime in Dugan's restaurant.

" 'Twas one night in September when I got Mame to take

a walk after supper when the things were all cleared away. We strolled out a distance and sat on a pile of lumber at the edge of town. Such opportunities was seldom, so I spoke my piece, explaining how the Brazilian diamonds and the fire kindler were laying up sufficient treasure to guarantee the happiness of two, and that both of 'em together couldn't equal the light from somebody's eyes, and that the name of Dugan should be changed to Peters, or reasons why not would be in order.

"Mame didn't say anything right away. Directly she gave a kind of shudder, and I began to learn something.

"'Jeff,' she says, 'I'm sorry you spoke. I like you as well as any of them, but there isn't a man in the world I'd ever marry, and there never will be. Do you know what a man is in my eye? He's a tomb. He's a sarcophagus for the interment of Beafsteakpork-chopsliver'nbaconhamandeggs. He's that and nothing more. For two years I've watched men eat, eat, eat, until they represent nothing on earth to me but ruminant bipeds. They're absolutely nothing but something that goes in front of a knife and fork and plate at the table. They're fixed that way in my mind and memory. I've tried to overcome it, but I can't. I've heard girls rave about their sweethearts, but I never could understand it. A man and a sausage grinder and a pantry awake in me exactly the same sentiments. I went to a matinée once to see an actor the girls were crazy about. I got interested enough to wonder whether he liked his steak rare, medium, or well done, and his eggs over or straight up. That was all. No, Jeff; I'll marry no man and see him sit at the breakfast table and eat, and come back to dinner and eat, and happen in again at supper to eat, eat, eat.'

"'But, Mame,' says I, 'it'll wear off. You've had too much of it. You'll marry some time, of course. Men don't eat always.'

"'As far as my observation goes, they do. No, I'll tell you what I'm going to do.' Mame turns, sudden, to animation and bright

39

eyes. 'There's a girl named Susie Foster in Terre Haute, a chum of mine. She waits in the railroad eating house there. I worked two years in a restaurant in that town. Susie has it worse than I do, because the men who eat at railroad stations gobble. They try to flirt and gobble at the same time. Whew! Susie and I have it all planned out. We're saving our money, and when we get enough we're going to buy a little cottage and five acres we know of, and live together, and grow violets for the Eastern market. A man better not bring his appetite within a mile of that ranch.'

"'Don't girls ever—' I commenced, but Mame heads me off, sharp.

"'No, they don't. They nibble a little bit sometimes; that's all.'

"'I thought the confect—'

"'For goodness' sake, change the subject,' says Mame.

"As I said before, that experience puts me wise that the feminine arrangement ever struggles after deceptions and illusions. Take England—beef made her; wieners elevated Germany; Uncle Sam owes his greatness to fried chicken and pie, but the young ladies of the Shetalkyou schools, they'll never believe it. Shakespeare, they allow, and Rubinstein, and the Rough Riders is what did the trick.

" 'Twas a situation calculated to disturb. I couldn't bear to give up Mame; and yet it pained me to think of abandoning the practice of eating. I had acquired the habit too early. For twenty-seven years I had been blindly rushing upon my fate, yielding to the insidious lures of that deadly monster, food. It was too late. I was a ruminant biped for keeps. It was lobster salad to a doughnut that my life was going to be blighted by it.

"I continued to board at the Dugan tent, hoping that Mame would relent. I had sufficient faith in true love to believe that since it has often outlived the absence of a square meal it might, in time, overcome the presence of one. I went on ministering to my fatal vice, although I felt that each time I shoved a potato into my mouth in Mame's presence I might be burying my fondest hopes.

"I think Collier must have spoken to Mame and got the same answer, for one day he orders a cup of coffee and a cracker, and sits nibbling the corner of it like a girl in the parlor, that's filled up in the kitchen, previous, on cold roast and fried cabbage. I caught on and did the same, and maybe we thought we'd made a hit! The next day we tried it again, and out comes old man Dugan fetching in his hands the fairy viands.

"'Kinder off yer feed, ain't ye, gents?' he asks, fatherly and some sardonic. 'Thought I'd spell Mame a bit, seein' the work was light, and my rheumatiz can stand the strain.'

"So back me and Collier had to drop to the heavy grub again. I noticed about that time that I was seized by a most uncommon and devastating appetite. I ate until Mame must have hated to see me darken the door. Afterward I found out that I had been made the victim of the first dark and irreligious trick played on me by Ed Collier. Him and me had been taking drinks together uptown regular, trying to drown our thirst for food. That man had bribed about ten bartenders to always put a big slug of Appletree's Anaconda Appetite Bitters in every one of my drinks. But the last trick he played me was hardest to forget.

"One day Collier failed to show up at the tent. A man told me he left town that morning. My only rival now was the bill of fare. A few days before he left Collier had presented me with a two-gallon jug of fine whisky which he said a cousin had sent him from Kentucky. I now have reason to believe that it contained Appletree's Anaconda Appetite Bitters almost exclusively. I continued to devour tons of provisions. In Mame's eyes I remained a mere biped, more ruminant than ever.

"About a week after Collier pulled his freight there came a kind of side-show to town, and hoisted a tent near the railroad.

41

I judged it was a sort of fake museum and curiosity business. I called to see Mame one night, and Ma Dugan said that she and Thomas, her younger brother, had gone to the show. That same thing happened for three nights that week. Saturday night I caught her on the way coming back, and got to sit on the steps a while and talk to her. I noticed she looked different. Her eyes were softer, and shiny like. Instead of a Mame Dugan to fly from the voracity of man and raise violets, she seemed to be a Mame more in line as God intended her, approachable, and suited to bask in the light of the Brazilians and the Kindler.

"'You seem to be right smart inveigled,' says I, 'with the Unparalleled Exhibition of the World's Living Curiosities and Wonders.'

"'It's a change,' says Mame.

"'You'll need another,' says I, 'if you keep on going every night.'

"'Don't be cross, Jeff,' says she; 'it takes my mind off business.'

"'Don't the curiosities eat?' I ask.

"'Not all of them. Some of them are wax.'

"'Look out, then, that you don't get stuck,' says I, kind of flip and foolish.

"Mame blushed. I didn't know what to think about her. My hopes raised some that perhaps my attentions had palliated man's awful crime of visibly introducing nourishment into his system. She talked some about the stars, referring to them with respect and politeness, and I driveled a quantity about united hearts, homes made bright by true affection, and the Kindler. Mame listened without scorn, and I says to myself, 'Jeff, old man, you're removing the hoodoo that has clung to the consumer of victuals; you're setting your heel upon the serpent that lurks in the gravy bowl.'

"Monday night I drop around. Mame is at the Unparalleled Exhibition with Thomas.

"'Now, may the curse of the forty-one seven-sided sea cooks,' says I, 'and the bad luck of the nine impenitent grasshoppers rest upon this self-same sideshow at once and forever more. Amen. I'll go to see it myself to-morrow night and investigate its baleful charm. Shall man that was made to inherit the earth be bereft of his sweetheart first by a knife and fork and then by a ten-cent circus?'

"The next night before starting out for the exhibition tent I inquire and find out that Mame is not at home. She is not at the circus with Thomas this time, for Thomas waylays me in the grass outside of the grub tent with a scheme of his own before I had time to eat supper.

"'What'll you give me, Jeff,' says he, 'if I tell you something?'

"'The value of it, son,' I says.

"'Sis is stuck on a freak,' says Thomas, 'one of the side-show freaks. I don't like him. She does. I overheard 'em talking. Thought maybe you'd like to know. Say, Jeff, does it put you wise two dollars' worth? There's a target rifle up town that—'

"I frisked my pockets and commenced to dribble a stream of halves and quarters into Thomas's hat. The information was of the pile-driver system of news, and it telescoped my intellects for a while. While I was leaking small change and smiling foolish on the outside, and suffering disturbances internally, I was saying, idiotically and pleasantly:

"'Thank you, Thomas—thank you—er—a freak, you said, Thomas. Now, could you make out the monstrosity's entitlements a little clearer, if you please, Thomas?'

"'This is the fellow,' says Thomas, pulling out a yellow handbill from his pocket and shoving it under my nose. 'He's the Champion Faster of the Universe. I guess that's why Sis got soft on him. He don't eat nothing. He's going to fast forty-nine days. This is the sixth. That's him.'

"I looked at the name Thomas pointed out—'Professor Eduardo Collieri.' 'Ah!' says I, in admiration, 'that's not so bad, Ed Collier. I give you credit for the trick. But I don't give you the girl until she's Mrs. Freak.'

"I hit the sod in the direction of the show. I came up to the rear of the tent, and, as I did so, a man wiggled out like a snake from under the bottom of the canvas, scrambled to his feet, and ran into me like a locoed bronco. I gathered him by the neck and investigated him by the light of the stars. It is Professor Eduardo Collieri, in human habiliments, with a desperate look in one eye and impatience in the other.

"'Hello, Curiosity,' says I. 'Get still a minute and let's have a look at your freakship. How do you like being the willopus-wallopus or the bim-bam from Borneo, or whatever name you are denounced by in the side-show business?'

"'Jeff Peters,' says Collier, in a weak voice. 'Turn me loose, or I'll slug you one. I'm in the extremest kind of a large hurry. Hands off!'

"'Tut, tut, Eddie,' I answers, holding him hard; 'let an old friend gaze on the exhibition of your curiousness. It's an eminent graft you fell onto, my son. But don't speak of assaults and battery, because you're not fit. The best you've got is a lot of nerve and a mighty empty stomach.' And so it was. The man was as weak as a vegetarian cat.

"'I'd argue this case with you, Jeff,' says he, regretful in his style, 'for an unlimited number of rounds if I had half an hour to train in and a slab of beefsteak two feet square to train with. Curse the man, I say, that invented the art of going foodless. May his soul in eternity be chained up within two feet of a bottomless pit of red-hot hash. I'm abandoning the conflict, Jeff; I'm deserting to the enemy. You'll find Miss Dugan inside contemplating the only living mummy and the informed hog. She's a fine girl, Jeff.

44

I'd have beat you out if I could have kept up the grubless habit a little while longer. You'll have to admit that the fasting dodge was aces-up for a while. I figured it out that way. But say, Jeff, it's said that love makes the world go around. Let me tell you, the announcement lacks verification. It's the wind from the dinner horn that does it. I love that Mame Dugan. I've gone six days without food in order to coincide with her sentiments. Only one bite did I have. That was when I knocked the tattooed man down with a war club and got a sandwich he was gobbling. The manager fined me all my salary; but salary wasn't what I was after. 'Twas that girl. I'd give my life for her, but I'd endanger my immortal soul for a beef stew. Hunger is a horrible thing, Jeff. Love and business and family and religion and art and patriotism are nothing but shadows of words when a man's starving!'

"In such language Ed Collier discoursed to me, pathetic. I gathered the diagnosis that his affections and his digestions had been implicated in a scramble and the commissary had won out. I never disliked Ed Collier. I searched my internal admonitions of suitable etiquette to see if I could find a remark of a consoling nature, but there was none convenient.

"'I'd be glad, now,' says Ed, 'if you'll let me go. I've been hard hit, but I'll hit the ration supply harder. I'm going to clean out every restaurant in town. I'm going to wade waist deep in sirloins and swim in ham and eggs. It's an awful thing, Jeff Peters, for a man to come to this pass—to give up his girl for something to eat—it's worse than that man Esau, that swapped his copyright for a partridge—but then, hunger's a fierce thing. You'll excuse me, now, Jeff, for I smell a pervasion of ham frying in the distance, and my legs are crying out to stampede in that direction.'

"'A hearty meal to you, Ed Collier,' I says to him, 'and no hard feelings. For myself, I am projected to be an unseldom eater, and I have condolence for your predicaments.'

"There was a sudden big whiff of frying ham smell on the breeze; and the Champion Faster gives a snort and gallops off in the dark toward fodder.

"I wish some of the cultured outfit that are always advertising the extenuating circumstances of love and romance had been there to see. There was Ed Collier, a fine man full of contrivances and flirtations, abandoning the girl of his heart and ripping out into the contiguous territory in the pursuit of sordid grub. 'Twas a rebuke to the poets and a slap at the best-paying element of fiction. An empty stomach is a sure antidote to an overfull heart.

"I was naturally anxious to know how far Mame was infatuated with Collier and his stratagems. I went inside the Unparalleled Exhibition, and there she was. She looked surprised to see me, but unguilty.

"'It's an elegant evening outside,' says I. 'The coolness is quite nice and gratifying, and the stars are lined out, first class, up where they belong. Wouldn't you shake these by-products of the animal kingdom long enough to take a walk with a common human who never was on a programme in his life?'

"Mame gave a sort of sly glance around, and I knew what that meant.

"'Oh,' says I, 'I hate to tell you; but the curiosity that lives on wind has flew the coop. He just crawled out under the tent. By this time he has amalgamated himself with half the delicatessen truck in town.'

"'You mean Ed Collier?' says Mame.

"'I do,' I answers; 'and a pity it is that he has gone back to crime again. I met him outside the tent, and he exposed his intentions of devastating the food crop of the world. 'Tis enormously sad when one's ideal descends from his pedestal to make a seventeen-year locust of himself.'

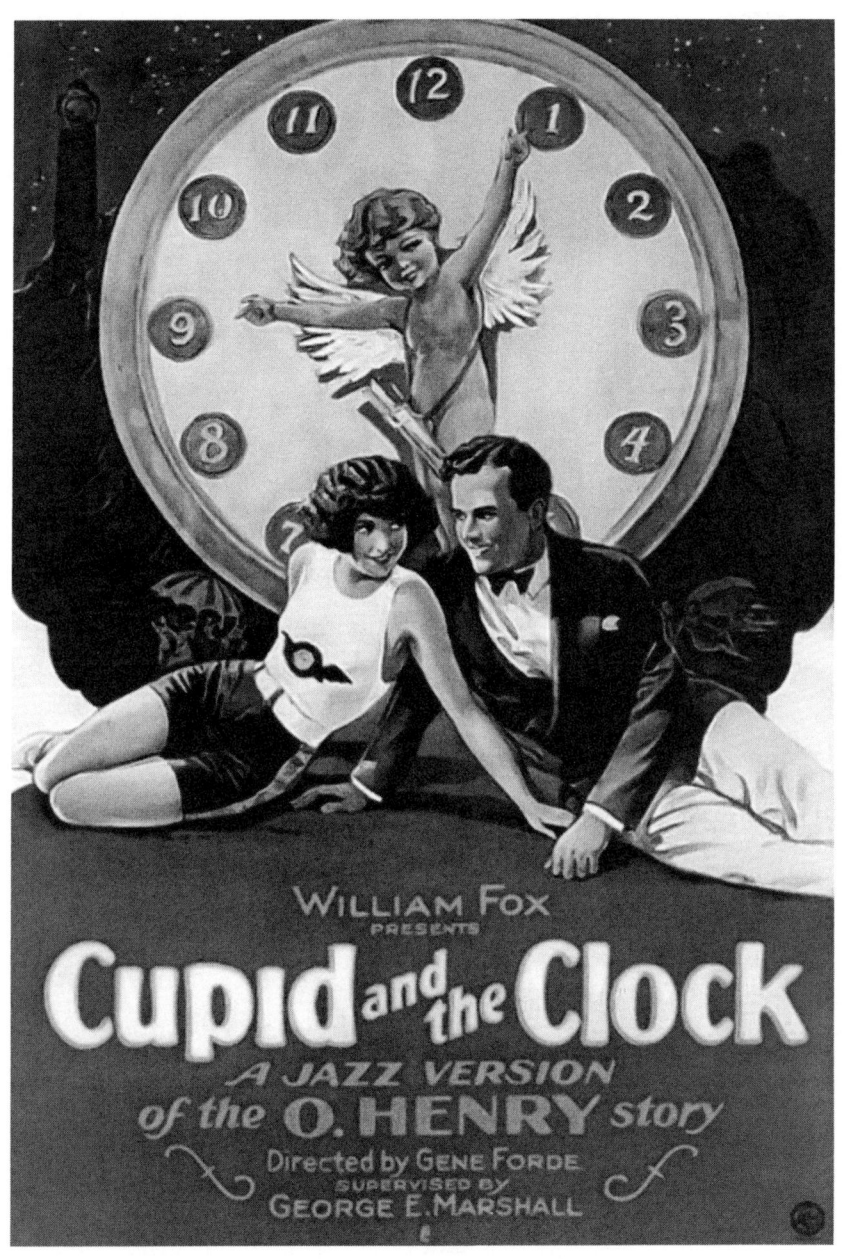

Cupid and the Clock (1927)
(From the O. Henry story "The Caliph, Cupid and the Clock")

Courtesy of Internet Movie Data Base (IMDb)

"Mame looked me straight in the eye until she had cork-screwed my reflections.

"'Jeff,' says she, 'it isn't quite like you to talk that way. I don't care to hear Ed Collier ridiculed. A man may do ridiculous things, but they don't look ridiculous to the girl he does 'em for. That was one man in a hundred. He stopped eating just to please me. I'd be hard-hearted and ungrateful if I didn't feel kindly toward him. Could you do what he did?'

"'I know,' says I, seeing the point, 'I'm condemned. I can't help it. The brand of the consumer is upon my brow. Mrs. Eve settled that business for me when she made the dicker with the snake. I fell from the fire into the frying-pan. I guess I'm the Champion Feaster of the Universe.' I spoke humble, and Mame mollified herself a little.

"'Ed Collier and I are good friends,' she said, 'the same as me and you. I gave him the same answer I did you—no marrying for me. I liked to be with Ed and talk with him.

There was something mighty pleasant to me in the thought that here was a man who never used a knife and fork, and all for my sake.'

"'Wasn't you in love with him?' I asks, all injudicious. 'Wasn't there a deal on for you to become Mrs. Curiosity?'

"'All of us do it sometimes. All of us get jostled out of the line of profitable talk now and then. Mame put on that little lemon *glacé* smile that runs between ice and sugar, and says, much too pleasant: 'You're short on credentials for asking that question, Mr. Peters. Suppose you do a forty-nine day fast, just to give you ground to stand on, and then maybe I'll answer it.'

"So, even after Collier was kidnapped out of the way by the revolt of his appetite, my own prospects with Mame didn't seem to be improved. And then business played out in Guthrie.

"I had stayed too long there. The Brazilians I had sold commenced to show signs of wear, and the Kindler refused to light up right frequent on wet mornings. There is always a time, in my business, when the star of success says, 'Move on to the next town.' I was travelling by wagon at that time so as not to miss any of the small towns; so I hitched up a few days later and went down to tell Mame good-bye. I wasn't abandoning the game; I intended running over to Oklahoma City and work it for a week or two. Then I was coming back to institute fresh proceedings against Mame.

"What do I find at the Dugans' but Mame all conspicuous in a blue travelling dress, with her little trunk at the door. It seems that sister Lottie Bell, who is a typewriter in Terre Haute, is going to be married next Thursday, and Mame is off for a week's visit to be an accomplice at the ceremony. Mame is waiting for a freight wagon that is going to take her to Oklahoma, but I condemns the freight wagon with promptness and scorn, and offers to deliver the goods myself. Ma Dugan sees no reason why not, as Mr. Freighter wants pay for the job; so, thirty minutes later Mame and I pull out in my light spring wagon with white canvas cover, and head due south.

"That morning was of a praiseworthy sort. The breeze was lively, and smelled excellent of flowers and grass, and the little cottontail rabbits entertained themselves with skylarking across the road. My two Kentucky bays went for the horizon until it come sailing in so fast you wanted to dodge it like a clothesline. Mame was full of talk and rattled on like a kid about her old home and her school pranks and the things she liked and the hateful ways of those Johnson girls just across the street, 'way up in Indiana. Not a word was said about Ed Collier or victuals or such solemn subjects. About noon Mame looks and finds that the lunch she had put up in a basket had been left behind. I could have managed quite a collation, but Mame didn't seem to be grieving over nothing to eat, so I made no lamentations. It was a sore subject with me, and I ruled provender in all its branches out of my conversation.

"I am minded to touch light on explanations how I came to lose the way. The road was dim and well grown with grass; and there was Mame by my side confiscating my intellects and attention. The excuses are good or they are not, as they may appear to you. But I lost it, and at dusk that afternoon, when we should have been in Oklahoma City, we were seesawing along the edge of nowhere in some undiscovered river bottom, and the rain was falling in large, wet bunches. Down there in the swamps we saw a little log house on a small knoll of high ground. The bottom grass and the chaparral and the lonesome timber crowded all around it. It seemed to be a melancholy little house, and you felt sorry for it. 'Twas that house for the night, the way I reasoned it. I explained to Mame, and she leaves it to me to decide. She doesn't become galvanic and prosecuting, as most women would, but she says it's all right; she knows I didn't mean to do it.

"We found the house was deserted. It had two empty rooms. There was a little shed in the yard where beasts had once been kept. In a loft of it was a lot of old hay. I put my horses in there and gave them some of it, for which they looked at me sorrowful, expecting apologies. The rest of the hay I carried into the house by armfuls, with a view to accommodations. I also brought in the patent kindler and the Brazilians, neither of which are guaranteed against the action of water.

"Mame and I sat on the wagon seats on the floor, and I lit a lot of the kindler on the hearth, for the night was chilly. If I was any judge, that girl enjoyed it. It was a change for her. It gave her a different point of view. She laughed and talked, and the kindler made a dim light compared to her eyes. I had a pocketful of cigars, and as far as I was concerned there had never been any fall of man. We were at the same old stand in the Garden of Eden. Out there somewhere in the rain and the dark was the river of Zion, and the angel with the flaming sword had not yet put up the keep-off-the-grass sign. I opened up a gross or two of the Brazilians and made Mame put them on—rings, brooches, necklaces, eardrops, bracelets, girdles, and lockets. She flashed and sparkled like a million-dollar princess until she had pink spots in her cheeks and almost cried for a looking-glass.

"When it got late I made a fine bunk on the floor for Mame with the hay and my lap robes and blankets out of the wagon, and persuaded her to lie down. I sat in the other room burning tobacco and listening to the pouring rain and meditating on the many vicissitudes that came to a man during the seventy years or so immediately preceding his funeral.

"I must have dozed a little while before morning, for my eyes were shut, and when I opened them it was daylight, and there stood Mame with her hair all done up neat and correct, and her eyes bright with admiration of existence.

"'Gee whiz, Jeff!' she exclaims, 'but I'm hungry. I could eat a—'

"I looked up and caught her eye. Her smile went back in and she gave me a cold look of suspicion. Then I laughed, and laid down on the floor to laugh easier. It seemed funny to me. By nature and geniality I am a hearty laugher, and I went the limit. When I came to, Mame was sitting with her back to me, all contaminated with dignity.

"'Don't be angry, Mame,' I says, 'for I couldn't help it. It's the funny way you've done up your hair. If you could only see it!'

"'You needn't tell stories, sir,' said Mame, cool and advised. 'My hair is all right. I know what you were laughing about. Why, Jeff, look outside,' she winds up, peeping through a chink between the logs. I opened the little wooden window and looked out. The entire river bottom was flooded, and the knob of land on which the house stood was an island in the middle of a rushing stream of yellow water a hundred yards wide. And it was still raining hard. All we could do was to stay there till the doves brought in the olive branch.

"I am bound to admit that conversations and amusements languished during that day. I was aware that Mame was getting a too prolonged one-sided view of things again, but I had no way to change it. Personally, I was wrapped up in the desire to eat. I had hallucinations of hash and visions of ham, and I kept saying to myself all the time, 'What'll you have to eat, Jeff?—what'll you order now, old man, when the waiter comes?' I picks out to myself all sorts of favorites from the bill of fare, and imagines them coming. I guess it's that way with all hungry men. They can't get their cogitations trained on anything but something to eat. It shows that the little table with the broken-legged caster and the imitation Worcester sauce and the napkin covering up the coffee stains is the paramount issue, after all, instead of the question of immortality or peace between nations.

"I sat there, musing along, arguing with myself quite heated as to how I'd have my steak—with mushrooms, or à la créole. Mame was on the other seat, pensive, her head leaning on her hand. 'Let the potatoes come home-fried,' I states in my mind, 'and brown the hash in the pan, with nine poached eggs on the side.' I felt, careful, in my own pockets to see if I could find a peanut or a grain or two of popcorn.

"Night came on again with the river still rising and the rain still falling. I looked at Mame and I noticed that desperate look on her face that a girl always wears when she passes an ice-cream lair. I knew that poor girl was hungry—maybe for the first time in her life. There was that anxious look in her eye that a woman has only when she has missed a meal or feels her skirt coming unfastened in the back.

"It was about eleven o'clock or so on the second night when we sat, gloomy, in our shipwrecked cabin. I kept jerking my mind away from the subject of food, but it kept flopping back again before I could fasten it. I thought of everything good to eat I had ever heard of. I went away back to my kidhood and remembered the hot biscuit sopped in sorghum and bacon gravy with partiality and respect. Then I trailed along up the years, pausing at green apples and salt, flapjacks and maple, lye hominy, fried chicken Old Virginia style, corn on the cob, spareribs and sweet potato pie, and wound up with Georgia Brunswick stew, which is the top notch of good things to eat, because it comprises 'em all.

"They say a drowning man sees a panorama of his whole life pass before him. Well, when a man's starving he sees the ghost of every meal he ever ate set out before him, and he invents new dishes that would make the fortune of a chef. If somebody would collect the last words of men who starved to death, they'd have to sift 'em mighty fine to discover the sentiment, but they'd compile into a cook book that would sell into the millions.

"I guess I must have had my conscience pretty well inflicted with culinary meditations, for, without intending to do so, I says, out loud, to the imaginary waiter, 'Cut it thick and have it rare, with the French fried, and six, soft-scrambled, on toast.'

"Mame turned her head quick as a wing. Her eyes were sparkling and she smiled sudden.

"'Medium for me,' she rattles out, 'with the Juliennes, and three, straight up. Draw one, and brown the wheats, double order to come. Oh, Jeff, wouldn't it be glorious! And then I'd like to have a half fry, and a little chicken curried with rice, and a cup custard with ice cream, and—'

"'Go easy,' I interrupts; 'where's the chicken liver pie, and the kidney sauté on toast, and the roast lamb, and—'

53

"'Oh,' cuts in Mame, all excited, 'with mint sauce, and the turkey salad, and stuffed olives, and raspberry tarts, and—'

"'Keep it going,' says I. 'Hurry up with the fried squash, and the hot corn pone with sweet milk, and don't forget the apple dumpling with hard sauce, and the cross-barred dew-berry pie—'

"Yes, for ten minutes we kept up that kind of restaurant repartee. We ranges up and down and backward and forward over the main trunk lines and the branches of the victual subject, and Mame leads the game, for she is apprised in the ramifications of grub, and the dishes she nominates aggravates my yearnings. It seems that there is a feeling that Mame will line up friendly again with food. It seems that she looks upon the obnoxious science of eating with less contempt than before.

"The next morning we find that the flood has subsided. I geared up the bays, and we splashed out through the mud, some precarious, until we found the road again. We were only a few miles wrong, and in two hours we were in Oklahoma City. The first thing we saw was a big restaurant sign, and we piled into there in a hurry. Here I finds myself sitting with Mame at table, with knives and forks and plates between us, and she not scornful, but smiling with starvation and sweetness.

" 'Twas a new restaurant and well stocked. I designated a list of quotations from the bill of fare that made the waiter look out toward the wagon to see how many more might be coming.

"There we were, and there was the order being served. 'Twas a banquet for a dozen, but we felt like a dozen. I looked across the table at Mame and smiled, for I had recollections. Mame was looking at the table like a boy looks at his first stem-winder. Then she looked at me, straight in the face, and two big tears came in her eyes. The waiter was gone after more grub.

"'Jeff,' she says, soft like, 'I've been a foolish girl. I've looked at things from the wrong side. I never felt this way before. Men get hungry every day like this, don't they? They're big and strong, and they do the hard work of the world, and they don't eat just to spite silly waiter girls in restaurants, do they, Jeff? You said once—that is, you asked me—you wanted me to—well, Jeff, if you still care—I'd be glad and willing to have you always sitting across the table from me. Now give me something to eat, quick, please.'

"So, as I've said, a woman needs to change her point of view now and then. They get tired of the same old sights—the same old dinner table, washtub, and sewing machine. Give 'em a touch of the various—a little travel and a little rest, a little tomfoolery along with the tragedies of keeping house, a little petting after the blowing-up, a little upsetting and a little jostling around—and everybody in the game will have chips added to their stack by the play."

Presidents' Day

Third Monday in February

Mt. Rushmore

(From left to right)

1st President George Washington (February 22, 1732 – December 14, 1799), 3rd President Thomas Jefferson (April 13, 1743 – July 4, 1826), 26th President Theodore Roosevelt Jr. (October 27, 1858 – January 6, 1919) and the 16th President Abraham Lincoln (February 12, 1809 – April 15, 1865). Photographed by Thomas Newland June 24, 2021.

Courtesy of Pexels

A Philistine in Bohemia

George Washington, with his right arm upraised, sits his iron horse at the lower corner of Union Square, forever signaling the Broadway cars to stop as they round the curve into Fourteenth Street. But the cars buzz on, heedless, as they do at the beck of a private citizen, and the great General must feel, unless his nerves are iron, that rapid transit gloria mundi.

Should the General raise his left hand as he has raised his right it would point to a quarter of the city that forms a haven for the oppressed and suppressed of foreign lands. In the cause of national or personal freedom they have found a refuge here, and the patriot who made it for them sits his steed, overlooking their district, while he listens through his left ear to vaudeville that caricatures the posterity of his protégés. Italy, Poland, the former Spanish possessions and the polyglot tribes of Austria-Hungary have spilled here a thick lather of their effervescent sons. In the eccentric cafés and lodging-houses of the vicinity they hover over their native wines and political secrets. The colony changes with much frequency. Faces disappear from the haunts to be replaced by others. Whither do these uneasy birds flit? For half of the answer observe carefully the suave foreign air and foreign courtesy of the next waiter who serves your table d'hôte. For the other half, perhaps if the barber shops had tongues (and who will dispute it?) they could tell their share.

Titles are as plentiful as finger rings among these transitory exiles. For lack of proper exploitation a stock of title goods large enough to supply the trade of upper Fifth Avenue is here condemned to a mere pushcart traffic. The new-world landlords who entertain these offshoots of nobility are not dazzled by coronets and crests. They have doughnuts to sell instead of daughters. With them it is a serious matter of trading in flour and sugar instead of pearl powder and bonbons.

These assertions are deemed fitting as an introduction to the tale, which is of plebeians and contains no one with even the ghost of a title.

Katy Dempsey's mother kept a furnished-room house in this oasis of the aliens. The business was not profitable. If the two scraped together enough to meet the landlord's agent on rent day and negotiate for the ingredients of a daily Irish stew they called it success. Often the stew lacked both meat and potatoes. Sometimes it became as bad as consommé with music.

In this moldy old house Katy waxed plump and pert and wholesome and as beautiful and freckled as a tiger lily. She was the good fairy who was guilty of placing the damp clean towels and cracked pitchers of freshly laundered Croton in the lodgers' rooms.

You are informed (by virtue of the privileges of astronomical discovery) that the star lodger's name was Mr. Brunelli. His wearing a yellow tie and paying his rent promptly distinguished him from the other lodgers. His raiment was splendid, his complexion olive, his mustache fierce, his manners a prince's, his rings and pins as magnificent as those of a traveling dentist.

He had breakfast served in his room, and he ate it in a red dressing gown with green tassels. He left the house at noon and returned at midnight. Those were mysterious hours, but there was nothing mysterious about Mrs. Dempsey's lodgers except the things that were not mysterious. One of Mr. Kipling's poems is addressed to "Ye who hold the unwritten clue to all save all unwritten things." The same "readers" are invited to tackle the foregoing assertion.

Mr. Brunelli, being impressionable and a Latin, fell to conjugating the verb "amare," with Katy in the objective case, though not because of antipathy. She talked it over with her mother.

"Sure, I like him," said Katy. "He's more politeness than twinty candidates for Alderman, and lie makes me feel like a queen whin he walks at me side. But what is he, I dinno? I've me suspicions. The marnin'll coom whin he'll throt out the picture av his baronial halls and ax to have the week's rint hung up in the ice chist along wid all the rist of 'em."

"'Tis thrue," admitted Mrs. Dempsey, "that he seems to be a sort iv Italian, and too coolchured in his spache for a rale gentleman. But ye may be misjudgin' him. Ye should niver suspect any wan of bein' of noble descint that pays cash and pathronizes the laundry rig'lar."

"He's the same thricks of spakin' and blarneyin' wid his hands," sighed Katy, "as the Frinch nobleman at Mrs. Toole's that ran away wid Mr. Toole's Sunday pants and left the photograph of the Bastille, his grandfather's chat-taw, as security for tin weeks' rint."

Mr. Brunelli continued his calorific wooing. Katy continued to hesitate. One day he asked her out to dine and she felt that a dénouement was in the air. While they are on their way, with Katy in her best muslin, you must take as an entr'acte a brief peep at New York's Bohemia.

'Tonio's restaurant is in Bohemia. The very location of it is secret. If you wish to know where it is ask the first person you meet. He will tell you in a whisper. 'Tonio discountenances custom; he keeps his house-front black and forbidding; he gives you a pretty bad dinner; he locks his door at the dining hour; but he knows spaghetti as the boarding-house knows cold veal; and—he has deposited many dollars in a certain Banco di—something with many gold vowels in the name on its windows.

To this restaurant Mr. Brunelli conducted Katy. The house was dark and the shades were lowered; but Mr. Brunelli touched an electric button by the basement door, and they were admitted.

Along a long, dark, narrow hallway they went and then through a shining and spotless kitchen that opened directly upon a back yard.

The walls of houses hemmed three sides of the yard; a high, board fence, surrounded by cats, the other. A wash of clothes was suspended high upon a line stretched from diagonal corners. Those were property clothes, and were never taken in by 'Tonio. They were there that wits with defective pronunciation might make puns in connection with the ragout.

A dozen and a half little tables set upon the bare ground were crowded with Bohemia-hunters, who flocked there because 'Tonio pretended not to want them and pretended to give them a good dinner. There was a sprinkling of real Bohemians present who came for a change because they were tired of the real Bohemia, and a smart shower of the men who originate the bright sayings of Congressmen and the little nephew of the well-known general passenger agent of the Evansville and Terre Haute Railroad Company.

Here is a bon mot that was manufactured at 'Tonio's:

"A dinner at 'Tonio's," said a Bohemian, "always amounts to twice the price that is asked for it."

Let us assume that an accommodating voice inquires:

"How so?"

"The dinner costs you 40 cents; you give 10 cents to the waiter, and it makes you feel like 30 cents."

Most of the diners were confirmed table d'hôters—gastro-nomic adventurers, forever seeking the El Dorado of a good claret, and consistently coming to grief in California.

Mr. Brunelli escorted Katy to a little table embowered with shrubbery in tubs, and asked her to excuse him for a while.

Katy sat, enchanted by a scene so brilliant to her. The grand ladies, in splendid dresses and plumes and sparkling rings; the fine gentlemen who laughed so loudly, the cries of "Garsong!" and "We, monseer," and "Hello, Mame!" that distinguish Bohemia; the lively chatter, the cigarette smoke, the interchange of bright smiles and eye-glances—all this display and magnificence over-powered the daughter of Mrs. Dempsey and held her motionless.

Mr. Brunelli stepped into the yard and seemed to spread his smile and bow over the entire company. And everywhere there was a great clapping of hands and a few cries of "Bravo!" and " 'Tonio! 'Tonio!" whatever those words might mean. Ladies waved their napkins at him, gentlemen almost twisted their necks off, trying to catch his nod.

When the ovation was concluded Mr. Brunelli, with a final bow, stepped nimbly into the kitchen and flung off his coat and waistcoat.

Flaherty, the nimblest "garsong" among the waiters, had been assigned to the special service of Katy. She was a little faint from hunger, for the Irish stew on the Dempsey table had been particularly weak that day. Delicious odors from unknown dishes tantalized her. And Flaherty began to bring to her table course after course of ambrosial food that the gods might have pronounced excellent.

But even in the midst of her Lucullian repast Katy laid down her knife and fork. Her heart sank as lead, and a tear fell upon her filet mignon. Her haunting suspicions of the star lodger arose again, fourfold. Thus courted and admired and smiled

Union Square circa 1870.

George Washington, a bronze equestrian statue by Henry Kirke Brown
(February 24, 1814 – July 10, 1886) was dedicated in 1856.

upon by that fashionable and gracious assembly, what else could Mr. Brunelli be but one of those dazzling titled patricians, glorious of name but shy of rent money, concerning whom experience had made her wise? With a sense of his ineligibility growing within her there was mingled a torturing conviction that his personality was becoming more pleasing to her day by day. And why had he left her to dine alone?

But here he was coming again, now coatless, his snowy shirt-sleeves rolled high above his Jeffriesonian elbows, a white yachting cap perched upon his jetty curls.

" 'Tonio! 'Tonio!" shouted many, and "The spaghetti! The spaghetti!" shouted the rest.

Never at 'Tonio's did a waiter dare to serve a dish of spaghetti until 'Tonio came to test it, to prove the sauce and add the needful dash of seasoning that gave it perfection.

From table to table moved 'Tonio, like a prince in his palace, greeting his guests. White, jewelled hands signalled him from every side.

A glass of wine with this one and that, smiles for all, a jest and repartee for any that might challenge—truly few princes could be so agreeable a host! And what artist could ask for further appreciation of his handiwork? Katy did not know that the proudest consummation of a New Yorker's ambition is to shake hands with a spaghetti chef or to receive a nod from a Broadway head-waiter.

At last the company thinned, leaving but a few couples and quartettes lingering over new wine and old stories. And then came Mr. Brunelli to Katy's secluded table, and drew a chair close to hers.

Katy smiled at him dreamily. She was eating the last spoonful of a raspberry roll with Burgundy sauce.

"You have seen!" said Mr. Brunelli, laying one hand upon his collar bone. "I am Antonio Brunelli! Yes; I am the great 'Tonio! You have not suspect that! I loave you, Katy, and you shall marry with me. Is it not so? Call me 'Antonio,' and say that you will be mine."

Katy's head drooped to the shoulder that was now freed from all suspicion of having received the knightly accolade.

"Oh, Andy," she sighed, "this is great! Sure, I'll marry wid ye. But why didn't ye tell me ye was the cook? I was near turnin' ye down for bein' one of thim foreign counts!"

Mardi Gras

February/March

47 days before Easter

Promotional poster for the Mobile Mardi Gras Carnival,
February 26th & 27th 1900.

Courtesy Library of Congress

Blind Man's Holiday

Alas for the man and for the artist with the shifting point of perspective! Life shall be a confusion of ways to the one; the landscape shall rise up and confound the other. Take the case of Lorison. At one time he appeared to himself to be the feeblest of fools; at another he conceived that he followed ideals so fine that the world was not yet ready to accept them. During one mood he cursed his folly; possessed by the other, he bore himself with a serene grandeur akin to greatness: in neither did he attain the perspective.

Generations before, the name had been "Larsen." His race had bequeathed him its fine-strung, melancholy temperament, its saving balance of thrift and industry.

From his point of perspective he saw himself an outcast from society, forever to be a shady skulker along the ragged edge of respectability; a denizen *des trois-quartz de monde*, that pathetic spheroid lying between the *haut* and the *demi*, whose inhabitants envy each of their neighbors, and are scorned by both. He was self-condemned to this opinion, as he was self-exiled, through it, to this quaint Southern city a thousand miles from his former home. Here he had dwelt for longer than a year, knowing but few, keeping in a subjective world of shadows which was invaded at times by the perplexing bulks of jarring realities. Then he fell in love with a girl whom he met in a cheap restaurant, and his story begins.

The Rue Chartres, in New Orleans, is a street of ghosts. It lies in the quarter where the Frenchman, in his prime, set up his translated pride and glory; where, also, the arrogant don had swaggered, and dreamed of gold and grants and ladies' gloves. Every flagstone has its grooves worn by footsteps going royally to the wooing and the fighting. Every house has a princely heartbreak; each doorway its untold tale of gallant promise and slow decay.

By night the Rue Chartres is now but a murky fissure, from which the groping wayfarer sees, flung against the sky, the tangled filigree of Moorish iron balconies. The old houses of monsieur stand yet, indomitable against the century, but their essence is gone. The street is one of ghosts to whosoever can see them.

A faint heartbeat of the street's ancient glory still survives in a corner occupied by the Café Carabine d'Or. Once men gathered there to plot against kings, and to warn presidents. They do so yet, but they are not the same kind of men. A brass button will scatter these; those would have set their faces against an army. Above the door hangs the sign board, upon which has been depicted a vast animal of unfamiliar species. In the act of firing upon this monster is represented an unobtrusive human levelling an obtrusive gun, once the color of bright gold. Now the legend above the picture is faded beyond conjecture; the gun's relation to the title is a matter of faith; the menaced animal, wearied of the long aim of the hunter, has resolved itself into a shapeless blot.

The place is known as "Antonio's," as the name, white upon the red-lit transparency, and gilt upon the windows, attests. There is a promise in "Antonio"; a justifiable expectancy of savory things in oil and pepper and wine, and perhaps an angel's whisper of garlic. But the rest of the name is "O'Riley." Antonio O'Riley!

The Carabine d'Or is an ignominious ghost of the Rue Chartres. The café where Bienville and Conti dined, where a prince has broken bread, is become a "family ristaurant."

Its customers are working men and women, almost to a unit. Occasionally you will see chorus girls from the cheaper theatres, and men who follow avocations subject to quick vicissitudes; but at Antonio's—name rich in Bohemian promise, but tame in fulfillment—manners debonair and gay are toned down to the "family" standard. Should you light a cigarette, mine host will touch you on the "arrum" and remind you that the proprieties are menaced. "Antonio" entices and beguiles from fiery legend without, but "O'Riley" teaches decorum within.

It was at this restaurant that Lorison first saw the girl. A flashy fellow with a predatory eye had followed her in, and had advanced to take the other chair at the little table where she stopped, but Lorison slipped into the seat before him. Their acquaintance began, and grew, and now for two months they had sat at the same table each evening, not meeting by appointment, but as if by a series of fortuitous and happy accidents. After dining, they would take a walk together in one of the little city parks, or among the panoramic markets where exhibits a continuous vaudeville of sights and sounds. Always at eight o'clock their steps led them to a certain street corner, where she prettily but firmly bade him good night and left him. "I do not live far from here," she frequently said, "and you must let me go the rest of the way alone."

But now Lorison had discovered that he wanted to go the rest of the way with her, or happiness would depart, leaving, him on a very lonely corner of life. And at the same time that he made the discovery, the secret of his banishment from the society of the good laid its finger in his face and told him it must not be.

Man is too thoroughly an egoist not to be also an egotist; if he love, the object shall know it. During a lifetime he may conceal it through stress of expediency and honor, but it shall bubble from his dying lips, though it disrupt a neighborhood. It is known, however, that most men do not wait so long to disclose their passion. In the case of Lorison, his particular ethics positively forbade him to declare his sentiments, but he must needs dally with the subject, and woo by innuendo at least.

On this night, after the usual meal at the Carabine d'Or, he strolled with his companion down the dim old street toward the river.

The Rue Chartres perishes in the old Place d'Armes. The ancient Cabildo, where Spanish justice fell like hail, faces it, and the Cathedral, another provincial ghost, overlooks it. Its center is a little, iron-railed park of flowers and immaculate graveled walks, where citizens take the air of evenings. Pedestalled high above it, the general sits his cavorting steed, with his face turned stonily down the river toward English Turn, whence come no more Britons to bombard his cotton bales.

Often the two sat in this square, but to-night Lorison guided her past the stone-stepped gate, and still riverward. As they walked, he smiled to himself to think that all he knew of her—except that be loved her—was her name, Norah Greenway, and that she lived with her brother. They had talked about everything except themselves. Perhaps her reticence had been caused by his.

They came, at length, upon the levee, and sat upon a great, prostrate beam. The air was pungent with the dust of commerce. The great river slipped yellowly past. Across it Algiers lay, a longitudinous black bulk against a vibrant electric haze sprinkled with exact stars.

The girl was young and of the piquant order. A certain

bright melancholy pervaded her; she possessed an untarnished, pale prettiness doomed to please. Her voice, when she spoke, dwarfed her theme. It was the voice capable of investing little subjects with a large interest. She sat at ease, bestowing her skirts with the little womanly touch, serene as if the begrimed pier were a summer garden. Lorison poked the rotting boards with his cane.

He began by telling her that he was in love with some one to whom he durst not speak of it. "And why not?" she asked, accepting swiftly his fatuous presentation of a third person of straw.

"My place in the world," he answered, "is none to ask a woman to share. I am an outcast from honest people; I am wrongly accused of one crime, and am, I believe, guilty of another."

Thence he plunged into the story of his abdication from society. The story, pruned of his moral philosophy, deserves no more than the slightest touch. It is no new tale, that of the gambler's declension. During one night's sitting he lost, and then had imperiled a certain amount of his employer's money, which, by accident, he carried with him. He continued to lose, to the last wager, and then began to gain, leaving the game winner to a somewhat formidable sum. The same night his employer's safe was robbed. A search was had; the winnings of Lorison were found in his room, their total forming an accusative nearness to the sum purloined. He was taken, tried and, through incomplete evidence, released, smutched with the sinister *devoirs* of a disagreeing jury.

"It is not in the unjust accusation," he said to the girl, "that my burden lies, but in the knowledge that from the moment I staked the first dollar of the firm's money I was a criminal—no matter whether I lost or won. You see why it is impossible for me to speak of love to her."

"It is a sad thing," said Norah, after a little pause, "to think what very good people there are in the world."

"Good?" said Lorison.

"I was thinking of this superior person whom you say you love. She must be a very poor sort of creature."

"I do not understand."

"Nearly," she continued, "as poor a sort of creature as yourself."

"You do not understand," said Lorison, removing his hat and sweeping back his fine, light hair. "Suppose she loved me in return, and were willing to marry me. Think, if you can, what would follow. Never a day would pass but she would be reminded of her sacrifice. I would read a condescension in her smile, a pity even in her affection, that would madden me. No. The thing would stand between us forever. Only equals should mate. I could never ask her to come down upon my lower plane."

An arc light faintly shone upon Lorison's face. An illumination from within also pervaded it. The girl saw the rapt, ascetic look; it was the face either of Sir Galahad or Sir Fool.

"Quite starlike," she said, "is this unapproachable angel. Really too high to be grasped."

"By me, yes."

She faced him suddenly. "My dear friend, would you prefer your star fallen?" Lorison made a wide gesture.

"You push me to the bald fact," he declared; "you are not in sympathy with my argument. But I will answer you so. If I could reach my particular star, to drag it down, I would not do it; but if it were fallen, I would pick it up, and thank Heaven for the privilege."

They were silent for some minutes. Norah shivered, and thrust her hands deep into the pockets of her jacket. Lorison uttered a remorseful exclamation.

"I'm not cold," she said. "I was just thinking. I ought to tell you something. You have selected a strange confidante. But you cannot expect a chance acquaintance, picked up in a doubtful restaurant, to be an angel."

"Norah!" cried Lorison.

"Let me go on. You have told me about yourself. We have been such good friends. I must tell you now what I never wanted you to know. I am—worse than you are. I was on the stage . . . I sang in the chorus . . . I was pretty bad, I guess . . . I stole diamonds from the prima donna . . . they arrested me . . . I gave most of them up, and they let me go . . . I drank wine every night . . . a great deal . . . I was very wicked, but—"

Lorison knelt quickly by her side and took her hands.

"Dear Norah!" he said, exultantly. "It is you, it is you I love! You never guessed it, did you? 'Tis you I meant all the time. Now I can speak. Let me make you forget the past. We have both suffered; let us shut out the world, and live for each other. Norah, do you hear me say I love you?"

"In spite of—"

"Rather say because of it. You have come out of your past noble and good. Your heart is an angel's. Give it to me."

"A little while ago you feared the future too much to even speak."

"But for you; not for myself. Can you love me?"

She cast herself, wildly sobbing, upon his breast.

"Better than life—than truth itself—than everything."

"And my own past," said Lorison, with a note of solicitude—"can you forgive and—"

"I answered you that," she whispered, "when I told you I loved you." She leaned away, and looked thoughtfully at him. "If I had not told you about myself, would you have—would you—"

"No," he interrupted; "I would never have let you know I loved you. I would never have asked you this—Norah, will you be my wife?"

She wept again.

"Oh, believe me; I am good now—I am no longer wicked! I will be the best wife in the world. Don't think I am—bad any more. If you do I shall die, I shall die!"

While he was consoling, her, she brightened up, eager and impetuous. "Will you marry me to-night?" she said. "Will you prove it that way. I have a reason for wishing it to be to-night. Will you?"

Of one of two things was this exceeding frankness the outcome: either of importunate brazenness or of utter innocence. The lover's perspective contained only the one.

"The sooner," said Lorison, "the happier I shall be."

"What is there to do?" she asked. "What do you have to get? Come! You should know."

Her energy stirred the dreamer to action.

"A city directory first," he cried, gayly, "to find where the man lives who gives licenses to happiness. We will go together and rout him out. Cabs, cars, policemen, telephones and ministers shall aid us."

"Father Rogan shall marry us," said the girl, with ardor. "I will take you to him."

———————————————

An hour later the two stood at the open doorway of an immense, gloomy brick building in a narrow and lonely street. The license was tight in Norah's hand.

"Wait here a moment," she said, "till I find Father Rogan."

She plunged into the black hallway, and the lover was left standing, as it were, on one leg, outside. His impatience was not greatly taxed. Gazing curiously into what seemed the hallway to Erebus, he was presently reassured by a stream of light that bisected the darkness, far down the passage. Then he heard her call, and fluttered lampward, like the moth. She beckoned him through a doorway into the room whence emanated the light. The room was bare of nearly everything except books, which had subjugated all its space. Here and there little spots of territory had been reconquered. An elderly, bald man, with a superlatively calm, remote eye, stood by a table with a book in his hand, his finger still marking a page. His dress was somber and appertained to a religious order. His eye denoted an acquaintance with the perspective.

"Father Rogan," said Norah, "this is *he*."

"The two of ye," said Father Rogan, "want to get married?"

They did not deny it. He married them. The ceremony was quickly done. One who could have witnessed it, and felt its scope, might have trembled at the terrible inadequacy of it to rise to the dignity of its endless chain of results.

Afterward the priest spake briefly, as if by rote, of certain other civil and legal addenda that either might or should, at a later time, cap the ceremony. Lorison tendered a fee, which was declined, and before the door closed after the departing couple Father Rogan's book popped open again where his finger marked it.

In the dark hall Norah whirled and clung to her companion, tearful.

"Will you never, never be sorry?"

At last she was reassured.

At the first light they reached upon the street, she asked the time, just as she had each night. Lorison looked at his watch. Half-past eight.

Lorison thought it was from habit that she guided their steps toward the corner where they always parted. But, arrived there, she hesitated, and then released his arm. A drug store stood on the corner; its bright, soft light shone upon them.

"Please leave me here as usual to-night," said Norah, sweetly. "I must—I would rather you would. You will not object? At six to-morrow evening I will meet you at Antonio's. I want to sit with you there once more. And then—I will go where you say." She gave him a bewildering, bright smile, and walked swiftly away.

Surely it needed all the strength of her charm to carry off this astounding behavior. It was no discredit to Lorison's strength of mind that his head began to whirl. Pocketing his hands, he rambled vacuously over to the druggist's windows, and began assiduously to spell over the names of the patent medicines therein displayed.

As soon as he had recovered his wits, he proceeded along the street in an aimless fashion. After drifting for two or three squares, he flowed into a somewhat more pretentious thoroughfare, a way much frequented by him in his solitary ramblings. For here was a row of shops devoted to traffic in goods of the widest range of choice—handiworks of art, skill and fancy, products of nature and labor from every zone.

Here, for a time, he loitered among the conspicuous windows, where was set, emphasized by congested floods of light, the cunningest spoil of the interiors. There were few passers, and of this Lorison was glad. He was not of the world. For a long time he had touched his fellow man only at the gear of a levelled cog-wheel—at right angles, and upon a different axis. He had dropped into a distinctly new orbit. The stroke of ill fortune had acted upon him, in effect, as a blow delivered upon the apex of a certain ingenious toy, the musical top, which, when thus buffeted while spinning, gives forth, with scarcely retarded motion, a complete change of key and chord.

Strolling along the pacific avenue, he experienced singular, supernatural calm, accompanied by an unusual activity of brain. Reflecting upon recent affairs, he assured himself of his happiness in having won for a bride the one he had so greatly desired, yet he wondered mildly at his dearth of active emotion. Her strange behavior in abandoning him without valid excuse on his bridal eve aroused in him only a vague and curious speculation. Again, he found himself contemplating, with complaisant serenity, the incidents of her somewhat lively career. His perspective seemed to have been queerly shifted.

As he stood before a window near a corner, his ears were assailed by a waxing clamor and commotion. He stood close to the window to allow passage to the cause of the hubbub—a procession of human beings, which rounded the corner and headed in his direction. He perceived a salient hue of blue and a glitter of brass about a central figure of dazzling white and silver, and a ragged wake of black, bobbing figures.

Two ponderous policemen were conducting between them a woman dressed as if for the stage, in a short, white, satiny skirt reaching to the knees, pink stockings, and a sort of sleeveless bodice bright with relucent, armor-like scales. Upon her curly, light hair was perched, at a rollicking angle, a shining tin helmet. The costume was to be instantly recognized as one of those amazing conceptions to which competition has harried the inventors of the spectacular ballet. One of the officers bore a long cloak upon his arm, which, doubtless, had been intended to veil the candid attractions of their effulgent prisoner, but, for some reason, it had not been called into use, to the vociferous delight of the tail of the procession.

Compelled by a sudden and vigorous movement of the woman, the parade halted before the window by which Lorison stood. He saw that she was young, and, at the first glance, was deceived by a sophistical prettiness of her face, which waned before a more judicious scrutiny. Her look was bold and reckless, and upon her countenance, where yet the contours of youth survived, were the finger-marks of old age's credentialed courier, Late Hours.

The young woman fixed her unshrinking gaze upon Lorison, and called to him in the voice of the wronged heroine in straits:

"Say! You look like a good fellow; come and put up the bail, won't you? I've done nothing to get pinched for. It's all a mistake. See how they're treating me! You won't be sorry, if you'll help me out of this. Think of your sister or your girl being dragged along the streets this way! I say, come along now, like a good fellow."

It may be that Lorison, in spite of the unconvincing bathos of this appeal, showed a sympathetic face, for one of the officers left the woman's side, and went over to him.

"It's all right, Sir," he said, in a husky, confidential tone; "she's the right party. We took her after the first act at the Green Light Theatre, on a wire from the chief of police of Chicago. It's only a square or two to the station. Her rig's pretty bad, but she refused to change clothes—or, rather," added the officer, with a smile, "to put on some. I thought I'd explain matters to you so you wouldn't think she was being imposed upon."

"What is the charge?" asked Lorison.

"Grand larceny. Diamonds. Her husband is a jeweler in Chicago. She cleaned his show case of the sparklers, and skipped with a comic-opera troupe."

The policeman, perceiving that the interest of the entire group of spectators was centered upon himself and Lorison—their conference being regarded as a possible new complication—was fain to prolong the situation—which reflected his own importance—by a little afterpiece of philosophical comment.

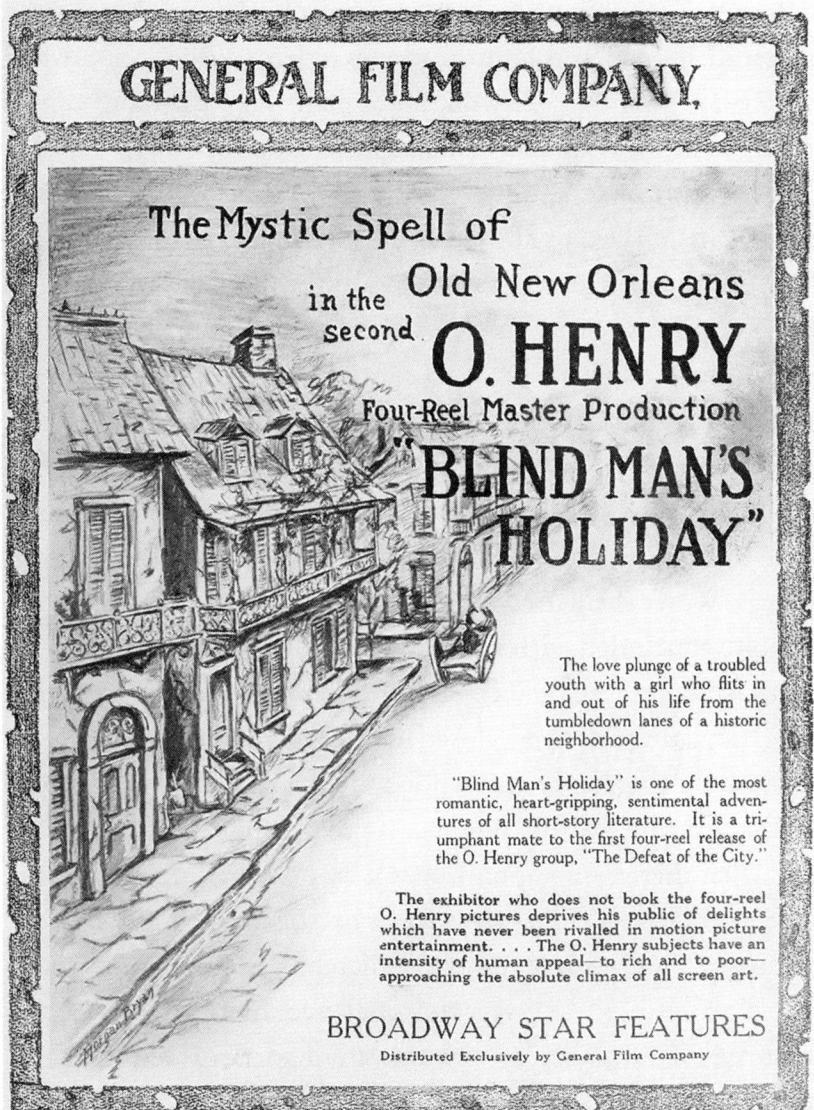

Promotional poster for 1917 silent film four-reeler "Blind Man's Holiday"

"A gentleman like you, Sir," he went on affably, "would never notice it, but it comes in my line to observe what an immense amount of trouble is made by that combination—I mean the stage, diamonds and light-headed women who aren't satisfied with good homes. I tell you, Sir, a man these days and nights wants to know what his women folks are up to."

The policeman smiled a good night, and returned to the side of his charge, who had been intently watching Lorison's face during the conversation, no doubt for some indication of his intention to render succor. Now, at the failure of the sign, and at the movement made to continue the ignominious progress, she abandoned hope, and addressed him thus, pointedly:

"You damn chalk-faced quitter! You was thinking of giving me a hand, but you let the cop talk you out of it the first word. You're a dandy to tie to. Say, if you ever get a girl, she'll have a picnic. Won't she work you to the queen's taste! Oh, my!"

She concluded with a taunting, shrill laugh that rasped Lorison like a saw. The policemen urged her forward; the delighted train of gaping followers closed up the rear; and the captive Amazon, accepting her fate, extended the scope of her maledictions so that none in hearing might seem to be slighted.

Then there came upon Lorison an overwhelming revulsion of his perspective. It may be that he had been ripe for it, that the abnormal condition of mind in which he had for so long existed was already about to revert to its balance; however, it is certain that the events of the last few minutes had furnished the channel, if not the impetus, for the change.

The initial determining influence had been so small a thing as the fact and manner of his having been approached by the officer. That agent had, by the style of his accost, restored the loiterer to his former place in society. In an instant he had been transformed from a somewhat rancid prowler along the fishy side streets of gentility into an honest gentleman, with whom even so lordly a guardian of the peace might agreeably exchange the compliments.

This, then, first broke the spell, and set thrilling in him a resurrected longing for the fellowship of his kind, and the rewards of the virtuous. To what end, he vehemently asked himself, was this fanciful self-accusation, this empty renunciation, this moral squeamishness through which he had been led to abandon what was his heritage in life, and not beyond his deserts? Technically, he was uncondemned; his sole guilty spot was in thought rather than deed, and cognizance of it unshared by others. For what good, moral or sentimental, did he slink, retreating like the hedgehog from his own shadow, to and fro in this musty Bohemia that lacked even the picturesque?

But the thing that struck home and set him raging was the part played by the Amazonian prisoner. To the counterpart of that astounding belligerent—identical at least, in the way of experience—to one, by her own confession, thus far fallen, had he, not three hours since, been united in marriage. How desirable and natural it had seemed to him then, and how monstrous it seemed now! How the words of diamond thief number two yet burned in his ears: "If you ever get a girl, she'll have a picnic." What did that mean but that women instinctively knew him for one they could hoodwink? Still again, there reverberated the policeman's sapient contribution to his agony: "A man these days and nights wants to know what his women folks are up to." Oh, yes, he had been a fool; he had looked at things from the wrong standpoint.

But the wildest note in all the clamor was struck by pain's forefinger, jealousy. Now, at least, he felt that keenest sting—a mounting love unworthily bestowed. Whatever she might be, he loved her; he bore in his own breast his doom. A grating, comic flavor to his predicament struck him suddenly, and he laughed creakingly as he swung down the echoing pavement.

An impetuous desire to act, to battle with his fate, seized him. He stopped upon his heel, and smote his palms together triumphantly. His wife was—where? But there was a tangible link; an outlet more or less navigable, through which his derelict ship of matrimony might yet be safely towed—the priest!

Like all imaginative men with pliable natures, Lorison was, when thoroughly stirred, apt to become tempestuous. With a high and stubborn indignation upon him, be retraced his steps to the intersecting street by which he had come. Down this he hurried to the corner where he had parted with—an astringent grimace tinctured the thought—his wife. Thence still back he harked, following through an unfamiliar district his stimulated recollections of the way they had come from that preposterous wedding. Many times he went abroad, and nosed his way back to the trail, furious.

At last, when he reached the dark, calamitous building in which his madness had culminated, and found the black hallway, he dashed down it, perceiving no light or sound. But he raised his voice, hailing loudly; reckless of everything but that he should find the old mischief-maker with the eyes that looked too far away to see the disaster he had wrought. The door opened, and in the stream of light Father Rogan stood, his book in hand, with his finger marking the place.

"Ah!" cried Lorison. "You are the man I want. I had a wife of you a few hours ago. I would not trouble you, but I neglected to note how it was done. Will you oblige me with the information whether the business is beyond remedy?"

"Come inside," said the priest; "there are other lodgers in the house, who might prefer sleep to even a gratified curiosity."

Lorison entered the room and took the chair offered him. The priest's eyes looked a courteous interrogation.

"I must apologize again," said the young man, "for so soon

intruding upon you with my marital infelicities, but, as my wife has neglected to furnish me with her address, I am deprived of the legitimate recourse of a family row."

"I am quite a plain man," said Father Rogan, pleasantly; "but I do not see how I am to ask you questions."

"Pardon my indirectness," said Lorison; "I will ask one. In this room to-night you pronounced me to be a husband. You afterward spoke of additional rites or performances that either should or could be effected. I paid little attention to your words then, but I am hungry to hear them repeated now. As matters stand, am I married past all help?"

"You are as legally and as firmly bound," said the priest, "as though it had been done in a cathedral, in the presence of thousands. The additional observances I referred to are not necessary to the strictest legality of the act, but were advised as a precaution for the future—for convenience of proof in such contingencies as wills, inheritances and the like."

Lorison laughed harshly.

"Many thanks," he said. "Then there is no mistake, and I am the happy benedict. I suppose I should go stand upon the bridal corner, and when my wife gets through walking the streets she will look me up."

Father Rogan regarded him calmly.

"My son," he said, "when a man and woman come to me to be married I always marry them. I do this for the sake of other people whom they might go away and marry if they did not marry each other. As you see, I do not seek your confidence; but your case seems to me to be one not altogether devoid of interest. Very few marriages that have come to my notice have brought such well-expressed regret within so short a time. I will hazard one question: were you not under the impression that you loved the lady you married, at the time you did so?"

"Loved her!" cried Lorison, wildly. "Never so well as now, though she told me she deceived and sinned and stole. Never more than now, when, perhaps, she is laughing at the fool she cajoled and left, with scarcely a word, to return to God only knows what particular line of her former folly."

Father Rogan answered nothing. During the silence that succeeded, he sat with a quiet expectation beaming in his full, lambent eye.

"If you would listen—" began Lorison. The priest held up his hand.

"As I hoped," he said. "I thought you would trust me. Wait but a moment." He brought a long clay pipe, filled and lighted it.

"Now, my son," he said.

Lorison poured a twelve month's accumulated confidence into Father Rogan's ear. He told all; not sparing himself or omitting the facts of his past, the events of the night, or his disturbing conjectures and fears.

"The main point," said the priest, when he had concluded, "seems to me to be this—are you reasonably sure that you love this woman whom you have married?"

"Why," exclaimed Lorison, rising impulsively to his feet— "why should I deny it? But look at me—am I fish, flesh or fowl? That is the main point to me, I assure you."

"I understand you," said the priest, also rising, and laying down his pipe. "The situation is one that has taxed the endurance of much older men than you—in fact, especially much older men than you. I will try to relieve you from it, and this night. You shall see for yourself into exactly what predicament you have fallen, and how you shall, possibly, be extricated. There is no evidence so credible as that of the eyesight."

Father Rogan moved about the room, and donned a soft

black hat. Buttoning his coat to his throat, he laid his hand on the doorknob. "Let us walk," he said.

The two went out upon the street. The priest turned his face down it, and Lorison walked with him through a squalid district, where the houses loomed, awry and desolate-looking, high above them. Presently they turned into a less dismal side street, where the houses were smaller, and, though hinting of the most meagre comfort, lacked the concentrated wretchedness of the more populous byways.

At a segregated, two-story house Father Rogan halted, and mounted the steps with the confidence of a familiar visitor. He ushered Lorison into a narrow hallway, faintly lighted by a cobwebbed hanging lamp. Almost immediately a door to the right opened and a dingy Irishwoman protruded her head.

"Good evening to ye, Mistress Geehan," said the priest, unconsciously, it seemed, falling into a delicately flavored brogue. "And is it yourself can tell me if Norah has gone out again, the night, maybe?"

"Oh, it's yer blissid riverence! Sure and I can tell ye the same. The purty darlin' wint out, as usual, but a bit later. And she says: 'Mother Geehan,' says she, 'it's me last noight out, praise the saints, this noight is!' And, oh, yer riverence, the swate, beautiful drame of a dress she had this toime! White satin and silk and ribbons, and lace about the neck and arrums—'twas a sin, yer reverence, the gold was spint upon it."

The priest heard Lorison catch his breath painfully, and a faint smile flickered across his own clean-cut mouth.

"Well, then, Mistress Geehan," said he, "I'll just step upstairs and see the bit boy for a minute, and I'll take this gentleman up with me."

"He's awake, thin," said the woman. "I've just come down from sitting wid him the last hour, tilling him fine shtories of ould County Tyrone. 'Tis a greedy gossoon, it is, yer riverence, for me shtories."

"Small the doubt," said Father Rogan. "There's no rocking would put him to slape the quicker, I'm thinking."

Amid the woman's shrill protest against the retort, the two men ascended the steep stairway. The priest pushed open the door of a room near its top.

"Is that you already, sister?" drawled a sweet, childish voice from the darkness.

"It's only ould Father Denny come to see ye, darlin'; and a foine gentleman I've brought to make ye a gr-r-and call. And ye resaves us fast aslape in bed! Shame on yez manners!"

"Oh, Father Denny, is that you? I'm glad. And will you light the lamp, please? It's on the table by the door. And quit talking like Mother Geehan, Father Denny."

The priest lit the lamp, and Lorison saw a tiny, tousled-haired boy, with a thin, delicate face, sitting up in a small bed in a corner. Quickly, also, his rapid glance considered the room and its contents. It was furnished with more than comfort, and its adornments plainly indicated a woman's discerning taste. An open door beyond revealed the blackness of an adjoining room's interior.

The boy clutched both of Father Rogan's hands. "I'm so glad you came," he said; "but why did you come in the night? Did sister send you?"

"Off wid ye! Am I to be sint about, at me age, as was Terence McShane, of Ballymahone? I come on me own r-r-responsibility."

Lorison had also advanced to the boy's bedside. He was fond of children; and the wee fellow, laying himself down to sleep alone in that dark room, stirred his heart.

"Aren't you afraid, little man?" he asked, stooping down beside him.

"Sometimes," answered the boy, with a shy smile, "when the rats make too much noise. But nearly every night, when sister goes out, Mother Geehan stays a while with me, and tells me funny stories. I'm not often afraid, sir."

"This brave little gentleman," said Father Rogan, "is a scholar of mine. Every day from half-past six to half-past eight—when sister comes for him—he stops in my study, and we find out what's in the inside of books. He knows multiplication, division and fractions; and he's troubling me to begin wid the chronicles of Ciaran of Clonmacnoise, Corurac McCullenan and Cuan O'Lochain, the gr-r-reat Irish histhorians." The boy was evidently accustomed to the priest's Celtic pleasantries. A little, appreciative grin was all the attention the insinuation of pedantry received.

Lorison, to have saved his life, could not have put to the child one of those vital questions that were wildly beating about, unanswered, in his own brain. The little fellow was very like Norah; he had the same shining hair and candid eyes.

"Oh, Father Denny," cried the boy, suddenly, "I forgot to tell you! Sister is not going away at night any more! She told me so when she kissed me good night as she was leaving. And she said she was so happy, and then she cried. Wasn't that queer? But I'm glad; aren't you?"

"Yes, lad. And now, ye omadhaun, go to sleep, and say good night; we must be going."

"Which shall I do first, Father Denny?"

"Faith, he's caught me again! Wait till I get the sassenach into the annals of Tageruach, the hagiographer; I'll give him enough of the Irish idiom to make him more respectful."

The light was out, and the small, brave voice bidding them good night from the dark room. They groped downstairs, and tore away from the garrulity of Mother Geehan.

Again the priest steered them through the dim ways, but this time in another direction. His conductor was serenely silent, and Lorison followed his example to the extent of seldom speaking. Serene he could not be. His heart beat suffocatingly in his breast. The following of this blind, menacing trail was pregnant with he knew not what humiliating revelation to be delivered at its end.

They came into a more pretentious street, where trade, it could be surmised, flourished by day. And again the priest paused; this time before a lofty building, whose great doors and windows in the lowest floor were carefully shuttered and barred. Its higher apertures were dark, save in the third story, the windows of which were brilliantly lighted. Lorison's ear caught a distant, regular, pleasing thrumming, as of music above. They stood at an angle of the building. Up, along the side nearest them, mounted an iron stairway. At its top was an upright, illuminated parallelogram. Father Rogan had stopped, and stood, musing.

"I will say this much," he remarked, thoughtfully: "I believe you to be a better man than you think yourself to be, and a better man than I thought some hours ago. But do not take this," he added, with a smile, "as much praise. I promised you a possible deliverance from an unhappy perplexity. I will have to modify that promise. I can only remove the mystery that enhanced that perplexity. Your deliverance depends upon yourself. Come."

He led his companion up the stairway. Halfway up, Lorison caught him by the sleeve. "Remember," he gasped, "I love that woman."

"You desired to know."

"I—Go on."

The priest reached the landing at the top of the stairway. Lorison, behind him, saw that the illuminated space was the glass upper half of a door opening into the lighted room. The rhythmic music increased as they neared it; the stairs shook with the mellow vibrations.

Lorison stopped breathing when he set foot upon the highest step, for the priest stood aside, and motioned him to look through the glass of the door.

His eye, accustomed to the darkness, met first a blinding glare, and then he made out the faces and forms of many people, amid an extravagant display of splendid robings—billowy laces, brilliant-hued finery, ribbons, silks and misty drapery. And then he caught the meaning of that jarring hum, and he saw the tired, pale, happy face of his wife, bending, as were a score of others, over her sewing machine—toiling, toiling. Here was the folly she pursued, and the end of his quest.

But not his deliverance, though even then remorse struck him. His shamed soul fluttered once more before it retired to make room for the other and better one. For, to temper his thrill of joy, the shine of the satin and the glimmer of ornaments recalled the disturbing figure of the bespangled Amazon, and the base duplicate histories lit by the glare of footlights and stolen diamonds. It is past the wisdom of him who only sets the scenes, either to praise or blame the man. But this time his love overcame his scruples. He took a quick step, and reached out his hand for the doorknob. Father Rogan was quicker to arrest it and draw him back.

"You use my trust in you queerly," said the priest sternly. "What are you about to do?"

"I am going to my wife," said Lorison. "Let me pass."

"Listen," said the priest, holding him firmly by the arm. "I am about to put you in possession of a piece of knowledge of which, thus far, you have scarcely proved deserving. I do not think you ever will; but I will not dwell upon that. You see in that room the woman you married, working for a frugal living for herself, and a generous comfort for an idolized brother. This building belongs to the chief costumer of the city. For months the advance orders for the coming Mardi Gras festivals have kept the work going day and night. I myself secured employment here for Norah. She toils here each night from nine o'clock until daylight, and, besides, carries home with her some of the finer costumes, requiring more delicate needlework, and works there part of the day. Somehow, you two have remained strangely ignorant of each other's lives. Are you convinced now that your wife is not walking the streets?"

"Let me go to her," cried Lorison, again struggling, "and beg her forgiveness!"

"Sir," said the priest, "do you owe me nothing? Be quiet. It seems so often that Heaven lets fall its choicest gifts into hands that must be taught to hold them. Listen again. You forgot that repentant sin must not compromise, but look up, for redemption, to the purest and best. You went to her with the fine-spun sophistry that peace could be found in a mutual guilt; and she, fearful of losing what her heart so craved, thought it worth the price to buy it with a desperate, pure, beautiful lie. I have known her since the day she was born; she is as innocent and unsullied in life and deed as a holy saint. In that lowly street where she dwells she first saw the light, and she has lived there ever since, spending her days in generous self-sacrifice for others. Och, ye spalpeen!" continued Father Rogan, raising his finger in kindly anger at Lorison. "What for, I wonder, could she be after making a fool of hersilf, and shamin' her swate soul with lies, for the like of you!"

"Sir," said Lorison, trembling, "say what you please of me. Doubt it as you must, I will yet prove my gratitude to you, and my devotion to her. But let me speak to her once now, let me kneel for just one moment at her feet, and—"

"Tut, tut!" said the priest. "How many acts of a love drama do you think an old bookworm like me capable of witnessing? Besides, what kind of figures do we cut, spying upon the mysteries of midnight millinery! Go to meet your wife to-morrow, as she ordered you, and obey her thereafter, and maybe some time I shall get forgiveness for the part I have played in this night's work. Off wid yez down the shtairs, now! 'Tis late, and an ould man like me should be takin' his rest."

Saint Patrick's Day

March 17th

St. Patrick's Day Irish Beauty (vintage postcard)

Courtesy of Alamy

The Shamrock
and the Palm

On North Rampart Street one day, I met Clancy, whom I had not seen in months. Clancy is an American with an Irish diathesis and cosmopolitan proclivities. Many businesses have claimed him, but none for long. The roadster's blood is in his veins.

He greeted me with heartiness, and I thought I saw something in his eye that ought to be divulged. Sometimes, when Clancy has returned from his voyages into the informal and the egregious, he can be persuaded to oral construction. Now I thought I saw in him symptoms of voluntary discourse, so I hastily convoyed him to a little café nearby, where a fan buzzed, mitigating the torrid sultriness of the New Orleans summer.

" 'Tis very near the tropics, this weather to-day," said Clancy—apropos—I thought—of the season. But, it appeared, it had more to do with the story. I nodded confirmatorily.

" 'Tis elegant weather," continued Clancy, "for filibusterin'. 'Tis what I've been doin' for two months past, strugglin' to liberate a foreign people from a tyrant's clutch. 'Twas hard work. 'Tis strainin' to the back and grows corns on your hands."

"So," I said, "you've turned soldier of fortune in earnest. I hope you make it pay. To what country did you lend your aid?"

"Where's Kamchatka?" asked Clancy, irrelevantly, I thought.

"Why, off Siberia, up in the Arctic regions, I believe," I answered, somewhat doubtfully.

"I thought that was the cold one," said Clancy, with a nod. "I'm always gettin' the two names mixed. 'Twas Guatemala, then—the hot one—I've been filibusterin' with. Ye'll find that country on the map. 'Tis in the district known as the tropics. By the foresight of Providence, it lies on the coast, so the geography man could run the names of the towns off into the water. They're an inch long, small type, composed of Spanish dialects, and, 'tis my opinion of the same system and syntax that blew up the *Maine*. Yes, 'twas that country I sailed against, single-handed, and endeavored to liberate it from a tyrannical government with a single-barreled pickax, unloaded at that. Ye don't understand, of course. 'Tis a statement demandin' elucidation and apologies.

" 'Twas one morning about the first of June; I was standin' down on the wharf, lookin' about at the ships in the river. There was a little steamer moored right opposite me that seemed about ready to sail. The funnels of it were throwin' out smoke, and a gang of roustabouts were carryin' aboard a pile of boxes that was stacked up on the wharf. The boxes were about two feet square, and somethin' like four feet long, and they seemed to be pretty heavy.

"I walked over, careless, to the stack of boxes. I saw one of them had been broken in handlin'. 'Twas curiosity made me pull up the loose top and look inside. The box was packed full of Winchester rifles. 'So, so,' says I to myself; 'somebody's gettin' a twist on the neutrality laws. Somebody's aidin' with munitions of war. I wonder where the popguns are goin.'"

"I heard somebody cough, and I turned around. There stood a little, round, fat man with a brown face and white clothes, a first-class-looking little man, with a four-carat diamond on his

98

finger and his eye full of interrogations and respects. I judged he was a kind of foreigner—maybe from Russia or Japan or the archipelagoes.

" 'Hist!' says the round man, full of concealments and confidences. 'Will the señor respect the discoveryments he has made, that the mans on the ship shall not be acquaint? The señor will be a gentleman that shall not expose one thing that by accident occur.'

" 'Monseer,' says I—for I judged him to be a kind of Frenchman, that assortment of foreigners being doomed by nature to politeness and dialects—'receive my most exasperated assurances that your secret is safe with James Clancy. Furthermore, I will go so far as to remark, Veev la Liberty—veev it good and strong. Whenever you hear of a Clancy obstructin' the abolishment of existin' governments you may notify me by return mail.'

" 'The señor is good,' says the dark, fat man, smilin' under his black mustache. 'Wish you to come aboard my ship and drink of wine a glass?'

"Bein' a Clancy, in two minutes me and the foreigner man were seated at a table in the cabin of the steamer, with a bottle between us. I could hear the heavy boxes bein' dumped into the hold. I judged that cargo must consist of at least 2,000 Winchesters. Me and the brown man drank the bottle of stuff, and he called the steward to bring another. When you amalgamate a Clancy with the contents of a bottle you practically instigate secession. I had heard a good deal about these revolutions in them tropical localities, and I begun to want a hand in it.

" 'You goin' to stir things up in your country, ain't you, monseer?' says I, with a wink to let him know I was on.

" 'Yes, yes,' said the little man, pounding his fist on the table. 'A change of the greatest will occur. Too long have the people been oppressed with the promises and the never-to-happen things to become. The great work it shall be carry on. Yes. Our forces shall in the capital city strike of the soonest. *Carrambos!*

" '*Carrambos* is the word,' says I, beginning to invest myself with enthusiasm and more wine, 'likewise veeva, as I said before. May the shamrock of old—I mean the banana-vine or the pie-plant, or whatever the imperial emblem may be of your down-trodden country, wave forever.'

" 'A thousand thank-yous,' says the round man, 'for your emission of amicable utterances. What our cause needs of the very most is mans who will the work do, to lift it along. Oh, for one thousands strong, good mans to aid the General De Vega that he shall to his country bring those success and glory! It is hard—oh, so hard to find good mans to help in the work.'

" 'Monseer,' says I, leanin' over the table and graspin' his hand, 'I don't know where your country is, but me heart bleeds for it. The heart of a Clancy was never deaf to the sight of an oppressed people. The family is filibusterers by birth, and foreigners by trade. If you can use James Clancy's arms and his blood in denudin' your shores of the tyrant's yoke they're yours to command.'

"General De Vega was overcome with joy to confiscate my condolence of his conspiracies and predicaments. He tried to embrace me across the table, but his fatness, and the wine that was not in the bottles, prevented. Thus was I welcomed into the ranks of filibustery. Then the general man told me his country had the name of Guatemala, and was the greatest nation laved by any ocean whatever, anywhere. He looked at me with tears in his eyes, and from time to time he would emit the remark, 'Ah! big, strong, brave mans! That is what my country need.'

"General De Vega, as was the name by which he denounced himself, brought out a document for me to sign, which I did, makin' a fine flourish and curlycue with the tail of the 'y'.

" 'Your passage-money,' says the general, business-like, 'shall from your pay be deduct.'

" 'Twill not,' says I, haughty. 'I'll pay my own passage.' A hundred and eighty dollars I had in my inside pocket, and 'twas no common filibuster I was goin' to be, filibusterin' for me board and clothes.

"The steamer was to sail in two hours, and I went ashore to get some things together I'd need. When I came aboard I showed the general with pride the outfit. 'Twas a fine Chinchilla overcoat, Arctic overshoes, fur cap and earmuffs, with elegant fleece-lined gloves and woolen muffler.

" '*Carrambos!*' says the little general. 'What clothes are these that shall go to the tropic?' And then the little spalpeen laughs, and he calls the captain, and the captain calls the purser, and they pipe up the chief engineer, and the whole gang leans against the cabin and laughs at Clancy's wardrobe for Guatemala.

"I reflects a bit, serious, and asks the general again to denominate the terms by which his country is called. He tells me, and I see then that 'twas the t'other one, Kamchatka, I had in mind. Since then I've had difficulty in separatin' the two nations in name, climate and geographic disposition.

"I paid my passage—twenty-four dollars, first cabin—and ate at table with the officer crowd. Down on the lower deck was a gang of second-class passengers, about forty of them, seemin' to be Spaniards and the like. I wondered what so many of them were goin' along for.

"Well, then, in three days we sailed alongside that Guatemala. 'Twas a blue country, and not yellow as 'tis miscolored on the map. We landed at a town on the coast, where a train of cars was waitin' for us on a dinky little railroad. The boxes on the steamer were brought ashore and loaded on the cars. The gang of Spaniards got aboard, too, the general and me in the front car.

Yes, me and General De Vega headed the revolution, as it pulled out of the seaport town. That train travelled about as fast as a policeman goin' to a riot. It penetrated the most conspicuous lot of fuzzy scenery ever seen outside a geography. We run some forty miles in seven hours, and the train stopped. There was no more railroad. 'Twas a sort of camp in a damp gorge full of wildness and melancholies. They was gradin' and choppin' out the forests ahead to continue the road. 'Here,' says I to myself, 'is the romantic haunt of the revolutionists. Here will Clancy, by the virtue that is in a superior race and the inculcation of Fenian tactics, strike a tremendous blow for liberty.'

"They unloaded the boxes from the train and begun to knock the tops off. From the first one that was open I saw General De Vega take the Winchester rifles and pass them around to a squad of morbid, sore-toed soldiery. The other boxes was opened next, and, believe me or not, divil another gun was to be seen. Every other box in the load was full of pickaxes and spades.

"And then—sorrow be upon them tropics—the proud Clancy and the dishonored Spaniards, each one of them, had to shoulder a pick or a spade, and march away to work on that dirty little railroad. Yes; 'twas that the Spaniards shipped for, and 'twas that the filibusterin' Clancy signed for, though unbeknownst to himself at the time. In after days I found out about it. It seems 'twas hard to get hands to work on that road. The intelligent natives of the country was too lazy to work. Indeed, the saints know, 'twas unnecessary. By stretchin' out one hand, they could seize the most delicate and costly fruits of the earth, and, by stretchin' out the other, they could sleep for days at a time without hearin' a seven-o'clock whistle or the footsteps of the rent man upon the stairs. So, regular, the steamers travelled to the United States to seduce labor. Usually the imported spade-slinger died in two or three months from eatin' the over-ripe water and breathin' the violent tropical scenery. Wherefore they made them sign contracts for a year, when they hired them, and put an armed guard over the poor devils to keep them from runnin' away.

" 'Twas thus I was double-crossed by the tropics through a family failin' of goin' out of the way to hunt disturbances.

"They gave me a pick, and I took it, meditatin' an insurrection on the spot; but there was the guards handlin' the Winchesters careless, and I come to the conclusion that discretion was the best part of filibusterin'. There was about a hundred of us in the gang startin' out to work, and the word was given to move. I steps out of the ranks and goes up to that General De Vega man, who was smokin' a cigar and gazin' upon the scene with satisfactions and glory. He smiles at me polite and devilish. 'Plenty work,' says he, 'for big, strong mans in Guatemala. Yes. T'irty dollars in the month. Good pay. Ah, yes. You strong, brave man. Bimeby we push those railroad in the capital very quick. They want you go work now. *Adios*, strong mans.'

" 'Monseer,' says I, lingerin', 'will you tell a poor little Irishman this: When I set foot on your cockroachy steamer, and breathed liberal and revolutionary sentiments into your sour wine, did you think I was conspirin' to sling a pick on your contemptuous little railroad? And when you answered me with patriotic recitations, humping up the star-spangled cause of liberty, did you have meditations of reducin' me to the ranks of the stump-grubbin' Spaniards in the chain-gangs of your vile and grovelin' country?'

"The general man expanded his rotundity and laughed considerable. Yes, he laughed very long and loud, and I, Clancy, stood and waited.

" 'Comical mans!' he shouts, at last. 'So, you will kill me from the laughing. Yes; it is hard to find the brave, strong mans to aid my country. Revolutions? Did I speak of r-r-revolutions? Not one word. I say, big, strong mans is need in Guatemala. So. The mistake is of you. You have looked in those one box containing those gun for the guard. You think all boxes is contain gun? No. There is not war in Guatemala. But work? Yes. Good. T'irty dollar in the month. You shall shoulder one pickaxe, señor, and dig for the liberty and prosperity of Guatemala. Off to your work. The guard waits for you.'

" 'Little, fat, poodle dog of a brown man,' says I, quiet, but full of indignations and discomforts, 'things shall happen to you. Maybe not right away, but as soon as J. Clancy can formulate somethin' in the way of repartee.'

"The boss of the gang orders us to work. I tramps off with the Guineas, and I hears the distinguished patriot and kidnapper laughin' hearty as we go.

" 'Tis a sorrowful fact, for eight weeks I built railroads for that misbehavin' country. I filibustered twelve hours a day with a heavy pick and a spade, choppin' away the luxurious landscape that grew upon the right of way. We worked in swamps that smelled like there was a leak in the gas mains, trampin' down a fine assortment of the most expensive hot-house plants and vegetables. The scene was tropical beyond the wildest imagination of the geography man. The trees was all sky-scrapers; the underbrush was full of needles and pins; there was monkeys jumpin' around and crocodiles and pink-tailed mockin'-birds, and ye stood knee-deep in the rotten water and grabbled roots for the liberation of Guatemala. Of nights we would build smudges in camp to discourage the mosquitoes, and sit in the smoke, with the guards pacin' all around us. There was two hundred men workin' on the road—mostly Guineas, black men, Spaniards and Swedes. Three or four were Irish.

"One old man named Halloran—a man of Hibernian

entitlements and discretions, explained it to me. He had been workin' on the road a year. Most of them died in less than six months. He was dried up to gristle and bone, and shook with chills every third night.

" 'When you first come,' says he, 'ye think ye'll leave right away. But they hold out your first month's pay for your passage over, and by that time the tropics has its grip on ye. Ye're surrounded by a ragin' forest full of disreputable beasts—lions and baboons and anacondas—waitin' to devour ye. The sun strikes ye hard, and melts the marrow in your bones. Ye get similar to the lettuce-eaters the poetry-book speaks about. Ye forget the elevated sintiments of life, such as patriotism, revenge, disturbances of the peace and the dacint love of a clane shirt. Ye do your work, and ye swallow the kerosene ile and rubber pipestems dished up to ye by the Spanish cook for food. Ye light your pipeful, and say to yoursilf, "Nixt week I'll break away," and ye go to sleep and call yersilf a liar, for ye know ye'll never do it.'

" 'Who is this general man,' asks I, 'that calls himself De Vega?'

" 'Tis the man,' says Halloran, 'who is tryin' to complete the finishin' of the railroad. 'Twas the project of a private corporation, but it busted, and then the government took it up. De Vegy is a big politician, and wants to be prisident. The people want the railroad completed, as they're taxed mighty on account of it. The De Vegy man is pushin' it along as a campaign move.'

" 'Tis not my way,' says I, 'to make threats against any man, but there's an account to be settled between the railroad man and James O'Dowd Clancy.'

" 'Twas that way I thought, mesilf, at first,' Halloran says, with a big sigh, 'until I got to be a lettuce-eater. The fault's wid these tropics. They rejuices a man's system. 'Tis a land, as the poet says, "Where it always seems to be after dinner." I does me work and smokes me pipe and sleeps. There's little else in life,

105

anyway. Ye'll get that way yersilf, mighty soon. Don't be harbourin' any sintiments at all, Clancy.'

" 'I can't help it,' says I; 'I'm full of 'em. I enlisted in the revolutionary army of this dark country in good faith to fight for its liberty, honors and silver candlesticks; instead of which I am set to amputatin' its scenery and grubbin' its roots. 'Tis the general man will have to pay for it.'

"Two months I worked on that railroad before I found a chance to get away. One day a gang of us was sent back to the end of the completed line to fetch some picks that had been sent down to Port Barrios to be sharpened. They were brought on a hand-car, and I noticed, when I started away, that the car was left there on the track.

"That night, about twelve, I woke up Halloran and told him my scheme.

" 'Run away?' says Halloran. 'Good Lord, Clancy, do ye mean it? Why, I ain't got the nerve. It's too chilly, and I ain't slept enough. Run away? I told you, Clancy, I've eat the lettuce. I've lost my grip. 'Tis the tropics that's done it. 'Tis like the poet says: "Forgotten are our friends that we have left behind; in the hollow lettuce-land we will live and lay reclined." You better go on, Clancy. I'll stay, I guess. It's too early and cold, and I'm sleepy.'

"So I had to leave Halloran. I dressed quiet, and slipped out of the tent we were in. When the guard came along I knocked him over, like a ninepin, with a green cocoanut I had, and made for the railroad. I got on that hand-car and made it fly. 'Twas yet a while before daybreak when I saw the lights of Port Barrios about a mile away. I stopped the hand-car there and walked to the town. I stepped inside the corporations of that town with care and hesitations. I was not afraid of the army of Guatemala, but me soul quaked at the prospect of a hand-to-hand struggle with its employment bureau. 'Tis a country that hires its help easy and keeps 'em long. Sure I can fancy Missis America and Missis Guatemala passin' a bit of gossip some fine, still night across the mountains. 'Oh, dear,' says Missis America, 'and it's a lot of trouble I'm havin' ag'in with the help, señora, ma'am.' 'Laws, now!' says Missis Guatemala, 'you don't say so, ma'am! Now, mine never think of leavin' me—te-he! ma'am,' snickers Missis Guatemala.

"I was wonderin' how I was goin' to move away from them tropics without bein' hired again. Dark as it was, I could see a steamer ridin' in the harbor, with smoke emergin' from her stacks. I turned down a little grass street that run down to the water. On the beach I found a little brown man just about to shove off in a skiff.

" 'Hold on, Señor,' says I, 'savve English?'

" 'Heap plenty, yes,' says he, with a pleasant grin.

" 'What steamer is that?' I asks him, 'and where is it going? And what's the news, and the good word and the time of day?'

" 'That steamer the *Conchita*,' said the brown man, affable and easy, rollin' a cigarette. 'Him come from New Orleans for load banana. Him got load last night. I think him sail in one, two hour. Verree nice day we shall be goin' have. You hear some talkee 'bout big battle, maybe so? You think catchee General De Vega, señor? Yes? No?'

" 'How's that, Señor?' says I. 'Big battle? What battle? Who wants catchee General De Vega? I've been up at my old gold mines in the interior for a couple of months, and haven't heard any news.'

" 'Oh,' says the brown man, proud to speak the English, 'verree great revolution in Guatemala one week ago. General De Vega, him try be president. Him raise armee—one—five—ten thousand mans for fight at the government. Those one government send five—forty—hundred thousand soldier to suppress revolution. They fight big battle yesterday at Lomagrande—that about nineteen or fifty mile in the mountain. That government soldier wheep General De Vega—oh, most bad. Five hundred—nine hundred—two thousand of his mans is kill. That revolution is smash suppress—bust—very quick. General De Vega, him r-r-run away fast on one big mule. Yes, carrambos! The general, him r-r-run away, and his armee is kill. That government soldier, they try find General De Vega verree much. They want catchee him for shoot. You think they catchee that general, señor?'

" 'Saints grant it!' says I. ' 'Twould be the judgment of Providence for settin' the warlike talent of a Clancy to gradin' the tropics with a pick and shovel. But 'tis not so much a question of insurrections now, me little man, as 'tis of the hired-man problem. 'Tis anxious I am to resign a situation of responsibility and trust with the white wings department of your great and degraded country. Row me in your little boat out to that steamer, and I'll give ye five dollars—sinker pacers—sinker pacers,' says I, reducin' the offer to the language and denomination of the tropic dialects.

" '*Cinco pesos*,' repeats the little man. 'Five dollee, you give?'

" 'Twas not such a bad little man. He had hesitations at first, sayin' that passengers leavin' the country had to have papers and passports, but at last he took me out alongside the steamer.

"Day was just breakin' as we struck her, and there wasn't a soul to be seen on board. The water was very still, and the brown man gave me a lift from the boat, and I climbed onto the steamer where her side was sliced to the deck for loadin' fruit. The hatches was open, and I looked down and saw the cargo of bananas that filled the hold to within six feet of the top. I thinks to myself, 'Clancy, you better go as a stowaway. It's safer. The steamer men might hand you back to the employment bureau. The tropic'll get you, Clancy, if you don't watch out.'

"So I jumps down easy among the bananas, and digs out a hole to hide in among the bunches. In an hour or so I could hear the engines goin', and feel the steamer rockin', and I knew we were off to sea. They left the hatches open for ventilation, and pretty soon it was light enough in the hold to see fairly well. I got to feelin' a bit hungry, and thought I'd have a light fruit lunch, by way of refreshment. I creeped out of the hole I'd made and stood up straight. Just then I saw another man crawl up about ten feet away and reach out and skin a banana and stuff it into his mouth. 'Twas a dirty man, black-faced and ragged and disgraceful of aspect. Yes, the man was a ringer for the pictures of the fat Weary Willie in the funny papers. I looked again, and saw it was my general man—De Vega, the great revolutionist, mule-rider and pickaxe importer. When he saw me the general hesitated with his mouth filled with banana and his eyes the size of cocoanuts.

" 'Hist!' I says. 'Not a word, or they'll put us off and make us walk. "Veev la Liberty!" I adds, capperin' the sentiment by shovin' a banana into the source of it. I was certain the general wouldn't recognize me. The nefarious work of the tropics had left me lookin' different. There was half an inch of roan whiskers coverin' me face, and me costume was a pair of blue overalls and a red shirt.

" 'How you come in the ship, señor?' asked the general as soon as he could speak.

" 'By the back door—whist!' says I. ' 'Twas a glorious blow for liberty we struck,' I continues; 'but we was overpowered by numbers. Let us accept our defeat like brave men and eat another banana.'

" 'Were you in the cause of liberty fightin', señor?' says the general, sheddin' tears on the cargo.

" 'To the last,' says I. ' 'Twas I led the last desperate charge against the minions of the tyrant. But it made them mad, and we was forced to retreat. 'Twas I, general, procured the mule upon which you escaped. Could you give that ripe bunch a little boost this way, general? It's a bit out of my reach. Thanks.'

" 'Say you so, brave patriot?' said the general, again weepin'. 'Ah, *Dios!* And I have not the means to reward your devotion. Barely did I my life bring away. *Carrambos!* what a devil's animal was that mule, señor! Like ships in one storm was I dashed about. The skin on myself was ripped away with the thorns and vines. Upon the bark of a hundred trees did that beast of the infernal bump, and cause outrage to the legs of mine. In the night to Port Barrios I came. I dispossess myself of that mountain of mule and hasten along the water shore. I find a little boat to be tied. I launch myself and row to the steamer. I cannot see any mans on board, so I climbed one rope which hang at the side. I then myself hide in the bananas. Surely, I say, if the ship captains view me, they shall throw me again to those Guatemala. Those things are not good. Guatemala will shoot General De Vega. Therefore, I am hide and remain silent. Life itself is glorious. Liberty, it is pretty good; but so good as life I do not think.'

"Three days, as I said, was the trip to New Orleans. The general man and me got to be cronies of the deepest dye. Bananas we ate until they were distasteful to the sight and an eyesore to the palate, but to bananas alone was the bill of fare reduced. At night I crawls out, careful, on the lower deck, and gets a bucket of fresh water.

"That General De Vega was a man inhabited by an engorgement of words and sentences. He added to the monotony of the voyage by divestin' himself of conversation. He believed I was a revolutionist of his own party, there bein', as he told me, a good many Americans and other foreigners in its ranks. 'Twas a braggart and a conceited little gabbler it was, though he considered himself a hero. 'Twas on himself he wasted all his regrets at the failin' of his plot. Not a word did the little balloon have to say about the other misbehavin' idiots that had been shot, or run themselves to death in his revolution.

"The second day out he was feelin' pretty braggy and uppish for a stowed-away conspirator that owed his existence to a mule and stolen bananas. He was tellin' me about the great railroad he had been buildin', and he relates what he calls a comic incident about a fool Irishman he inveigled from New Orleans to sling a pick on his little morgue of a narrow-gauge line. 'Twas sorrowful to hear the little, dirty general tell the opprobrious story of how he put salt upon the tail of that reckless and silly bird, Clancy. Laugh, he did, hearty and long. He shook with laughin', the black-faced rebel and outcast, standin' neck-deep in bananas, without friends or country.

" 'Ah, señor,' he snickers, 'to the death you would have laughed at that drollest Irish. I say to him: "Strong, big mans is need very much in Guatemala." "I will blows strike for your down-pressed country," he say. "That shall you do," I tell him. Ah! it was an Irish so comic. He sees one box break upon the wharf that contain for the guard a few gun. He think there is gun in all the box. But that is all pickaxe. Yes. Ah! señor, could you the face of that Irish have seen when they set him to the work!'

" 'Twas thus the ex-boss of the employment bureau contributed to the tedium of the trip with merry jests and anecdote. But now and then he would weep upon the bananas and make oration about the lost cause of liberty and the mule.

" 'Twas a pleasant sound when the steamer bumped against the pier in New Orleans. Pretty soon we heard the pat-a-pat of hundreds of bare feet, and the Spaniard gang that unloads the fruit jumped on the deck and down into the hold. Me and the general worked a while at passin' up the bunches, and they thought we were part of the gang. After about an hour we managed to slip off the steamer onto the wharf.

" 'Twas a great honor on the hands of an obscure Clancy, havin' the entertainment of the representative of a great foreign filibusterin' power. I first bought for the general and myself many long drinks and things to eat that were not bananas. The general man trotted along at my side, leavin' all the arrangements to me. I led him up to Lafayette Square and set him on a bench in the little park. Cigarettes I had bought for him, and he humped himself down on the seat like a little, fat, contented hobo. I look him over as he sets there, and what I see pleases me. Brown by nature and instinct, he is now brindled with dirt and dust. Praise to the mule, his clothes is mostly strings and flaps. Yes, the looks of the general man is agreeable to Clancy.

"I asks him, delicate, if, by any chance, he brought away anybody's money with him from Guatemala. He sighs and humps his shoulders against the bench. Not a cent. All right. Maybe, he tells me, some of his friends in the tropic outfit will send him funds later. The general was as clear a case of no visible means as I ever saw.

"I told him not to move from the bench, and then I went up to the corner of Poydras and Carondelet. Along there is O'Hara's beat. In five minutes along comes O'Hara, a big, fine man, red-faced, with shinin' buttons, swingin' his club. 'Twould be a fine thing for Guatemala to move into O'Hara's precinct. 'Twould be a fine bit of recreation for Danny to suppress revolutions and uprisin's once or twice a week with his club.

" 'Is 5046 workin' yet, Danny?' says I, walkin' up to him.

" 'Overtime,' says O'Hara, lookin' over me suspicious. 'Want some of it?'

"Fifty-forty-six is the celebrated city ordinance authorizin' arrest, conviction and imprisonment of persons that succeed in concealin' their crimes from the police.

" 'Don't ye know Jimmy Clancy?' says I. 'Ye pink-gilled monster.' So, when O'Hara recognized me beneath the scandalous exterior bestowed upon me by the tropics, I backed him into a doorway and told him what I wanted, and why I wanted it. 'All right, Jimmy,' says O'Hara. 'Go back and hold the bench. I'll be along in ten minutes.'

"In that time O'Hara strolled through Lafayette Square and spied two Weary Willies disgracin' one of the benches. In ten minutes more J. Clancy and General De Vega, late candidate for the presidency of Guatemala, was in the station house. The general is badly frightened, and calls upon me to proclaim his distinguishments and rank.

"'The man,' says I to the police, 'used to be a railroad man. He's on the bum now. 'Tis a little bughouse he is, on account of losin' his job.'

" '*Carrambos!*' says the general, fizzin' like a little soda-water fountain, 'you fought, señor, with my forces in my native country. Why do you say the lies? You shall say I am the General De Vega, one soldier, one *caballero*—'

"'Railroader,' says I again. 'On the hog. No good. Been livin' for three days on stolen bananas. Look at him. Ain't that enough?'

"Twenty-five dollars or sixty days, was what the recorder gave the general. He didn't have a cent, so he took the time. They let me go, as I knew they would, for I had money to show, and O'Hara knew me. Sixty days. 'Twas just so long that I slung a pick for the great country of Kam—Guatemala."

Clancy paused. There was a look of happy content on his deeply sunburned face.

"Would you just step around the corner a minute with me?" he asked. "If ye don't mind, I'll walk with ye there, and show ye Exhibit A. I go around there myself, every ten minutes, to look at it, and the time's about up now."

I walked with him to the corner of Ursulines and down the street a little way. A gang of men, under guard from the parish prison, was at work cleaning the very rubbishy street, thus working out the fines they were unable to pay otherwise.

Clancy stopped me on the sidewalk opposite a little, rotund, dark-featured man of foreign aspect, who was struggling feverishly with a heavy, iron rake. The heat was almost tropical, and the little man showed vast areas of dampness through his tattered clothes.

"Hey, monseer!" Called Clancy, sharply. The little man looked up and scowled darkly. "Fat, strong mans," shouted Clancy, cheerily, "is needed in New Orleans. Yes. To carry on the good work. *Carrambos!* Erin go bragh!"

Easter

March 22nd - April 25

(Varies by year)

Flower Vendor's Easter display, New York City, circa 1900.

Courtesy of Alamy

The Red Roses of Tonia

A trestle burned down on the International Railroad. The south-bound from San Antonio was cut off for the next forty-eight hours. On that train was Tonia Weaver's Easter hat.

Espirition, the Mexican, who had been sent forty miles in a buckboard from the Espinosa Ranch to fetch it, returned with a shrugging shoulder and hands empty except for a cigarette. At the small station, Nopal, he had learned of the delayed train and, having no commands to wait, turned his ponies toward the ranch again.

Now, if one supposes that Easter, the Goddess of Spring, cares any more for the after-church parade on Fifth Avenue than she does for her loyal outfit of subjects that assemble at the meeting-house at Cactus, Tex., a mistake has been made. The wives and daughters of the ranchmen of the Frio country put forth Easter blossoms of new hats and gowns as faithfully as is done anywhere, and the Southwest is, for one day, a mingling of prickly pear, Paris, and paradise. And now it was Good Friday, and Tonia Weaver's Easter hat blushed unseen in the desert air of an impotent express car, beyond the burned trestle. On Saturday noon the Rogers girls, from the Shoestring Ranch, and Ella Reeves, from the Anchor-O, and Mrs. Bennet and Ida, from Green Valley, would convene at the Espinosa and pick up Tonia. With their Easter hats and frocks carefully wrapped and bundled against the dust, the fair aggregation would then merrily jog the ten miles to Cactus, where on the morrow they would array themselves, subjugate man, do homage to Easter, and cause jealous agitation among the lilies of the field.

Tonia sat on the steps of the Espinosa ranch house flicking gloomily with a quirt at a tuft of curly mesquite. She displayed a frown and a contumelious lip, and endeavored to radiate an aura of disagreeableness and tragedy.

"I hate railroads," she announced positively. "And men. Men pretend to run them. Can you give any excuse why a trestle should burn? Ida Bennet's hat is to be trimmed with violets. I shall not go one step toward Cactus without a new hat. If I were a man I would get one."

Two men listened uneasily to this disparagement of their kind. One was Wells Pearson, foreman of the Mucho Calor cattle ranch. The other was Thompson Burrows, the prosperous sheepman from the Quintana Valley. Both thought Tonia Weaver adorable, especially when she railed at railroads and menaced men. Either would have given up his epidermis to make for her an Easter hat more cheerfully than the ostrich gives up his tip or the aigrette lays down its life. Neither possessed the ingenuity to conceive a means of supplying the sad deficiency against the coming Sabbath. Pearson's deep brown face and sunburned light hair gave him the appearance of a schoolboy seized by one of youth's profound and insolvable melancholies. Tonia's plight grieved him through and through. Thompson Burrows was the more skilled and pliable. He hailed from somewhere in the East originally; and he wore neckties and shoes, and was made dumb by woman's presence.

"The big water-hole on Sandy Creek," said Pearson, scarcely hoping to make a hit, "was filled up by that last rain."

"Oh! Was it?" said Tonia sharply. "Thank you for the

information. I suppose a new hat is nothing to you, Mr. Pearson. I suppose you think a woman ought to wear an old Stetson five years without a change, as you do. If your old water-hole could have put out the fire on that trestle you might have some reason to talk about it."

"I am deeply sorry," said Burrows, warned by Pearson's fate, "that you failed to receive your hat, Miss Weaver—deeply sorry, indeed. If there was anything I could do—"

"Don't bother," interrupted Tonia, with sweet sarcasm. "If there was anything you could do, you'd be doing it, of course. There isn't."

Tonia paused. A sudden sparkle of hope had come into her eye. Her frown smoothed away. She had an inspiration.

"There's a store over at Lone Elm Crossing on the Nueces," she said, "that keeps hats. Eva Rogers got hers there. She said it was the latest style. It might have some left. But it's twenty-eight miles to Lone Elm."

The spurs of two men who hastily arose jingled; and Tonia almost smiled. The Knights, then, were not all turned to dust; nor were their rowels rust.

"Of course," said Tonia, looking thoughtfully at a white gulf cloud sailing across the cerulean dome, "nobody could ride to Lone Elm and back by the time the girls call by for me to-morrow. So, I reckon I'll have to stay at home this Easter Sunday."

And then she smiled.

"Well, Miss Tonia," said Pearson, reaching for his hat, as guileful as a sleeping babe. "I reckon I'll be trotting along back to Mucho Calor. There's some cutting out to be done on Dry Branch first thing in the morning; and me and Road Runner has got to be on hand. It's too bad your hat got sidetracked. Maybe they'll get that trestle mended yet in time for Easter."

"I must be riding, too, Miss Tonia," announced Burrows, looking at his watch. "I declare, it's nearly five o'clock! I must be out at my lambing camp in time to help pen those crazy ewes."

Tonia's suitors seemed to have been smitten with a need for haste. They bade her a ceremonious farewell, and then shook each other's hands with the elaborate and solemn courtesy of the Southwesterner.

"Hope I'll see you again soon, Mr. Pearson," said Burrows.

"Same here," said the cowman, with the serious face of one whose friend goes upon a whaling voyage. "Be gratified to see you ride over to Mucho Calor any time you strike that section of the range."

Pearson mounted Road Runner, the soundest cow-pony on the Frio, and let him pitch for a minute, as he always did on being mounted, even at the end of a day's travel.

"What kind of a hat was that, Miss Tonia," he called, "that you ordered from San Antone? I can't help but be sorry about that hat."

"A straw," said Tonia; "the latest shape, of course; trimmed with red roses. That's what I like—red roses."

"There's no color more becoming to your complexion and hair," said Burrows, admiringly.

"It's what I like," said Tonia. "And of all the flowers, give me red roses. Keep all the pinks and blues for yourself. But what's the use, when trestles burn and leave you without anything? It'll be a dry old Easter for me!"

Pearson took off his hat and drove Road Runner at a gallop into the chaparral east of the Espinosa ranch house.

As his stirrups rattled against the brush Burrows's long-legged sorrel struck out down the narrow stretch of open prairie to the southwest.

Tonia hung up her quirt and went into the sitting-room.

"I'm mighty sorry, daughter, that you didn't get your hat," said her mother.

"Oh, don't worry, mother," said Tonia, coolly. "I'll have a new hat, all right, in time to-morrow."

———————

When Burrows reached the end of the strip of prairie he pulled his sorrel to the right and let him pick his way daintily across a sacuista flat through which ran the ragged, dry bed of an arroyo. Then up a gravelly hill, matted with bush, the horse scrambled, and at length emerged, with a snort of satisfaction into a stretch of high, level prairie, grassy and dotted with the lighter green of mesquites in their fresh spring foliage. Always to the right Burrows bore, until in a little while he struck the old Indian trail that followed the Nueces southward, and that passed, twenty-eight miles to the southeast, through Lone Elm.

Here Burrows urged the sorrel into a steady lope. As he settled himself in the saddle for a long ride he heard the drumming of hoofs, the hollow "thwack" of chaparral against wooden stirrups, the whoop of a Comanche; and Wells Pearson burst out of the brush at the right of the trail like a precocious yellow chick from a dark green Easter egg.

Except in the presence of awing femininity melancholy found no place in Pearson's bosom. In Tonia's presence his voice was as soft as a summer bullfrog's in his reedy nest. Now, at his gleesome yawp, rabbits, a mile away, ducked their ears, and sensitive plants closed their fearful fronds.

"Moved your lambing camp pretty far from the ranch, haven't you, neighbor?" asked Pearson, as Road Runner fell in at the sorrel's side.

"Twenty-eight miles," said Burrows, looking a little grim. Pearson's laugh woke an owl one hour too early in his water-elm on the river bank, half a mile away.

"All right for you, sheepman. I like an open game, myself. We're two locoed he-milliners hat-hunting in the wilderness. I notify you. Burr, to mind your corrals. We've got an even start, and the one that gets the headgear will stand some higher at the Espinosa."

"You've got a good pony," said Burrows, eyeing Road Runner's barrel-like body and tapering legs that moved as regularly as the pistonrod of an engine. "It's a race, of course; but you're too much of a horseman to whoop it up this soon. Say we travel together till we get to the home stretch."

"I'm your company," agreed Pearson, "and I admire your sense. If there's hats at Lone Elm, one of 'em shall set on Miss Tonia's brow to-morrow, and you won't be at the crowning. I ain't bragging, Burr, but that sorrel of yours is weak in the fore-legs."

"My horse against yours," offered Burrows, "that Miss Tonia wears the hat I take her to Cactus to-morrow."

"I'll take you up," shouted Pearson. "But oh, it's just like horse-stealing for me! I can use that sorrel for a lady's animal when—when somebody comes over to Mucho Calor, and—"

Burrows' dark face glowered so suddenly that the cowman broke off his sentence. But Pearson could never feel any pressure for long.

"What's all this Easter business about, Burr?" he asked, cheerfully. "Why do the women folks have to have new hats by the almanac or bust all cinches trying to get 'em?"

"It's a seasonable statute out of the testaments," explained Burrows. "It's ordered by the Pope or somebody. And it has something to do with the Zodiac I don't know exactly, but I think it was invented by the Egyptians."

"It's an all-right jubilee if the heathens did put their brand on it," said Pearson; "or else Tonia wouldn't have anything to do with it. And they pull it off at church, too. Suppose there ain't but one hat in the Lone Elm store, Burr!"

"Then," said Burrows, darkly, "the best man of us'll take it back to the Espinosa."

"Oh, man!" cried Pearson, throwing his hat high and catching it again, "there's nothing like you come off the sheep ranges before. You talk good and collateral to the occasion. And if there's more than one?"

"Then," said Burrows, "we'll pick our choice and one of us'll get back first with his and the other won't."

"There never was two souls," proclaimed Pearson to the stars, "that beat more like one heart than yourn and mine. Me and you might be riding on a unicorn and thinking out of the same piece of mind."

At a little past midnight the riders loped into Lone Elm. The half a hundred houses of the big village were dark. On its only street the big wooden store stood barred and shuttered.

In a few moments the horses were fastened and Pearson was pounding cheerfully on the door of old Sutton, the storekeeper.

The barrel of a Winchester came through a cranny of a solid window shutter followed by a short inquiry.

"Wells Pearson, of the Mucho Calor, and Burrows, of Green Valley," was the response. "We want to buy some goods in the store. Sorry to wake you up but we must have 'em. Come on out, Uncle Tommy, and get a move on you."

Uncle Tommy was slow, but at length they got him behind his counter with a kerosene lamp lit, and told him of their dire need.

"Easter hats?" said Uncle Tommy, sleepily. "Why, yes, I believe I have got just a couple left. I only ordered a dozen this spring. I'll show 'em to you."

Now, Uncle Tommy Sutton was a merchant, half asleep or awake. In dusty pasteboard boxes under the counter he had two left-over spring hats. But, alas! for his commercial probity on that early Saturday morn—they were hats of two springs ago, and a woman's eye would have detected the fraud at half a glance. But to the unintelligent gaze of the cowpuncher and the sheepman they seemed fresh from the mint of contemporaneous April.

The hats were of a variety once known as "cart-wheels." They were of stiff straw, colored red, and flat brimmed. Both were exactly alike, and trimmed lavishly around their crowns with full blown, immaculate, artificial white roses.

"That all you got, Uncle Tommy?" said Pearson. "All right. Not much choice here, Burr. Take your pick."

"They're the latest styles" lied Uncle Tommy. "You'd see 'em on Fifth Avenue, if you was in New York."

Uncle Tommy wrapped and tied each hat in two yards of dark calico for a protection. One Pearson tied carefully to his calfskin saddle-thongs; and the other became part of Road Runner's burden. They shouted thanks and farewells to Uncle Tommy, and cantered back into the night on the home stretch.

The horsemen jockeyed with all their skill. They rode more slowly on their way back. The few words they spoke were not unfriendly. Burrows had a Winchester under his left leg slung over his saddle horn. Pearson had a six shooter belted around him. Thus men rode in the Frio country.

At half-past seven in the morning they rode to the top of a hill and saw the Espinosa Ranch, a white spot under a dark patch of live-oaks, five miles away.

The sight roused Pearson from his drooping pose in the saddle. He knew what Road Runner could do. The sorrel was lathered, and stumbling frequently; Road Runner was pegging away like a donkey engine.

Pearson turned toward the sheepman and laughed. "Good-bye, Burr," he cried, with a wave of his hand. "It's a race now. We're on the home stretch."

He pressed Road Runner with his knees and leaned toward the Espinosa. Road Runner struck into a gallop, with tossing head and snorting nostrils, as if he were fresh from a month in pasture.

Pearson rode twenty yards and heard the unmistakable sound of a Winchester lever throwing a cartridge into the barrel. He dropped flat along his horse's back before the crack of the rifle reached his ears.

It is possible that Burrows intended only to disable the horse—he was a good enough shot to do that without endangering his rider. But as Pearson stooped the ball went through his shoulder and then through Road Runner's neck. The horse fell and the cowman pitched over his head into the hard road, and neither of them tried to move.

Burrows rode on without stopping.

In two hours Pearson opened his eyes and took inventory. He managed to get to his feet and staggered back to where Road Runner was lying. Road Runner was lying there, but he appeared to be comfortable. Pearson examined him and found that the bullet had "creased" him. He had been knocked out temporarily, but not seriously hurt. But he was tired, and he lay there on Miss Tonia's hat and ate leaves from a mesquite branch that obligingly hung over the road.

Pearson made the horse get up. The Easter hat, loosed from the saddle-thongs, lay there in its calico wrappings, a shapeless thing from its sojourn beneath the solid carcass of Road Runner. Then Pearson fainted and fell head long upon the poor hat again, crumpling it under his wounded shoulders.

It is hard to kill a cowpuncher. In half an hour he revived—long enough for a woman to have fainted twice and tried ice-cream for a restorer. He got up carefully and found Road Runner who was busy with the near-by grass. He tied the unfortunate hat to the saddle again, and managed to get himself there, too, after many failures.

At noon a gay and fluttering company waited in front of the Espinosa Ranch. The Rogers girls were there in their new buckboard, and the Anchor-O outfit and the Green Valley folks— mostly women. And each and every one wore her new Easter hat, even upon the lonely prairies, for they greatly desired to shine forth and do honor to the coming festival.

At the gate stood Tonia, with undisguised tears upon her cheeks. In her hand she held Burrow's Lone Elm hat, and it was at its white roses, hated by her, that she wept. For her friends were telling her, with the ecstatic joy of true friends, that cart-wheels could not be worn, being three seasons passed into oblivion.

"Put on your old hat and come, Tonia," they urged. "For Easter Sunday?" she answered. "I'll die first." And wept again.

The hats of the fortunate ones were curved and twisted into the style of spring's latest proclamation.

A strange being rode out of the brush among them, and there sat his horse languidly. He was stained and disfigured with the green of the grass and the limestone of rocky roads.

"Hallo, Pearson," said Daddy Weaver. "Look like you've been breaking a mustang. What's that you've got tied to your saddle—a pig in a poke?"

"Oh, come on, Tonia, if you're going," said Betty Rogers. "We mustn't wait any longer. We've saved a seat in the buckboard for you. Never mind the hat. That lovely muslin you've got on looks sweet enough with any old hat."

Pearson was slowly untying the queer thing on his saddle. Tonia looked at him with a sudden hope. Pearson was a man who created hope. He got the thing loose and handed it to her. Her quick fingers tore at the strings.

"Best I could do," said Pearson slowly. "What Road Runner and me done to it will be about all it needs."

"Oh, oh! it's just the right shape," shrieked Tonia. "And red roses! Wait till I try it on!"

She flew in to the glass, and out again, beaming, radiating, blossomed.

"Oh, don't red become her?" chanted the girls in recitative. "Hurry up, Tonia!"

Tonia stopped for a moment by the side of Road Runner.

"Thank you, thank you, Wells," she said, happily. "It's just what I wanted. Won't you come over to Cactus to-morrow and go to church with me?"

"If I can," said Pearson. He was looking curiously at her hat, and then he grinned weakly. Tonia flew into the buckboard like a bird. The vehicles sped away for Cactus.

"What have you been doing, Pearson?" asked Daddy Weaver. "You ain't looking so well as common."

"Me?" said Pearson. "I've been painting flowers. Them roses was white when I left Lone Elm. Help me down, Daddy Weaver, for I haven't got any more paint to spare."

Cinco de Mayo

May 5th

The single illustration by Kay Sims Campbell rejected for the "lost" O. Henry story "Joe and Billy," published by Southwest Classics Press in 2004. The image was deemed "too menacing" for the book's intended demographic and was reworked for inclusion in the book. In 2016, the *J.C. Elkins O. Henry Literary Discussion Group* traveled to Paint Rock, Texas to visit Campbell Ranch to see the Solar Markers during the autumnal equinox and to read "He Also Serves." During the visit, Kay Sims Campbell gifted the original (color) illustration to editor Michael Wenzel.

Courtesy of Michael Wenzel

He Also Serves

If I could have a thousand years—just one little thousand years—more of life, I might, in that time, draw near enough to true Romance to touch the hem of her robe. Up from ships men come, and from waste places and forest and road and garret and cellar to maunder to me in strangely distributed words of the things they have seen and considered. The recording of their tales is no more than a matter of ears and fingers. There are only two fates I dread—deafness and writer's cramp. The hand is yet steady; let the ear bear the blame if these printed words be not in the order they were delivered to me by Hunky Magee, true camp-follower of fortune.

Biography shall claim you but an instant—I first knew Hunky when he was head-waiter at Chubb's little beefsteak restaurant and café on Third Avenue. There was only one waiter besides.

Then, successively, I caromed against him in the little streets of the Big City after his trip to Alaska, his voyage as cook with a treasure-seeking expedition to the Caribbean, and his failure as a pearl-fisher in the Arkansas River. Between these dashes into the land of adventure he usually came back to Chubb's for a while. Chubb's was a port for him when gales blew too high; but when you dined there and Hunky went for your steak you never knew whether he would come to anchor in the kitchen or in the Malayan Archipelago. You wouldn't care for his

131

description—he was soft of voice and hard of face, and rarely had to use more than one eye to quell any approach to a disturbance among Chubb's customers.

One night I found Hunky standing at a corner of Twenty-third Street and Third Avenue after an absence of several months. In ten minutes we had a little round table between us in a quiet corner, and my ears began to get busy. I leave out my sly ruses and feints to draw Hunky's word-of-mouth blows—it all came to something like this:

"Speaking of the next election," said Hunky, "did you ever know much about Indians? No? I don't mean the Cooper, Beadle, cigar-store, or Laughing Water kind—I mean the modern Indian—the kind that takes Greek prizes in colleges and scalps the half-back on the other side in football games. The kind that eats macaroons and tea in the afternoons with the daughter of the professor of biology, and fills up on grasshoppers and fried rattlesnake when they get back to the ancestral wickiup.

"Well, they ain't so bad. I like 'em better than most foreigners that have come over in the last few hundred years. One thing about the Indian is this: when he mixes with the white race he swaps all his own vices for them of the pale-faces—and he retains all his own virtues. Well, his virtues are enough to call out the reserves whenever he lets 'em loose. But the imported foreigners adopt our virtues and keep their own vices—and it's going to take our whole standing army some day to police that gang.

"But let me tell you about the trip I took to Mexico with High Jack Snakefeeder, a Cherokee twice removed, a graduate of a Pennsylvania college and the latest thing in pointed-toed, rubber-heeled, patent kid moccasins and Madras hunting-shirt with turned-back cuffs. He was a friend of mine. I met him in Tahlequah when I was out there during the land boom, and we got thick. He had got all there was out of colleges and had come back to lead his people out of Egypt. He was a man of first-class style and wrote essays, and had been invited to visit rich guys' houses in Boston and such places.

"There was a Cherokee girl in Muscogee that High Jack was foolish about. He took me to see her a few times. Her name was Florence Blue Feather—but you want to clear your mind of all ideas of squaws with nose-rings and army blankets. This young lady was whiter than you are, and better educated than I ever was. You couldn't have told her from any of the girls shopping in the swell Third Avenue stores. I liked her so well that I got to calling on her now and then when High Jack wasn't along, which is the way of friends in such matters. She was educated at the Muscogee College, and was making a specialty of—let's see—eth—yes, ethnology. That's the art that goes back and traces the descent of different races of people, leading up from jelly-fish through monkeys and to the O'Briens. High Jack had took up that line too, and had read papers about it before all kinds of riotous assemblies—Chautauquas and Choctaws and chowder-parties, and such. Having a mutual taste for musty information like that was what made 'em like each other, I suppose. But I don't know! What they call congeniality of tastes ain't always it. Now, when Miss Blue Feather and me was talking together, I listened to her affidavits about the first families of the Land of Nod being cousins german (well, if the Germans don't nod, who does?) to the mound-builders of Ohio with incomprehension and respect. And when I'd tell her about the Bowery and Coney Island, and sing her a few songs that I'd heard the Jamaicans sing at their church lawn-parties, she didn't look much less interested than she did when High Jack would tell her that he had a pipe that the first inhabitants of America originally arrived here on stilts after a freshet at Tenafly, New Jersey.

"But I was going to tell you more about High Jack.

"About six months ago I get a letter from him, saying he'd been commissioned by the Minority Report Bureau of Ethnology at Washington to go down to Mexico and translate some excavations or dig up the meaning of some shorthand notes on some ruins—or something of that sort. And if I'd go along he could squeeze the price into the expense account.

"Well, I'd been holding a napkin over my arm at Chubb's about long enough then, so I wired High Jack 'Yes'; and he sent me a ticket, and I met him in Washington, and he had a lot of news to tell me. First of all, was that Florence Blue Feather had suddenly disappeared from her home and environments.

"'Run away?' I asked.

" 'Vanished,' says High Jack. 'Disappeared like your shadow when the sun goes under a cloud. She was seen on the street, and then she turned a corner and nobody ever seen her afterward. The whole community turned out to look for her, but we never found a clue.'

" 'That's bad—that's bad,' says I. 'She was a mighty nice girl, and as smart as you find 'em.'

"High Jack seemed to take it hard. I guess he must have esteemed Miss Blue Feather quite highly. I could see that he'd referred the matter to the whiskey-jug. That was his weak point—and many another man's. I've noticed that when a man loses a girl he generally takes to drink either just before or just after it happens.

"From Washington we railroaded it to New Orleans, and there took a tramp steamer bound for Belize. And a gale pounded us all down the Caribbean, and nearly wrecked us on the Yucatan coast opposite a little town without a harbor called Boca de Coacoyula. Suppose the ship had run against that name in the dark!

" 'Better fifty years of Europe than a cyclone in the bay,' says

High Jack Snakefeeder. So we get the captain to send us ashore in a dory when the squall seemed to cease from squalling.

"'We will find ruins here or make 'em,' says High. 'The Government doesn't care which we do. An appropriation is an appropriation.'

"Boca de Coacoyula was a dead town. Them biblical towns we read about—Tired and Siphon—after they was destroyed, they must have looked like Forty-second Street and Broadway compared to this Boca place. It still claimed 1300 inhabitants as estimated and engraved on the stone court-house by the census-taker in 1597. The citizens were a mixture of Indians and other Indians; but some of 'em was light-colored, which I was surprised to see. The town was huddled up on the shore, with woods so thick around it that a subpoena-server couldn't have reached a monkey ten yards away with the papers. We wondered what kept it from being annexed to Kansas; but we soon found out that it was Major Bing.

"Major Bing was the ointment around the fly. He had the cochineal, sarsaparilla, log-wood, annatto, hemp, and all other dye-woods and pure food adulteration concessions cornered. He had five-sixths of the Boca de Thingama-jiggers working for him on shares. It was a beautiful graft. We used to brag about Morgan and E. H. and others of our wisest when I was in the provinces— but now no more. That peninsula has got our little country turned into a submarine without even the observation tower showing.

"Major Bing's idea was this. He had the population go forth into the forest and gather these products. When they brought 'em in he gave 'em one-fifth for their trouble. Sometimes they'd strike and demand a sixth. The Major always gave in to 'em.

"The Major had a bungalow so close on the sea that the nine-inch tide seeped through the cracks in the kitchen floor. Me and him and High Jack Snakefeeder sat on the porch and drank rum from noon till midnight. He said he had piled up

$300,000 in New Orleans banks, and High and me could stay with him forever if we would. But High Jack happened to think of the United States, and began to talk ethnology.

"'Ruins!' says Major Bing. 'The woods are full of 'em. I don't know how far they date back, but they was here before I came.'

"High Jack asks what form of worship the citizens of that locality are addicted to.

" 'Why,' says the Major, rubbing his nose, 'I can't hardly say. I imagine it's infidel or Aztec or Nonconformist or something like that. There's a church here—a Methodist or some other kind—with a parson named Skidder. He claims to have converted the people to Christianity. He and me don't assimilate except on state occasions. I imagine they worship some kind of gods or idols yet. But Skidder says he has 'em in the fold.'

"A few days later High Jack and me, prowling around, strikes a plain path into the forest, and follows it a good four miles. Then a branch turns to the left. We go a mile, maybe, down that, and run up against the finest ruin you ever saw—solid stone with trees and vines and under-brush all growing up against it and in it and through it. All over it was chiseled carvings of funny beasts and people that would have been arrested if they'd ever come out in vaudeville that way. We approached it from the rear.

"High Jack had been drinking too much rum ever since we landed in Boca. You know how an Indian is—the palefaces fixed his clock when they introduced him to firewater. He'd brought a quart along with him.

" 'Hunky,' says he, 'we'll explore the ancient temple. It may be that the storm that landed us here was propitious. The Minority Report Bureau of Ethnology,' says he, 'may yet profit by the vagaries of wind and tide.'

"We went in the rear door of the bum edifice. We struck a kind of alcove without bath. There was a granite davenport, and a stone wash-stand without any soap or exit for the water, and some hardwood pegs drove into holes in the wall, and that was all. To go out of that furnished apartment into a Harlem hall bedroom would make you feel like getting back home from an amateur violoncello solo at an East Side Settlement house.

"While High was examining some hieroglyphics on the wall that the stone-masons must have made when their tools slipped, I stepped into the front room. That was at least thirty by fifty feet, stone floor, six little windows like square port-holes that didn't let much light in.

"I looked back over my shoulder, and sees High Jack's face three feet away.

" 'High,' says I, 'of all the—'

"And then I noticed he looked funny, and I turned around.

"He'd taken off his clothes to the waist, and he didn't seem to hear me. I touched him, and came near beating it. High Jack had turned to stone. I had been drinking some rum myself.

" 'Ossified!' I says to him, loudly. 'I knew what would happen if you kept it up.'

"And then High Jack comes in from the alcove when he hears me conversing with nobody, and we have a look at Mr. Snakefeeder No. 2. It's a stone idol, or god, or revised statute or something, and it looks as much like High Jack as one green pea looks like itself. It's got exactly his face and size and color, but it's steadier on its pins. It stands on a kind of rostrum or pedestal, and you can see it's been there ten million years.

" 'He's a cousin of mine,' sings High, and then he turns solemn.

" 'Hunky,' he says, putting one hand on my shoulder and one on the statue's, 'I'm in the holy temple of my ancestors.'

" 'Well, if looks goes for anything,' says I, 'you've struck a twin. Stand side by side with buddy, and let's see if there's any difference.'

"There wasn't. You know an Indian can keep his face as still as an iron dog's when he wants to, so when High Jack froze his features you couldn't have told him from the other one.

"'There's some letters,' says I, 'on his nob's pedestal, but I can't make 'em out. The alphabet of this country seems to be composed of sometimes a, e, i, o, and u, but generally z's, l's, and t's.'

" 'I'm in the holy temple of my ancestors' "

Original illustration from "He Also Serves" by Maynard Dixon
(January 24, 1875 – November 11, 1946)

Collier's

October 31, 1908

Courtesy The Internet Archive

"The girl gives a little jump backwards, and her eyes fly open as big as doughnuts"

Original illustration from "He Also Serves" by Maynard Dixon
(January 24, 1875 – November 11, 1946)
Collier's
October 31, 1908

Courtesy The Internet Archive

"High Jack's ethnology gets the upper hand of his rum for a minute, and he investigates the inscription.

"'Hunky,' says he, 'this is a statue of Tlotopaxl, one of the most powerful gods of the ancient Aztecs.'

"'Glad to know him,' says I, 'but in his present condition he reminds me of the joke Shakespeare got off on Julius Caesar. We might say about your friend:

"'Imperious what's-his-name, dead and turned to stone—
No use to write or call him on the 'phone.'

"'Hunky,' says High Jack Snakefeeder, looking at me funny, 'do you believe in reincarnation?'

"'It sounds to me,' says I, 'like either a clean-up of the slaughter-houses or a new kind of Boston pink. I don't know.'

"'I believe,' says he, 'that I am the reincarnation of Tlotopaxl. My researches have convinced me that the Cherokees, of all the North American tribes, can boast of the straightest descent from the proud Aztec race. That,' says he, 'was a favorite theory of mine and Florence Blue Feather's. And she—what if she—'

"High Jack grabs my arm and walls his eyes at me. Just then he looked more like his eminent co-Indian murderer, Crazy Horse.

"'Well,' says I, 'what if she, what if she, what if she? You're drunk,' says I. 'Impersonating idols and believing in—what was it?—recarnalization? Let's have a drink,' says I. 'It's as spooky here as a Brooklyn artificial-limb factory at midnight with the gas turned down.'

"Just then I heard somebody coming, and I dragged High Jack into the bedless bedchamber. There was peep-holes bored through the wall, so we could see the whole front part of the temple. Major Bing told me afterward that the ancient priests in charge used to rubber through them at the congregation.

"In a few minutes an old Indian woman came in with a big

oval earthen dish full of grub. She set it on a square block of stone in front of the graven image, and laid down and walloped her face on the floor a few times, and then took a walk for herself.

"High Jack and me was hungry, so we came out and looked it over. There was goat steaks and fried rice-cakes, and plantains and cassava, and broiled land-crabs and mangoes—nothing like what you get at Chubb's.

"We ate hearty—and had another round of rum.

"'It must be old Tecumseh's—or whatever you call him—birthday,' says I. 'Or do they feed him every day? I thought gods only drank vanilla on Mount Catawampus.'

"Then some more native parties in short kimonos that showed their aboriginees punctured the near-horizon, and me and High had to skip back into Father Axletree's private boudoir. They came by ones, twos, and threes, and left all sorts of offering—there was enough grub for Bingham's nine gods of war, with plenty left over for the Peace Conference at The Hague. They brought jars of honey, and bunches of bananas, and bottles of wine, and stacks of tortillas, and beautiful shawls worth one hundred dollars apiece that the Indian women weave of a kind of vegetable fiber like silk. All of 'em got down and wriggled on the floor in front of that hard-finish god, and then sneaked off through the woods again.

"'I wonder who gets this rake-off?' remarks High Jack.

"'Oh,' says I, 'there's priests or deputy idols or a committee of disarrangements somewhere in the woods on the job. Wherever you find a god you'll find somebody waiting to take charge of the burnt offerings.'

"And then we took another swig of rum and walked out to the parlor front door to cool off, for it was as hot inside as a summer camp on the Palisades.

"And while we stood there in the breeze we looks down the path and sees a young lady approaching the blasted ruin. She was bare-footed and had on a white robe, and carried a wreath of white flowers in her hand. When she got nearer we saw she had a long blue feather stuck through her black hair. And when she got nearer still me and High Jack Snakefeeder grabbed each other to keep from tumbling down on the floor; for the girl's face was as much like Florence Blue Feather's as his was like old King Toxicology's.

"And then was when High Jack's booze drowned his system of ethnology. He dragged me inside back of the statue, and says:

"'Lay hold of it, Hunky. We'll pack it into the other room. I felt it all the time,' says he. 'I'm the reconsideration of the god Locomotorataxia, and Florence Blue Feather was my bride a thousand years ago. She has come to seek me in the temple where I used to reign.'

"'All right,' says I. 'There's no use arguing against the rum question. You take his feet.'

"We lifted the three-hundred-pound stone god, and carried him into the back room of the café—the temple, I mean—and leaned him against the wall. It was more work than bouncing three live ones from an all-night Broadway joint on New-Year's Eve.

"Then High Jack ran out and brought in a couple of them Indian silk shawls and began to undress himself.

"'Oh, figs!' says I. 'Is it thus? Strong drink is an adder and sub-tractor, too. Is it the heat or the call of the wild that's got you?'

"But High Jack is too full of exaltation and cane-juice to reply. He stops the disrobing business just short of the Manhattan Beach rules, and then winds them red-and-white shawls around him, and goes out and stands on the pedestal as steady as any platinum deity you ever saw. And I looks through a peek-hole to see what he is up to.

"In a few minutes in comes the girl with the flower wreath.

Danged if I wasn't knocked a little silly when she got close, she looked so exactly much like Florence Blue Feather. 'I wonder,' says I to myself, 'if she has been reincarcerated, too? If I could see,' says I to myself, 'whether she has a mole on her left—' But the next minute I thought she looked one-eighth of a shade darker than Florence; but she looked good at that. And High Jack hadn't drunk all the rum that had been drank.

"The girl went up within ten feet of the bum idol, and got down and massaged her nose with the floor, like the rest did. Then she went nearer and laid the flower wreath on the block of stone at High Jack's feet. Rummy as I was, I thought it was kind of nice of her to think of offering flowers instead of household and kitchen provisions. Even a stone god ought to appreciate a little sentiment like that on top of the fancy groceries they had piled up in front of him.

"And then High Jack steps down from his pedestal, quiet, and mentions a few words that sounded just like the hieroglyphics carved on the walls of the ruin. The girl gives a little jump backward, and her eyes fly open as big as doughnuts; but she don't beat it.

"Why didn't she? I'll tell you why I think why. It don't seem to a girl so supernatural, unlikely, strange, and startling that a stone god should come to life for her. If he was to do it for one of them snub-nosed brown girls on the other side of the woods, now, it would be different—but her! I'll bet she said to herself: 'Well, goodness me! you've been a long time getting on your job. I've half a mind not to speak to you.'

"But she and High Jack holds hands and walks away out of the temple together. By the time I'd had time to take another drink and enter upon the scene they was twenty yards away, going up the path in the woods that the girl had come down. With the natural scenery already in place, it was just like a play to watch'em—she looking up at him, and him giving her back the best that an Indian can hand out in the way of a goo-goo eye. But there wasn't anything in that recarnification and revulsion to tintype for me.

"Hey! Injun!' I yells out to High Jack. 'We've got a board-bill due in town, and you're leaving me without a cent. Brace up and cut out the Neapolitan fisher-maiden, and let's go back home.'

"But on the two goes; without looking once back until, as you might say, the forest swallowed 'em up. And I never saw or heard of High Jack Snakefeeder from that day to this. I don't know if the Cherokees came from the Aspics; but if they did, one of 'em went back.

"All I could do was to hustle back to that Boca place and panhandle Major Bing. He detached himself from enough of his winnings to buy me a ticket home. And I'm back again on the job at Chubb's, sir, and I'm going to hold it steady. Come round, and you'll find the steaks as good as ever."

I wondered what Hunky Magee thought about his own story; so I asked him if he had any theories about reincarnation and transmogrification and such mysteries as he had touched upon.

"Nothing like that," said Hunky, positively. "What ailed High Jack was too much booze and education. They'll do an Indian up every time."

"But what about Miss Blue Feather?" I persisted.

"Say," said Hunky, with a grin, "that little lady that stole High Jack certainly did give me a jar when I first took a look at her, but it was only for a minute. You remember I told you High Jack said that Miss Florence Blue Feather disappeared from home about a year ago? Well, where she landed four days later was in as neat a five-room flat on East Twenty-third Street as you ever walked sideways through—and she's been Mrs. Magee ever since."

Mother's Day

Second Sunday in May

Arrangement in Grey and Black No. 1, best known under its colloquial name Whistler's Mother or Portrait of Artist's Mother.

James Abbott McNeill Whistler, 1871

The image has been used since the Victorian era as an icon for motherhood, affection for parents, and "family values." In 1934, the U.S. Post Office issued a stamp engraved with the portrait detail from Whistler's Mother, bearing the slogan "In memory and in honor of the mothers of America."

The Reformation
of Calliope

Calliope Catesby was in his humors again. Ennui was upon
him. This goodly promontory, the earth—particularly that portion of it known as Quicksand—was to him no more than a
pestilent congregation of vapors. Overtaken by the megrims,
the philosopher may seek relief in soliloquy; my lady find solace
in tears; the flaccid Easterner scold at the millinery bills of his
women folk. Such recourse was insufficient to the denizens of
Quicksand. Calliope, especially, was wont to express his ennui
according to his lights.

Over night Calliope had hung out signals of approaching
low spirits. He had kicked his own dog on the porch of the Occidental Hotel, and refused to apologize. He had become capri-
cious and fault-finding in conversation. While strolling about
he reached often for twigs of mesquite and chewed the leaves
fiercely. That was always an ominous act. Another symptom
alarming to those who were familiar with the different stages of
his doldrums was his increasing politeness and a tendency to use
formal phrases. A husky softness succeeded the usual penetrat-
ing drawl in his tones. A dangerous courtesy marked his manners. Later, his smile became crooked, the left side of his mouth
slanting upward, and Quicksand got ready to stand from under.

At this stage Calliope generally began to drink. Finally, about midnight, he was seen going homeward, saluting those whom he met with exaggerated but inoffensive courtesy. Not yet was Calliope's melancholy at the danger point. He would seat himself at the window of the room he occupied over Silvester's tonsorial parlors and there chant lugubrious and tuneless ballads until morning, accompanying the noises by appropriate maltreatment of a jangling guitar. More magnanimous than Nero, he would thus give musical warning of the forthcoming municipal upheaval that Quicksand was scheduled to endure.

A quiet, amiable man was Calliope Catesby at other times—quiet to indolence, and amiable to worthlessness. At best he was a loafer and a nuisance; at worst he was the Terror of Quicksand. His ostensible occupation was something subordinate in the real estate line; he drove the beguiled Easterner in buckboards out to look over lots and ranch property. Originally he came from one of the Gulf States, his lank six feet, slurring rhythm of speech, and sectional idioms giving evidence of his birthplace.

And yet, after taking on Western adjustments, this languid pine-box whittler, cracker barrel hugger, shady corner lounger of the cotton fields and sumac hills of the South became famed as a bad man among men who had made a life-long study of the art of truculence.

At nine the next morning Calliope was fit. Inspired by his own barbarous melodies and the contents of his jug, he was ready primed to gather fresh laurels from the diffident brow of Quicksand. Encircled and criss-crossed with cartridge belts, abundantly garnished with revolvers, and copiously drunk, he poured forth into Quicksand's main street. Too chivalrous to surprise and capture a town by silent sortie, he paused at the nearest corner and emitted his slogan—that fearful, brassy yell, so reminiscent of the steam piano, that had gained for him the classic appellation that had superseded his own baptismal name. Following close upon his vociferation came three shots from his forty-five by way of limbering up the guns and testing his aim. A yellow dog, the personal property of Colonel Swazey, the proprietor of the Occidental, fell feet upward in the dust with one farewell yelp. A Mexican who was crossing the street from the Blue Front grocery carrying in his hand a bottle of kerosene, was stimulated to a sudden and admirable burst of speed, still grasping the neck of the shattered bottle. The new gilt weather-cock on Judge Riley's lemon and ultramarine two-story residence shivered, flapped, and hung by a splinter, the sport of the wanton breezes. The artillery was in trim.

Calliope's hand was steady. The high, calm ecstasy of habitual battle was upon him, though slightly embittered by the sadness of Alexander in that his conquests were limited to the small world of Quicksand.

Down the street went Calliope, shooting right and left. Glass fell like hail; dogs vamosed; chickens flew, squawking; feminine voices shrieked concernedly to youngsters at large. The din was perforated at intervals by the *staccato* of the Terror's guns, and was drowned periodically by the brazen screech that Quicksand knew so well. The occasions of Calliope's low spirits were legal holidays in Quicksand. All along the main street in advance of his coming clerks were putting up shutters and closing doors. Business would languish for a space. The right of way was Calliope's, and as he advanced, observing the dearth of opposition and the few opportunities for distraction, his ennui perceptibly increased.

But some four squares farther down lively preparations were being made to minister to Mr. Catesby's love for interchange of compliments and repartee. On the previous night numerous messengers had hastened to advise Buck Patterson, the city marshal, of Calliope's impending eruption. The patience of that official, often strained in extending leniency toward the disturber's misdeeds, had been overtaxed. In Quicksand some indulgence was accorded the natural ebullition of human nature. Providing that the lives of the more useful citizens were not recklessly squandered, or too much property needlessly laid waste, the community sentiment was against a too strict enforcement of the law. But Calliope had raised the limit. His outbursts had been too frequent and too violent to come within the classification of a normal and sanitary relaxation of spirit.

Buck Patterson had been expecting and awaiting in his little ten-by-twelve frame office that preliminary yell announcing that Calliope was feeling blue. When the signal came the city marshal rose to his feet and buckled on his guns. Two deputy sheriffs and three citizens who had proven the edible qualities of fire also stood up, ready to bandy with Calliope's leaden jocularities.

"Gather that fellow in ," said Buck Patterson, setting forth the lines of the campaign. "Don't have no talk, but shoot as soon as you can get a show. Keep behind cover and bring him down. He's a nogood 'un. It's up to Calliope to turn up his toes this time, I reckon. Go to him all spraddled out, boys. And don't git too reckless, for what Calliope shoots at he hits."

Buck Patterson, tall, muscular, and solemn-faced, with his bright "City Marshal" badge shining on the breast of his blue flannel shirt, gave his posse directions for the onslaught upon Calliope. The plan was to accomplish the downfall of the Quicksand Terror without loss to the attacking party, if possible.

The splenetic Calliope, unconscious of retributive plots, was steaming down the channel, cannonading on either side, when he suddenly became aware of breakers ahead. The city marshal and one of the deputies rose up behind some dry-goods boxes half a square to the front and opened fire. At the same time the rest of the posse, divided, shelled him from two side streets up which they were cautiously maneuvering from a well-executed detour.

The first volley broke the lock of one of Calliope's guns, cut a neat underbit in his right ear, and exploded a cartridge in his crossbelt, scorching his ribs as it burst. Feeling braced up by this unexpected tonic to his spiritual depression, Calliope executed a fortissimo note from his upper register, and returned the fire like an echo. The upholders of the law dodged at his flash, but a trifle too late to save one of the deputies a bullet just above the elbow, and the marshal a bleeding cheek from a splinter that a ball tore from the box he had ducked behind.

And now Calliope met the enemy's tactics in kind. Choosing with a rapid eye the street from which the weakest and least accurate fire had come, he invaded it at a double-quick, abandoning the unprotected middle of the street. With rare cunning the opposing force in that direction—one of the deputies and two of the valorous volunteers—waited, concealed by beer barrels, until Calliope had passed their retreat, and then peppered him from the rear. In another moment they were reinforced by the marshal and his other men, and then Calliope felt that in order to successfully prolong the delights of the controversy he must find some means of reducing the great odds against him. His eye fell upon a structure that seemed to hold out this promise, providing he could reach it.

Not far away was the little railroad station, its building a strong box house, ten by twenty feet, resting upon a platform four feet above ground. Windows were in each of its walls. Something like a fort it might become to a man thus sorely pressed by superior numbers.

Calliope made a bold and rapid spurt for it, the marshal's crowd "smoking" him as he ran. He reached the haven in safety, the station agent leaving the building by a window, like a flying squirrel, as the garrison entered the door.

Patterson and his supporters halted under protection of a pile of lumber and held consultations. In the station was an unterrified desperado who was an excellent shot and carried an abundance of ammunition. For thirty yards on either side of the besieged was a stretch of bare, open ground. It was a sure thing that the man who attempted to enter that unprotected area would be stopped by one of Calliope's bullets.

The city marshal was resolved. He had decided that Calliope Catesby should no more wake the echoes of Quicksand with his strident whoop. He had so announced. Officially and personally he felt imperatively bound to put the soft pedal on that instrument of discord. It played bad tunes.

Standing near was a hand truck used in the manipulation of small freight. It stood by a shed full of sacked wool, a consignment from one of the sheep ranches. On this truck the marshal and his men piled three heavy sacks of wool. Stooping low, Buck Patterson started for Calliope's fort, slowly pushing this loaded truck before him for protection. The posse, scattering broadly, stood ready to nip the besieged in case he should show himself in an effort to repel the juggernaut of justice that was creeping upon him.

Only once did Calliope make demonstration. He fired from a window, and some tufts of wool spurted from the marshal's trustworthy bulwark. The return shots from the posse pattered against the window frame of the fort. No loss resulted on either side.

The marshal was too deeply engrossed in steering his protected battleship to be aware of the approach of the morning train until he was within a few feet of the platform. The train was coming up on the other side of it. It stopped only one minute at Quicksand. What an opportunity it would offer to

Calliope! He had only to step out the other door, mount the train, and away.

Abandoning his breastwork, Buck, with his gun ready, dashed up the steps and into the room, driving upon the closed door with one heave of his weighty shoulder. The members of the posse heard one shot fired inside, and then there was silence.

At length the wounded man opened his eyes. After a blank space he again could see and hear and feel and think. Turning his eyes about, he found himself lying on a wooden bench. A tall man with a perplexed countenance, wearing a big badge with "City Marshal" engraved upon it, stood over him. A little old woman in black, with a wrinkled face and sparkling black eyes, was holding a wet handkerchief against one of his temples. He was trying to get these facts fixed in his mind and connected with past events, when the old woman began to talk.

"There now, great, big, strong man! That bullet never tetched ye! Jest skeeted along the side of your head and sort of paralysed ye for a spell. I've heerd of sech things afore; cun-cussion is what they names it. Abel Wadkins used to kill squirrels that way— barkin' 'em, Abe called it. You jest been barked, sir, and you'll be all right in a little bit. Feel lots better already, don't ye! You just lay still a while longer and let me bathe your head. You don't know me, I reckon, and 'tain't surprisin' that you shouldn't. I come in on that train from Alabama to see my son. Big son, ain't he? Lands! you wouldn't hardly think he'd ever been a baby, would ye? This is my son, sir."

Half turning, the old woman looked up at the standing man, her worn face lighting with a proud and wonderful smile.

She reached out one veined and calloused hand and took one of her son's. Then smiling cheerily down at the prostrate man, she continued to dip the handkerchief, in the waiting-room tin washbasin and gently apply it to his temple. She had the benevolent garrulity of old age.

"I ain't seen my son before," she continued, "in eight years. One of my nephews, Elkanah Price, he's a conductor on one of them railroads and he got me a pass to come out here. I can stay a whole week on it, and then it'll take me back again. Jest think, now, that little boy of mine has got to be a officer—a city marshal of a whole town! That's somethin' like a constable, ain't it? I never knowed he was a officer; he didn't say nothin' about it in his letters. I reckon he thought his old mother'd be skeered about the danger he was in. But, laws! I never was much of a hand to git skeered. 'Tain't no use. I heard them guns a-shootin' while I was gettin' off them cars, and I see smoke a-comin' out of the depot, but I jest walked right along. Then I see son's face lookin' out through the window. I knowed him at oncet. He met me at the door, and squeezes me 'most to death. And there you was, sir, a-lyin' there jest like you was dead, and I 'lowed we'd see what might be done to help sot you up."

"I think I'll sit up now," said the concussion patient. "I'm feeling pretty fair by this time."

He sat, somewhat weakly yet, leaning against the wall. He was a rugged man, big-boned and straight. His eyes, steady and keen, seemed to linger upon the face of the man standing so still above him. His look wandered often from the face he studied to the marshal's badge upon the other's breast.

"Yes, yes, you'll be all right," said the old woman, patting his arm, "if you don't get to cuttin' up agin, and havin' folks shooting at you. Son told me about you, sir, while you was layin' senseless on the floor. Don't you take it as meddlesome fer an old woman with a son as big as you to talk about it. And you mustn't hold no grudge ag'in' my son for havin' to shoot at ye. A officer has got to take up for the law—it's his duty—and them that acts bad and lives wrong has to suffer. Don't blame my son any, sir—'taint his fault. He's always been a good boy—good when he was growin' up, and kind and 'bedient and well-behaved. Won't you let me advise you, sir, not to do so no more? Be a good man, and leave liquor alone and live peaceably and goodly. Keep away from bad company and work honest and sleep sweet."

The black-mitted hand of the old pleader gently touched the breast of the man she addressed. Very earnest and candid her old, worn face looked. In her rusty black dress and antique bonnet she sat, near the close of a long life, and epitomized the experience of the world. Still the man to whom she spoke gazed above her head, contemplating the silent son of the old mother.

"What does the marshal say?" he asked. "Does he believe the advice is good? Suppose the marshal speaks up and says if the talk's all right?"

The tall man moved uneasily. He fingered the badge on his breast for a moment, and then he put an arm around the old woman and drew her close to him. She smiled the unchanging mother smile of three-score years, and patted his big brown hand with her crooked, mittened fingers while her son spake.

"I says this," he said, looking squarely into the eyes of the other man, "that if I was in your place I'd follow it. If I was a drunken, desp'rate character, without shame or hope, I'd follow it. If I was in your place and you was in mine I'd say: 'Marshal, I'm willin' to swear if you'll give me the chance I'll quit the racket. I'll drop the tanglefoot and the gun play, and won't play hoss no more. I'll be a good citizen and go to work and quit my foolishness. So help me God!' That's what I'd say to you if you was marshal and I was in your place."

"Hear my son talkin'," said the old woman softly. "Hear him, sir. You promise to be good and he won't do you no harm.

Forty-one year ago his heart first beat ag'in' mine, and it's beat true ever since."

The other man rose to his feet, trying his limbs and stretching his muscles.

"Then," said he, "if you was in my place and said that, and I was marshal, I'd say: 'Go free, and do your best to keep your promise.'"

"Lawsy!" exclaimed the old woman, in a sudden flutter, "ef I didn't clear forget that trunk of mine! I see a man settin' it on the platform jest as I seen son's face in the window, and it went plum out of my head. There's eight jars of home-made quince jam in that trunk that I made myself. I wouldn't have nothin' happen to them jars for a red apple."

Away to the door she trotted, spry and anxious, and then Calliope Catesby spoke out to Buck Patterson:

"I just couldn't help it, Buck. I seen her through the window a-comin' in. She never had heard a word 'bout my tough ways. I didn't have the nerve to let her know I was a worthless cuss bein' hunted down by the community. There you was lyin' where my shot laid you, like you was dead. The idea struck me sudden, and I just took your badge off and fastened it onto myself, and I fastened my reputation onto you. I told her I was the marshal and you was a holy terror. You can take your badge back now, Buck."

With shaking fingers Calliope began to unfasten the disc of metal from his shirt.

"Easy there!" said Buck Patterson. "You keep that badge right where it is, Calliope Catesby. Don't you dare to take it off till the day your mother leaves this town. You'll be city marshal of Quicksand as long as she's here to know it. After I stir around town a bit and put 'em on I'll guarantee that nobody won't give the thing away to her. And say, you leather-headed, rip-roarin', low-down son of a locoed cyclone, you follow that advice she give me! I'm goin' to take some of it myself, too."

"Buck," said Calliope feelingly, "ef I don't I hope I may—"

"Shut up," said Buck. "She's a-comin' back."

Memorial Day

Last Monday in May

Vintage Memorial Day placard honoring the fallen of previous wars.

Courtesy crashingnightingale.com

The Flag Paramount

A dozen quarts of champagne, in conjunction with an informal sitting of the President and his cabinet, led to the establishment of the navy and the appointment of Felipe Carrera as its admiral. The wine had been sent by the Mogul Banana Company of New Orleans as a token of amicable relations—and certain consummated deals—between that company and the republic.

Next to the champagne the credit of the appointment belonged to Don Sabas Placido, the newly appointed Minister of War.

The session had been signally tedious; the business and the wine prodigiously dry. A sudden, prankish humor of Don Sabas impelling him to the deed, spiced the grave matters of state with a whiff of agreeable playfulness.

In the order of business had come a bulletin from the department of Orilla del Mar, reporting the seizure by the custom-house officers at the coast town of Solitas of the sloop *Estrella de Noche* and her cargo of dry goods, patent medicines, granulated sugar and three-star brandy. Also six Martini rifles and ten thousand Havana cigars. Caught in the act of smuggling, the sloop and cargo was now, according to law, the property of the republic.

The Collector of Customs, in making his statement, departed from conventional forms so far as to suggest that the confiscated vessel be converted to the use of the government. The prize was the first capture to the credit of the department for ten years. It often happened that government officials required transportation from point to point along the coast, and means were usually lacking. Furthermore, the sloop could act as a coast guard to discourage the pernicious art of smuggling. The Collector would also venture to name one to whom the charge of the boat could be safely entrusted—a young man, Felipe Carrera, not, be it understood, one of extreme wisdom, but loyal, and the best sailor along the coast.

It was upon this hint that the Minister of War executed his little piece of drollery that so enlivened the tedium of executive session.

In the constitution of this small, maritime banana republic was a forgotten section providing for the maintenance of a navy. The champagne was bubbling trickily in the veins of the mercurial statesmen. A formidable document was prepared, encrusted with chromatic seals and jaunty with fluttering ribbons, bearing the florid signatures of state, and conferring upon el Señor Don Felipe Carrera the title of Admiral of the marine fleet and force of the republic. Thus, within the space of a few minutes and the dominion of a dozen extra dry, the country rose to a place among naval powers, and Felipe Carrera became entitled to a salute of twenty-one guns whenever he should enter port.

The Southern races are lacking in that particular humor that finds entertainment in natural misfortunes. Owing to this defect, they are not moved to laughter at the deformed, the feeble-minded, or the insane. Felipe Carrera was but half-witted. Therefore, the people of Solitas called him "*el pobrecito loco*," saying that God had sent but half of him to earth, retaining the other. A somber youth, glowering and speaking only at the rarest times, Felipe was but negatively *loco*. He generally refused to answer all questions when on shore. He seemed to know that he was badly handicapped on land where so many kinds of under-standing are needed, but on the water few sailors whom God had entirely and carefully completed could handle a sailboat as well. He could sail a sloop five points nearer to the wind's eye than the best of them. He owned no boat, but worked among the crews of the schooners and sloops that skimmed the coast, trading, and freighting fruit out to the steamers where there was no harbor. It was through his famous boldness and skill as a sailor, as well as the pity felt for his mental imperfections that he was recommended by the Collector as a suitable custodian of the captured sloop.

When the outcome of Señor Placido's little pleasantry arrived in the form of the imposing commission, the Collector wondered and then smiled. He sent for Felipe, placed the document in his hands, explaining carefully to him the high honor that the government had granted him. Without a word, the newly created Admiral took his commission, and departed.

The next morning he came again to the Collector, and as he passed through the village streets many were the compassionate exclamations of "*pobrecito muchacho*," but never a laugh or a smile.

Somewhere, Felipe had raked together a pitiful semblance of a military uniform—a pair of red trousers, a dingy blue jacket embroidered with yellow braid, and an old fatigue cap abandoned by one of the British soldiers in Belize. In the latter he had fastened the gaudy feathers of a parrot's tail. Buckled around his waist was an ancient ship's cutlass contributed by Pedro Lafitte, the barber, who proudly asserted its inheritance from his ancestor, the illustrious buccaneer.

At the Admiral's heels tagged his newly shipped crew—three grinning, glossy black Caribs, bare to the waist; the sand in the streets spurting in a shower from the spring of their naked feet.

With becoming dignity, Felipe demanded his vessel of the Collector. And now, a fresh honor awaited him. The Collector's wife, a thin, little, yellow woman who read novels in a hammock all day, had found, in an old book, an engraving of a flag purporting to be the naval flag of the republic. Perhaps it had been so designed by the founders of the nation; but, as no navy had ever been established, oblivion had claimed its flag. With her own tawny hands she had made a flag after this pattern—a red cross upon a blue and white ground. Having a little of the romance that abounded in her novels, she presented it to Felipe with the words: "Brave sailor. This flag is of your country. It you will defend with the life. Go with God."

For the next month or two the navy had its troubles. Even the Admiral was perplexed to know what to do without orders, but none came. The sloop was re-christened "*El Nacional*," re-painted, and swung idly at anchor. When Felipe's little store of money was exhausted, he went to the Collector and raised the question of finances.

"Salaries!" exclaimed the Collector, with his hands raised. "*Qué* salaries! Not one *centavo* have I received of my own for seven months. The pay of an Admiral, you ask? *Quien sabe?* Should it be less than three thousand *pesos*? *Mira!* You will see a revolution in this country very soon. A good sign of it is when they call for *pesos, pesos, pesos*; and pay none out."

Felipe left the Collector with a look almost of content in his somber face. A revolution would mean fighting, and then the government would need his services. It was rather humiliating to be an admiral without anything to do, and have a hungry crew begging for *reales* to buy plantains and bread to eat.

When he returned to where the good-natured Caribs were hopefully waiting, they sprang up and saluted, as he had taught them.

"Come, *muchachos*," said the Admiral. "The government is poor. It has no money at present. We will earn what we need to live upon. Soon"—his heavy eyes almost lighted up—"our help may be gladly sought for."

Thereafter *El Nacional* turned out with the other coast craft and freighted bananas and oranges out to the fruit steamers who could not come nearer than a mile offshore, there being no harbor at Solitas. Surely, a self-supporting navy deserves red letters in the budget of any nation!

There was a little telegraph office in Solitas whence a little telegraph line ran over the big mountains to the capital. After earning enough at freighting to keep his crew in provisions and pay for a week or two, Felipe would infest this office, looking like the chorus of an insolvent comic opera troupe besieging the manager's den. Sprawled in a favorite corner, upon the floor, in his fast decaying uniform, with his prodigious saber, distributed between his red legs, he awaited, day after day, and week after week, the long delayed orders from his government, Each day he would inquire, gravely and expectantly, for dispatches. The operator would pretend to make a search, and reply:

"Not yet, it seems, *Señor el Almirante—Poco tiempo!*"

At the answer the Admiral would plump himself down, with a rattle, in his corner to await the infrequent click of the little instrument on the table. Outside, in the shade of the lime trees in the *calle*, the crew chewed sugar cane, or slumbered, well content to serve a country content with so little service.

One day in early summer the revolution predicted by the Collector flamed out suddenly. It had long been smoldering. At the head of the insurgents appeared that Hector and learned Theban of the Central American republics, Don Sabas Placido. A traveler, a soldier, a poet, a scientist, a statesman, and a connoisseur—the wonder was that he could content himself with the petty, remote life of his native country.

"It is a whim of Placido's," said a friend who knew him well, "to take up political intrigue. It is not otherwise than if he had come upon a new *tempo* in music, a new bacillus in the air, a new scent, or rhyme, or explosive. He will squeeze the revolution dry of sensations, and, a week afterward, forget it, skimming the seas of the world in his brigantine to add to his already world-famous collection of—*por Dios!*—everything—from postage stamps to *maquinas de vapor.*"

But the æsthetic Placido seemed to be creating a lively row, for a mere dilettante. The admired of the people, they had risen almost in a body to seat him in the place of the inclement President Prados. There was sharp fighting in the capital, where (contrary to arrangements) the army had rallied to the defense of the incumbent. There was, also, lively skirmishing in most of the coast towns. It was rumored that the revolution was aided by a powerful concern in the States—the Mogul Banana Company. Two of their steamers, the *Traveler* and the *Salvador*, were known to have conveyed insurgent troops from point to point along the coast.

At the first note of war the Admiral of the naval fleet and force made sail for Belize, where he traded a hastily collected cargo for cartridges for the five Martini rifles, the armament of *El Nacional*. Then back he hurried, to be prepared for his country's call. As yet, there had been no actual uprising in Solitas. Military law ruled, and the ferment was bottled for the time. There was a report that everywhere the revolutionists were encountering defeat. In the capital the President's forces triumphed, and there was a rumor that the leaders of the revolt had been forced to flee, hotly pursued.

In the little telegraph office at Solitas there was always a gathering of officials and loyal citizens, awaiting news from the seat of government. One morning the telegraph key began clicking, and presently the operator called, loudly: "One telegram for *el Almirante*, Don Señor Felipe Carrera!"

166

There was a shuffling sound; a great rattling of tin scabbard, and the Admiral, prompt at his spot of waiting, leaped across the room to receive it.

The message was handed to him. Slowly spelling it out, he found it to be his first official order—thus running:

"Proceed immediately with your vessel to mouth of Rio Ruiz; transport beef and provisions to barracks at Alforan. Martinez, General."

Small glory, to be sure, in this, his country's first call. But it had called, and joy surged in the Admiral's breast. He drew his cutlass belt to another buckle hole, roused his dozing crew, and in a quarter of an hour *El Nacional* was tacking swiftly down coast in a stiff landward breeze.

The Rio Ruiz is a small river, emptying into the sea ten miles below Solitas. That portion of the coast is wild and solitary. Through a gorge in the Cordilleras rushes the Rio Ruiz, cold and bubbling, to glide, at the last, with breadth and leisure, through an alluvial morass into the sea.

In two hours *El Nacional* entered the river's mouth. The banks were crowded with a disposition of formidable trees. The sumptuous undergrowth of the tropics overflowed the land, and drowned itself in the shallow waters. Silently the sloop entered there, and met a deeper silence. Brilliant with greens and ochres and floral scarlets, the umbrageous mouth of the Rio Ruiz furnished no sound or movement save of the seagoing water as it curled against the prow of the vessel. Small chance there seemed of wresting beef or provisions from that empty solitude.

The Admiral decided to cast anchor, and, at the chain's rattle, the forest was stimulated to instant and resounding uproar. The mouth of the Rio Ruiz had only been taking a morning nap. Parrots and baboons screeched and barked in the trees; a whirring and a hissing and a booming marked the awakening of animal life; a dark blue bulk was visible for an instant, as a startled tapir fought his way through the vines.

The navy, under orders, hung in the mouth of the little river for hours. The crew served the dinner of shark's fin soup, plantains, crab gumbo and sour claret. The Admiral, with a three-feet telescope, closely scanned the impervious foliage fifty yards away.

It was nearly sunset when a reverberating "hallo-o-o" came from the forest to their left. It was answered, and three men, mounted upon mules, crashed through the tropic tangle to within a dozen yards of the river's bank. There they dismounted; and one, unbuckling his belt, struck each mule a violent blow with his sword scabbard, so that they, with a fling of heels, dashed back again into the forest.

Those were strange-looking men to be convoying beef and provisions. One was a large and exceedingly active man, of striking presence. He was of the purest Spanish type, with curling dark hair, gray besprinkled, blue, sparkling eyes, and the pronounced air of a *caballero grande*. The other two were small, brown-faced men, wearing white military uniforms, high riding boots and swords. The clothes of all were drenched, bespattered and rent by the thicket. Some stress of circumstance must have driven them, *diable à quatre*, through flood, mire and jungle.

"*O-hé! Señor Almirante*," called the large man. "Send to us your boat."

The dory was lowered, and Felipe, with one of the Caribs, rowed toward the left bank.

The large man stood near the water's brink, waist deep in the curling vines. As he gazed upon the scarecrow figure in the stern of the dory a sprightly interest beamed upon his mobile face. Months of wageless and thankless service had dimmed the admiral's splendor. His red trousers were patched and ragged.

Most of the bright buttons and yellow braid were gone from his jacket. The visor of his cap was torn, and depended almost to his eyes. The admiral's feet were bare.

"Dear admiral," cried the large man, and his voice was like a blast from a horn, "I kiss your hands. I knew we could build upon your fidelity. You had our dispatch—from General Martinez. A little nearer with your boat, dear Admiral. Upon these evils of shifting vines we stand with the smallest security."

Felipe regarded him with a stolid face.

"Provisions and beef for the barracks at Alforan," he quoted.

"No fault of the butchers, *Almirante mio*, that the beef awaits you not. But you are come in time to save the cattle. Get us aboard your vessel, señor, at once. You first, *caballeros—á priesa*. Come back for me. The boat is too small."

The dory conveyed the two officers to the sloop, and returned for the large man.

"Have you so gross a thing as food, good admiral?" he cried, when aboard. "And, perhaps, coffee? Beef and provisions! *Nombre de Dios!* a little longer and we could have eaten one of those mules that you, Colonel Rafael, saluted so feelingly with your sword scabbard at parting. Let us have food; and then we will sail—for the barracks at Alforan—no?"

The Caribs prepared a meal, to which the three passengers of *El Nacional* set themselves with famished delight. About sunset, as was its custom, the breeze veered and swept back from the mountains, cool and steady, bringing a taste of the stagnant lagoons and mangrove swamps that guttered the lowlands. The mainsail of the sloop was hoisted and swelled to it, and at that moment they heard shouts and a waxing clamor from the bosky profundities of the wood.

"The butchers, my dear admiral," said the large man, smiling, "too late for the slaughter."

Further than his orders to his crew, the admiral was saying nothing. The topsail and jib were spread, and the sloop glided out of the estuary. The large man and his companions had bestowed themselves with what comfort they could about the bare deck. Belike, the thing big in their minds had been their departure from that critical shore; and now that the hazard was so far reduced their thoughts were loosed to the consideration of further deliverance. But when they saw the sloop turn and fly up coast again they relaxed, satisfied with the course the admiral had taken.

The large man sat at ease, his spirited blue eye engaged in the contemplation of the navy's commander. He was trying to estimate this somber and fantastic lad, whose impenetrable stolidity puzzled him. Himself a fugitive, his life sought, and chafing under the smart of defeat and failure, it was characteristic of him to transfer instantly his interest to the study of a thing new to him. It was like him, too, to have conceived and risked all upon this last desperate and madcap scheme—this message to a poor, crazed *fanatico* cruising about with his grotesque uniform and his farcical title. But his companions had been at their wits' end; escape had seemed incredible; and now he was pleased with the success of the plan they had called crack-brained and precarious.

The brief, tropic twilight seemed to slide swiftly into the pearly splendor of a moonlit night. And now the lights of Solitas appeared, distributed against the darkening shore to their right. The admiral stood, silent, at the tiller; the Caribs, like black panthers, held the sheets, leaping noiselessly at his short commands. The three passengers were watching intently the sea before them, and when at length they came in sight of the bulk of a steamer lying a mile out from the town, with her lights radiating deep into the water, they held a sudden voluble and close-headed converse. The sloop was speeding as if to strike midway between ship and shore.

"The Admiral had drawn his cutlass, and was darting upon him."

Ainslee's

January 1902

Original illustration by Charles Grunwald
(1867 – November 22, 1910)

The large man suddenly separated from his companions and approached the scarecrow at the helm.

"My dear admiral," he said, "the government has been exceedingly remiss. I feel all the shame for it that only its ignorance of your devoted service has prevented it from sustaining. An inexcusable oversight has been made. A vessel, a uniform and a crew worthy of your fidelity shall be furnished you. But just now, dear admiral, there is business of moment afoot. The steamer lying there is the *Salvador*. I and my friends desire to be conveyed to her, where we are sent on the government's business. Do us the favor to shape your course accordingly."

Without replying, the admiral gave a sharp command, and put the tiller hard to port. *El Nacional* swerved, and headed straight as an arrow's course for the shore.

"Do me the favor," said the large man, a trifle restively, "to acknowledge, at least, that you catch the sound of my words." It was possible that the fellow might be lacking in senses as well as intellect.

The admiral emitted a croaking, harsh laugh, and spake.

"They will stand you," he said, "with your face to a wall and shoot you dead. That is the way they kill traitors. I knew you when you stepped into my boat. I have seen your picture in a book. You are Sabas Placido, traitor to your country. With your face to a wall. So, you will die. I am the Admiral, and I will take you to them. With your face to a wall. Yes."

Don Sabas half turned and waved his hand, with a ringing laugh, toward his fellow fugitives. "To you, *caballeros*, I have related the history of that *banquete* when we issued that O! so ridiculous commission. Of a truth our jest has been turned against us. Behold the Frankenstein's monster we have created!"

Don Sabas glanced toward the shore. The lights of Solitas were drawing nearer. He could see the beach, the warehouse of the *Bodega Nacional*, the long, low *cuartel* occupied by the soldiers, and, behind that, gleaming in the moonlight, a stretch of high 'dobe wall. He had seen men stood with their faces to that wall and shot dead.

Again he addressed the extravagant figure at the helm.

"It is true," he said, "that I am fleeing the country. But, receive the assurance that I care very little for that. Courts and camps everywhere are open to Sabas Placido. *Vaya!* what is this molehill of a republic—this pig's head of a country—to a man like me? I am a *paisano* of everywhere. In *Roma, Londres, Vienna, Nuevo York, Madrid* you will hear them say: 'Welcome back, Don Sabas.' Come! *tonto*—baboon of a boy—Admiral, whatever you call yourself, turn your boat. Put us on board the *Salvador*, and here is your pay—five hundred *pesos* in money of the *Estados Unidos*—more than your lying government will pay you in twenty years."

Don Sabas pressed a plump purse against the boy's hand. The Admiral gave no heed to the words or the movement. Braced against the helm, he was holding the sloop dead on her shoreward course. His dull face was lit almost to intelligence by some internal conceit that seemed to afford him joy, and found utterance in another parrot-like cackle.

"That is why they do it," he said—"so that you will not see the guns. They fire—*boum!*—and you fall dead. With your face to the wall. Yes."

The admiral called a sudden order to his crew. The lithe, silent Caribs made fast the sheets they held, and slipped down the hatchway into the hold of the sloop. When the last one had disappeared, Don Sabas, like a big, brown leopard, leaped, closed and fastened the hatch and stood, smiling.

"No rifles, if you please, dear Admiral. It was a whimsey of mine once to compile a dictionary of the Carib *lengua*. So, I understood your order. Perhaps now you will—"

He cut short his words, for he heard the dull "swish" of iron scraping along tin. The admiral had drawn his cutlass, and was darting upon him. The blade descended, and it was only by a display of surprising agility that the large man escaped, with only a bruised shoulder, the glancing weapon. He was drawing his pistol as he sprang, and the next instant he shot the Admiral down.

Don Sabas stooped over him, and rose again.

"*En el corazon,*" he said briefly. "Señores, the navy is abolished."

Colonel Rafael sprang to the helm; the other officer hastened to loose the mainsail sheets. The boom swung round; *El Nacional* described a fluent curve and began to tack industriously for the *Salvador*.

"Strike that flag, señor," called Colonel Rafael. "Our friends on the steamer will wonder why we are sailing under it."

"Well said," cried Don Sabas. Advancing to the mast he lowered the flag to the deck, where lay its too loyal supporter. Thus ended the Minister of War's little piece of after-dinner drollery, and by the same hand that began it.

Suddenly Don Sabas gave a great cry of joy, and ran down the slanting deck to the side of Colonel Rafael. Across his arm he carried the flag of the extinguished navy.

"*Mire! mire! señor. Ah, Dios!* Already can I hear that great bear of an *Oestreicher* shout, '*Du hast mein herz gebrochen!*' *Mire!* Of my friend, Herr Grunitz, of *Vienna*, you have heard me relate. That man has travelled to Ceylon for an orchid— to Patagonia for a head-dress—to Benares for a slipper—to Mozambique for a spearhead to add to his famous collections. Thou knowest, also, *amigo* Rafael, that I have been a gatherer of curios. My collection of battle flags of the world's navies was the most complete in existence until last year. Then Herr Grunitz secured two, O! such rare specimens. One of a Barbary state, and one of the Makarooroos, a tribe on the west coast of Africa. I have not those, but they can be procured. But this flag, señor—do you know what it is? Name of God! do you know? See that red cross upon the blue and white ground! You never saw it before? *Seguramente no.* It is the naval flag of your country. *Mire!* This rotten tub we stand upon is its navy—that dead cockatoo lying there was its commander—that stroke of cutlass and single pistol shot a sea battle. All a piece of absurd foolery, I grant you—but authentic. There has never been another flag like this, and there never will be another. No. It is unique in the whole world. Yes. Think of what that means to a collector of flags! Do you know, *Coronel mio*, how many golden crowns Herr Grunitz would give for this flag? Ten thousand, likely. Well, a hundred thousand would not buy it. Beautiful flag! Only flag! Little devil of a most heaven-born flag! *O-hé!* old grumbler beyond the ocean. Wait till Don Sabas comes again to the Königin Strasse. He will let you kneel and touch the folds of it with one finger. *O-hé!* old spectacled ransacker of the world!"

Forgotten was the impotent revolution, the danger, the loss, the gall of defeat. Possessed solely by the inordinate and unparalleled passion of the collector, he strode up and down the little deck, clasping to his breast with one hand the paragon of a flag. He snapped his fingers triumphantly toward the east. He shouted the paean to his prize in trumpet tones, as though he would make old Grunitz hear.

They were waiting, on the *Salvador*, to welcome them. The sloop came close alongside the steamer where her sides were sliced almost to the lower deck for the loading of fruit. The sailors of the *Salvador* grappled and held her there.

Captain McLeod leaned over the side.

"Well, señor, the jig is up, I'm told."

"The jig is up?" Don Sabas looked perplexed for a moment.

"That revolution—*ah*—*si*." With a shrug of his shoulders he dismissed the matter.

The captain learned of the escape and the imprisoned crew.

"Caribs?" he said; "no harm in them." He slipped down into the sloop and kicked loose the hasp of the hatch. The black fellows came tumbling up, sweating but grinning.

"Hey! black boys!" said the captain, in a dialect of his own; "you sabe, catchy boat and vamos back same place quick."

They saw him point to themselves, the sloop and Solitas. "Yas, yas!" they cried, with broader grins and many nods.

The four—Don Sabas, the two officers and the captain—moved to quit the sloop. Don Sabas lagged a little behind, looking at the still form of the late Admiral, sprawled in his paltry trappings.

"*Pobrecito loco*," he said softly.

He was a brilliant cosmopolite and a *cognoscente* of high rank; but, after all, he was of the same race and blood and instinct of this people. Even as the simple *gente* of Solitas had said it, so said Don Sabas. Without a smile, he looked, and said, "The poor little crazed one!"

Stooping he raised the limp shoulders, drew the priceless and induplicable flag under them and over the breast, pinning it there with the diamond star of the Order of San Carlos that he took from the collar of his own coat.

He followed after the others, and stood with them upon the deck of the *Salvador*. The sailors that steadied *El Nacional* shoved her off. The jabbering Caribs hauled away at the rigging; the sloop headed for the shore; and Herr Grunitz's collection of naval flags was still the finest in the world.

Flag Day

June 14th

Raising the Flag on Iwo Jima

February 19, 1945

Pulitzer Prize winning photograph taken by Joseph John Rosenthal
(October 9, 1911 –August 20, 2006)

Public Domain. Courtesy of Wikimedia Commons

The Fourth in Salvador

On a summer's day, while the city was rocking with the din and red uproar of patriotism, Billy Casparis told me this story. In his way, Billy is Ulysses, Jr. Like Satan, he comes from going to and fro upon the earth and walking up and down in it. To-morrow morning while you are cracking your breakfast egg he may be off with his little alligator grip to boom a town site in the middle of Lake Okeechobee or to trade horses with the Patagonians.

We sat at a little, round table, and between us were glasses holding big lumps of ice, and above us leaned an artificial palm. And because our scene was set with the properties of the one they recalled to his mind, Billy was stirred to narrative.

"It reminds me," said he, "of a Fourth I helped to celebrate down in Salvador. 'Twas while I was running an ice factory down there, after I unloaded that silver mine I had in Colorado. I had what they called a 'conditional concession.' They made me put up a thousand dollars cash forfeit that I would make ice continuously for six months. If I did that I could draw down my ante. If I failed to do so the government took the pot. So the inspectors kept dropping in, trying to catch me without the goods.

"One day when the thermometer was at 110, the clock at half-past one, and the calendar at July third, two of the little, brown, oily nosers in red trousers slid in to make an inspection. Now, the factory hadn't turned out a pound of ice in three weeks, for a couple of reasons. The Salvador heathen wouldn't buy it; they said it made things cold they put it in. And I couldn't make any more, because I was broke. All I was holding on for was to get down my thousand so I could leave the country. The six months would be up on the sixth of July.

"Well, I showed 'em all the ice I had. I raised the lid of a darkish vat, and there was an elegant 100-pound block of ice, beautiful and convincing to the eye. I was about to close down the lid again when one of those brunette sleuths flops down on his red knees and lays a slanderous and violent hand on my guarantee of good faith. And in two minutes more they had dragged out on the floor that fine chunk of molded glass that had cost me fifty dollars to have shipped down from Frisco.

"'Ice-y?' says the fellow that played me the dishonorable trick; 'verree warm ice-y. Yes. The day is that hot, señor. Yes. Maybeso it is of desirableness to leave him out to get the cool. Yes.'

"'Yes,' says I, 'yes,' for I knew they had me. 'Touching's believing, ain't it, boys? Yes. Now there's some might say the seats of your trousers are sky blue, but 'tis my opinion they are red. Let's apply the tests of the laying on of hands and feet.' And so I hoisted both those inspectors out the door on the toe of my shoe, and sat down to cool off on my block of disreputable glass.

"And, as I live without oats, while I sat there, homesick for money and without a cent to my ambition, there came on the breeze the most beautiful smell my nose had entered for a year. God knows where it came from in that backyard of a country— it was a bouquet of soaked lemon peel, cigar stumps, and stale beer—exactly the smell of Goldbrick Charley's place on Fourteenth Street where I used to play pinochle of afternoons with the third-rate actors. And that smell drove my troubles through me and clinched 'em at the back. I began to long for my country and feel sentiments about it; and I said words about Salvador that you wouldn't think could come legitimate out of an ice factory.

"And while I was sitting there, down through the blazing sunshine in his clean, white clothes comes Maximilian Jones, an American interested in rubber and rosewood.

"'Great carrambos!' says I, when he stepped in, for I was in a bad temper, 'didn't I have catastrophes enough? I know what you want. You want to tell me that story again about Johnny Ammiger and the widow on the train. You've told it nine times already this month.'

"'It must be the heat,' says Jones, stopping in at the door, amazed. 'Poor Billy. He's got bugs. Sitting on ice, and calling his best friends pseudonyms. Hi!—*muchacho!*' Jones called my force of employees, who was sitting in the sun, playing with his toes, and told him to put on his trousers and run for the doctor.

"'Come back,' says I. 'Sit down, Maxy, and forget it. 'Tis not ice you see, nor a lunatic upon it. 'Tis only an exile full of home-sickness sitting on a lump of glass that's just cost him a thousand dollars. Now, what was it Johnny said to the widow first? I'd like to hear it again, Maxy—honest. Don't mind what I said.'

"Maximilian Jones and I sat down and talked. He was about as sick of the country as I was, for the grafters were squeezing him for half the profits of his rosewood and rubber. Down in the bottom of a tank of water I had a dozen bottles of sticky Frisco beer; and I fished these up, and we fell to talking about home and the flag and Hail Columbia and home-fried potatoes; and the drivel we contributed would have sickened any man enjoying those blessings. But at that time we were out of 'em. You can't appreciate home till you've left it, money till it's spent, your wife till she's joined a woman's club, nor Old Glory till you see it hanging on a broomstick on the shanty of a consul in a foreign town.

"And sitting there me and Maximilian Jones, scratching at our prickly heat and kicking at the lizards on the floor, became afflicted with a dose of patriotism and affection for our country. There was me, Billy Casparis, reduced from a capitalist to a pauper by over-addiction to my glass (in the lump), declares my troubles off for the present and myself to be an uncrowned sovereign of the greatest country on earth. And Maximilian Jones pours out whole drug stores of his wrath on oligarchies and potentates in red trousers and calico shoes. And we issues a declaration of interference in which we guarantee that the fourth day of July shall be celebrated in Salvador with all the kinds of salutes, explosions, honors of war, oratory, and liquids known to tradition. Yes, neither me nor Jones breathed with soul so dead. There shall be ruckuses in Salvador, we say, and the monkeys had better climb the tallest cocoanut trees and the fire department get out its red sashes and two tin buckets.

"About this time into the factory steps a native man incriminated by the name of General Mary Esperanza Dingo. He was some pumpkin both in politics and color, and the friend of me and Jones. He was full of politeness and a kind of intelligence, having picked up the latter and managed to preserve the former during a two years' residence in Philadelphia studying medicine. For a Salvadorian he was not such a calamitous little man, though he always would play jack, queen, king, ace, deuce for a straight.

"General Mary sits with us and has a bottle. While he was in the States he had acquired a synopsis of the English language and the art of admiring our institutions. By and by the General gets up and tiptoes to the doors and windows and other stage entrances, remarking 'Hist!' at each one. They all do that in Salvador before they ask for a drink of water or the time of day, being conspirators from the cradle and matinee idols by proclamation.

"'Hist!' says General Dingo again, and then he lays his chest on the table quite like Gaspard the Miser. 'Good friends, señores, to-morrow will be the great day of Liberty and Independence. The hearts of Americans and Salvadorians should beat together. Of your history and your great Washington I know. Is it not so?'

"Now, me and Jones thought that nice of the General to remember when the Fourth came. It made us feel good. He must have heard the news going round in Philadelphia about that disturbance we had with England.

"'Yes,' says me and Maxy together, 'we knew it. We were talking about it when you came in. And you can bet your bottom concession that there'll be fuss and feathers in the air to-morrow. We are few in numbers, but the welkin may as well reach out to push the button, for it's got to ring.'

"'I, too, shall assist,' says the General, thumping his collar-bone. 'I, too, am on the side of Liberty. Noble Americans, we will make the day one to be never forgotten.'

"'For us American whisky,' says Jones—'none of your Scotch smoke or anisada or Three Star Hennessey to-morrow. We'll borrow the consul's flag; old man Billfinger shall make orations, and we'll have a barbecue on the plaza.'

"'Fireworks,' says I, 'will be scarce; but we'll have all the cartridges in the shops for our guns. I've got two navy sixes I brought from Denver.'

"'There is one cannon,' said the General; 'one big cannon that will go "BOOM!" And three hundred men with rifles to shoot.'

"'Oh, say!' says Jones, 'Generalissimo, you're the real silk elastic. We'll make it a joint international celebration. Please, General, get a white horse and a blue sash and be grand marshal.'

"'With my sword,' says the General, rolling his eyes. 'I shall ride at the head of the brave men who gather in the name of Liberty.'

"'And you might,' we suggest, 'see the commandante and advise him that we are going to prize things up a bit. We Americans, you know, are accustomed to using municipal regulations for gun wadding when we line up to help the eagle scream. He might suspend the rules for one day. We don't want to get in the calaboose for spanking his soldiers if they get in our way, do you see?'

"'Hist!' says General Mary. 'The commandant is with us, heart and soul. He will aid us. He is one of us.'

"We made all the arrangements that afternoon. There was a Georgian in Salvador who had drifted down there from a busted-up colored colony that had been started on some possumless land in Mexico. As soon as he heard us say 'barbecue' he wept for joy and groveled on the ground. He dug his trench on the plaza, and got half a beef on the coals for an all-night roast. Me and Maxy went to see the rest of the Americans in the town and they all sizzled like a seidlitz with joy at the idea of solemnizing an old-time Fourth.

"There were six of us all together—Martin Dillard, a coffee planter; Henry Barnes, a railroad man; old man Billfinger, an educated tintype taker; me and Jonesy, and Jerry, the boss of the barbecue. There was also an Englishman in town named Sterrett, who was there to write a book on Domestic Architecture of the Insect World. We felt some bashfulness about inviting a Britisher to help crow over his own country, but we decided to risk it, out of our personal regard for him.

"We found Sterrett in pajamas working at his manuscript with a bottle of brandy for a paper weight.

"'Englishman,' says Jones, 'let us interrupt your disquisition on bug houses for a moment. To-morrow is the Fourth of July. We don't want to hurt your feelings, but we're going to commemorate the day when we licked you by a little refined debauchery and nonsense—something that can be heard above five miles off. If you are broad-gauged enough to taste whisky at your own wake, we'd be pleased to have you join us.'

"'Do you know,' says Sterrett, setting his glasses on his nose, 'I like your cheek in asking me if I'll join you; blast me if I don't. You might have known I would, without asking. Not as a traitor to my own country, but for the intrinsic joy of a blooming row.'

"On the morning of the Fourth I woke up in that old shanty of an ice factory feeling sore. I looked around at the wreck of all I possessed, and my heart was full of bile. From where I lay on my cot I could look through the window and see the consul's old ragged Stars and Stripes hanging over his shack. 'You're all kinds of a fool, Billy Casparis,' I says to myself; 'and of all your crimes against sense it does look like this idea of celebrating the Fourth should receive the award of demerit. Your business is busted up, your thousand dollars is gone into the kitty of this corrupt country on that last bluff you made, you've got just fifteen Chili dollars left, worth forty-six cents each at bedtime last night and steadily going down. To-day you'll blow in your last cent hurrahing for that flag, and to-morrow you'll be living on bananas from the stalk and screwing your drinks out of your friends. What's the flag done for you? While you were under it you worked for what you got. You wore your finger nails down skinning suckers, and salting mines, and driving bears and alligators off your town lot additions. How much does patriotism count for on deposit when the little man with the green eye-shade in the savings-bank adds up your book? Suppose you were to get pinched over here in this irreligious country for some little crime or other, and appealed to your country for protection—what would it do for you? Turn your appeal over to a committee of one railroad man, an army officer, a member of each labor union, and a colored man to investigate whether any of your ancestors were ever related to a cousin of Mark Hanna, and then file the papers in the Smithsonian Institution until after the next election. That's the kind of a sidetrack the Stars and Stripes would switch you onto.'

"You can see that I was feeling like an indigo plant; but after I washed my face in some cool water, and got out my navys and ammunition, and started up to the Saloon of the Immaculate Saints where we were to meet, I felt better. And when I saw those other American boys come swaggering into the trysting place—cool, easy, conspicuous fellows, ready to risk any kind of a one-card draw, or to fight grizzlies, fire, or extradition, I began to feel glad I was one of 'em. So, I says to myself again: 'Billy, you've got fifteen dollars and a country left this morning—blow in the dollars and blow up the town as an American gentleman should on Independence Day.'

"It is my recollection that we began the day along conventional lines. The six of us—for Sterrett was along—made progress among the cantinas, divesting the bars as we went of all strong drink bearing American labels. We kept informing the atmosphere as to the glory and preeminence of the United States and its ability to subdue, outjump, and eradicate the other nations of the earth. And, as the findings of American labels grew more plentiful, we became more contaminated with patriotism. Maximilian Jones hopes that our late foe, Mr. Sterrett, will not take offense at our enthusiasm. He sets down his bottle and shakes Sterrett's hand. 'As white man to white man,' says he, 'denude our uproar of the slightest taint of personality. Excuse us for Bunker Hill, Patrick Henry, and Waldorf Astor, and such grievances as might lie between us as nations.'

" 'Fellow hoodlums,' says Sterrett, 'on behalf of the Queen I ask you to cheese it. It is an honor to be a guest at disturbing the peace under the American flag. Let us chant the passionate strains of "Yankee Doodle" while the señor behind the bar mitigates the occasion with another round of cochineal and aqua fortis.'

"Old Man Billfinger, being charged with a kind of rhetoric, makes speeches every time we stop. We explained to such citizens as we happened to step on that we were celebrating the dawn of our own private brand of liberty, and to please enter such inhumanities as we might commit on the list of unavoidable casualties.

"About eleven o'clock our bulletins read: 'A considerable rise in temperature, accompanied by thirst and other alarming symptoms.' We hooked arms and stretched our line across the narrow streets, all of us armed with Winchesters and navys for purposes of noise and without malice. We stopped on a street corner and fired a dozen or so rounds, and began a serial assortment of United States whoops and yells, probably the first ever heard in that town.

"When we made that noise things began to liven up. We heard a pattering up a side street, and here came General Mary Esperanza Dingo on a white horse with a couple of hundred brown boys following him in red undershirts and bare feet, dragging guns ten feet long. Jones and me had forgot all about General Mary and his promise to help us celebrate. We fired another salute and gave another yell, while the General shook hands with us and waved his sword.

"'Oh, General,' shouts Jones, 'this is great. This will be a real pleasure to the eagle. Get down and have a drink.'

"'Drink?' says the general. 'No. There is no time to drink. *Viva la Libertad!*'

"'Don't forget *E Pluribus Unum*,' says Henry Barnes.

"'*Viva* it good and strong,' says I. 'Likewise, *viva* George Washington. God save the Union, and,' I says, bowing to Sterrett, 'don't discard the Queen.'

"'Thanks,' says Sterrett. 'The next round's mine. All in to the bar. Army, too.'

"But we were deprived of Sterrett's treat by a lot of gunshots several squares sway, which General Dingo seemed to think he ought to look after. He spurred his old white plug up that way, and the soldiers scuttled along after him.

" 'Mary is a real tropical bird,' says Jones. 'He's turned out the infantry to help us do honor to the Fourth. We'll get that cannon he spoke of after a while and fire some window-breakers with it. But just now I want some of that barbecued beef. Let us on to the plaza.'

"There we found the meat gloriously done, and Jerry waiting, anxious. We sat around on the grass, and got hunks of it on our tin plates. Maximilian Jones, always made tender-hearted by drink, cried some because George Washington couldn't be there to enjoy the day. 'There was a man I love, Billy,' he says, weeping on my shoulder. 'Poor George! To think he's gone, and missed the fireworks. A little more salt, please, Jerry.'

"From what we could hear, General Dingo seemed to be kindly contributing some noise while we feasted. There were guns going off around town, and pretty soon we heard that cannon go 'BOOM!' just as he said it would. And then men began to skim along the edge of the plaza, dodging in among the orange trees and houses. We certainly had things stirred up in Salvador. We felt proud of the occasion and grateful to General Dingo. Sterrett was about to take a bite off a juicy piece of rib when a bullet took it away from his mouth.

" 'Somebody's celebrating with ball cartridges,' says he, reaching for another piece. 'Little over-zealous for a non-resident patriot, isn't it?'

" 'Don't mind it,' I says to him. ' 'Twas an accident. They happen, you know, on the Fourth. After one reading of the

Declaration of Independence in New York I've known the S. R. O. sign to be hung out at all the hospitals and police stations.'

"But then Jerry gives a howl and jumps up with one hand clapped to the back of his leg where another bullet has acted over-zealous. And then comes a quantity of yells, and round a corner and across the plaza gallops General Mary Esperanza Dingo embracing the neck of his horse, with his men running behind him, mostly dropping their guns by way of discharging ballast. And chasing 'em all is a company of feverish little warriors wearing blue trousers and caps.

"'Assistance, amigos,' the General shouts, trying to stop his horse. 'Assistance, in the name of Liberty!'

"'That's the Compañia Azul, the President's bodyguard,' says Jones. 'What a shame! They've jumped on poor old Mary just because he was helping us to celebrate. Come on, boys, it's our Fourth;—do we let that little squad of A.D.T's break it up?'

"'I vote No,' says Martin Dillard, gathering his Winchester. 'It's the privilege of an American citizen to drink, drill, dress up, and be dreadful on the Fourth of July, no matter whose country he's in.'

"'Fellow citizens!' says old man Billfinger, 'In the darkest hour of Freedom's birth, when our brave forefathers promulgated the principles of undying liberty, they never expected that a bunch of blue jays like that should be allowed to bust up an anniversary. Let us preserve and protect the Constitution.'

"We made it unanimous, and then we gathered our guns and assaulted the blue troops in force. We fired over their heads, and then charged 'em with a yell, and they broke and ran. We were irritated at having our barbecue disturbed, and we chased 'em a quarter of a mile. Some of 'em we caught and kicked hard. The General rallied his troops and joined in the chase. Finally they scattered in a thick banana grove, and we couldn't flush a single one. So we sat down and rested.

"If I were to be put, severe, through the third degree, I wouldn't be able to tell much about the rest of the day. I mind that we pervaded the town considerable, calling upon the people to bring out more armies for us to destroy. I remember seeing a crowd somewhere, and a tall man that wasn't Billfinger making a Fourth of July speech from a balcony. And that was about all.

"Somebody must have hauled the old ice factory up to where I was, and put it around me, for there's where I was when I woke up the next morning. As soon as I could recollect my name and address I got up and held an inquest. My last cent was gone. I was all in.

"And then a neat black carriage drives to the door, and out steps General Dingo and a bay man in a silk hat and tan shoes.

"'Yes,' says I to myself, 'I see it now. You're the Chief de Policeos and High Lord Chamberlain of the Calaboosum; and you want Billy Casparis for excess of patriotism and assault with intent. All right. Might as well be in jail, anyhow.'

"But it seems that General Mary is smiling, and the bay man shakes my hand, and speaks in the American dialect.

"'General Dingo has informed me, Señor Casparis, of your gallant service in our cause. I desire to thank you with my person. The bravery of you and the other *señores Americanos* turned the struggle for liberty in our favor. Our party triumphed. The terrible battle will live forever in history.'

"'Battle?' says I; 'what battle?' and I ran my mind back along history, trying to think.

"'Señor Casparis is modest,' says General Dingo. 'He led his brave compadres into the thickest of the fearful conflict. Yes. Without their aid the revolution would have failed.'

"'Why, now,' says I, 'don't tell me there was a revolution yesterday. That was only a Fourth of—'

"But right there I abbreviated. It seemed to me it might be best.

"'After the terrible struggle,' says the bay man, 'President Bolano was forced to fly. To-day Caballo is President by proclamation. Ah, yes. Beneath the new administration I am the head of the Department of Mercantile Concessions. On my file I find one report, Señor Casparis, that you have not made ice in accord with your contract.' And here the bay man smiles at me, cute.

"'Oh, well,' says I, 'I guess the report's straight. I know they caught me. That's all there is to it.'

"'Do not say so,' says the bay man. He pulls off a glove and goes over and lays his hand on that chunk of glass.

"'Ice,' says he, nodding his head, solemn.

"General Dingo also steps over and feels of it.

"'Ice,' says the General; 'I'll swear to it.'

"'If Señor Casparis,' says the bay man, 'will present himself to the treasury on the sixth day of this month he will receive back the thousand dollars he did deposit as a forfeit. Adios, señor.'

"The General and the bay man bowed themselves out, and I bowed as often as they did.

"And when the carriage rolls away through the sand I bows once more, deeper than ever, till my hat touches the ground. But this time 'twas not intended for them. For, over their heads, I saw the old flag fluttering in the breeze above the consul's roof; and 'twas to it I made my profoundest salute."

Original illustration from "The Fourth in Salvador"
by Charles Henry White (1878 – 1918).

McClure's

July 1903

Austin History Center, Austin Public Library via University of North Texas
Libraries, The Portal to Texas History

Father's Day

Third Sunday in June

Athol, Margaret and William Porter, taken in the early 1890s.

The Church with
an Overshot Wheel

Lakelands is not to be found in the catalogues of fashionable summer resorts. It lies on a low spur of the Cumberland range of mountains on a little tributary of the Clinch River. Lakelands proper is a contented village of two dozen houses situated on a forlorn, narrow-gauge railroad line. You wonder whether the railroad lost itself in the pine woods and ran into Lakelands from fright and loneliness, or whether Lakelands got lost and huddled itself along the railroad to wait for the cars to carry it home. You wonder again why it was named Lakelands. There are no lakes, and the lands about are too poor to be worth mentioning.

Half a mile from the village stands the Eagle House, a big, roomy old mansion run by Josiah Rankin for the accommodation of visitors who desire the mountain air at inexpensive rates. The Eagle House is delightfully mismanaged. It is full of ancient instead of modern improvements, and it is altogether as comfortably neglected and pleasingly disarranged as your own home. But you are furnished with clean rooms and good and abundant fare: yourself and the piny woods must do the rest. Nature has provided a mineral spring, grape-vine swings, and croquet—even the wickets are wooden. You have Art to thank only for the fiddle-and-guitar music twice a week at the hop in the rustic pavilion.

The patrons of the Eagle House are those who seek recreation as a necessity, as well as a pleasure. They are busy people, who may be likened to clocks that need a fortnight's winding to insure a year's running of their wheels. You will find students there from the lower towns, now and then an artist, or a geologist absorbed in construing the ancient strata of the hills. A few quiet families spend the summers there; and often one or two tired members of that patient sisterhood known to Lakelands as "schoolmarms."

A quarter of a mile from the Eagle House was what would have been described to its guests as "an object of interest" in the catalogue, had the Eagle House issued a catalogue. This was an old, old mill that was no longer a mill. In the words of Josiah Rankin, it was "the only church in the United States, sah, with an overshot-wheel; and the only mill in the world, sah, with pews and a pipe organ." The guests of the Eagle House attended the old mill church each Sabbath, and heard the preacher liken the purified Christian to bolted flour ground to usefulness between the millstones of experience and suffering.

Every year about the beginning of autumn there came to the Eagle House one Abram Strong, who remained for a time an honored and beloved guest. In Lakelands he was called "Father Abram," because his hair was so white, his face so strong and kind and florid, his laugh so merry, and his black clothes and broad hat so priestly in appearance. Even new guests after three or four days' acquaintance gave him this familiar title.

Father Abram came a long way to Lakelands. He lived in a big, roaring town in the Northwest where he owned mills, not little mills with pews and an organ in them, but great, ugly, mountain-like mills that the freight trains crawled around all day like ants around an ant-heap. And now you must be told about Father Abram and the mill that was a church, for their stories run together.

In the days when the church was a mill, Mr. Strong was the miller. There was no jollier, dustier, busier, happier miller in all the land than he. He lived in a little cottage across the road from the mill. His hand was heavy, but his toll was light, and the mountaineers brought their grain to him across many weary miles of rocky roads.

The delight of the miller's life was his little daughter, Aglaia. That was a brave name, truly, for a flaxen-haired toddler; but the mountaineers love sonorous and stately names. The mother had encountered it somewhere in a book, and the deed was done. In her babyhood Aglaia herself repudiated the name, as far as common use went, and persisted in calling herself "Dums." The miller and his wife often tried to coax from Aglaia the source of this mysterious name, but without results. At last they arrived at a theory. In the little garden behind the cottage was a bed of rhododendrons in which the child took a peculiar delight and interest. It may have been that she perceived in "Dums" a kinship to the formidable name of her favorite flowers.

When Aglaia was four years old she and her father used to go through a little performance in the mill every afternoon, that never failed to come off, the weather permitting. When supper was ready her mother would brush her hair and put on a clean apron and send her across to the mill to bring her father home. When the miller saw her coming in the mill door he would come forward, all white with the flour dust, and wave his hand and sing an old miller's song that was familiar in those parts and ran something like this:

"The wheel goes round,
The grist is ground,
The dusty miller's merry.
He sings all day,
His work is play,
While thinking of his dearie."

Then Aglaia would run to him laughing, and call: "Da-da, come take Dums home;" and the miller would swing her to his shoulder and march over to supper, singing the miller's song. Every evening this would take place.

One day, only a week after her fourth birthday, Aglaia disappeared. When last seen she was plucking wild flowers by the side of the road in front of the cottage. A little while later her mother went out to see that she did not stray too far away, and she was already gone.

Of course every effort was made to find her. The neighbors gathered and searched the woods and the mountains for miles around. They dragged every foot of the mill race and the creek for a long distance below the dam. Never a trace of her did they find. A night or two before there had been a family of wanderers camped in a grove near by. It was conjectured that they might have stolen the child; but when their wagon was overtaken and searched she could not be found.

The miller remained at the mill for nearly two years; and then his hope of finding her died out. He and his wife moved to the Northwest. In a few years he was the owner of a modern mill in one of the important milling cities in that region. Mrs. Strong never recovered from the shock caused by the loss of Aglaia, and two years after they moved away the miller was left to bear his sorrow alone.

When Abram Strong became prosperous he paid a visit to Lakelands and the old mill. The scene was a sad one for him, but he was a strong man, and always appeared cheery and kindly. It was then that he was inspired to convert the old mill into a church. Lakelands was too poor to build one; and the still poorer mountaineers could not assist. There was no place of worship nearer than twenty miles.

The miller altered the appearance of the mill as little as possible. The big overshot-wheel was left in its place. The young people who came to the church used to cut their initials in its soft and slowly decaying wood. The dam was partly destroyed, and the clear mountain stream rippled unchecked down its rocky bed. Inside the mill the changes were greater. The shafts and millstones and belts and pulleys were, of course, all removed. There were two rows of benches with aisles between, and a little raised platform and pulpit at one end. On three sides overhead was a gallery containing seats, and reached by a stairway inside. There was also an organ—a real pipe organ—in the gallery, that was the pride of the congregation of the Old Mill Church. Miss Phœbe Summers was the organist. The Lakelands boys proudly took turns at pumping it for her at each Sunday's service. The Rev. Mr. Banbridge was the preacher, and rode down from Squirrel Gap on his old white horse without ever missing a service. And Abram Strong paid for everything. He paid the preacher $500 a year; and Miss Phœbe $200.

Thus, in memory of Aglaia, the old mill was converted into a blessing for the community in which she had once lived. It seemed that the brief life of the child had brought about more good than the three score years and ten of many. But Abram Strong set up yet another monument to her memory.

Out from his mills in the Northwest came the "Aglaia" flour, made from the hardest and finest wheat that could be raised. The country soon found out that the "Aglaia" flour had two prices. One was the highest market price, and the other was—nothing.

Wherever there happened a calamity that left people destitute—a fire, a flood, a tornado, a strike, or a famine, there would go hurrying a generous consignment of the "Aglaia" at its "nothing" price. It was given away cautiously and judiciously, but it was freely given, and not a penny could the hungry ones pay for it. There got to be a saying that whenever there was a disastrous fire in the poor districts of a city the fire chief's buggy reached the scene first, next the "Aglaia" flour wagon, and then the fire engines.

So this was Abram Strong's other monument to Aglaia. Perhaps to a poet the theme may seem too utilitarian for beauty; but to some the fancy will seem sweet and fine that the pure, white, virgin flour, flying on its mission of love and charity, might be likened to the spirit of the lost child whose memory it signalized.

There came a year that brought hard times to the Cumberlands. Grain crops everywhere were light, and there were no local crops at all. Mountain floods had done much damage to property. Even game in the woods was so scarce that the hunters brought hardly enough home to keep their folk alive. Especially about Lakelands was the rigor felt.

As soon as Abram Strong heard of this his messages flew; and the little narrow-gauge cars began to unload "Aglaia" flour there. The miller's orders were to store the flour in the gallery of the Old Mill Church; and that every one who attended the church was to carry home a sack of it.

Two weeks after that Abram Strong came for his yearly visit to the Eagle House, and became "Father Abram" again.

That season the Eagle House had fewer guests than usual. Among them was Rose Chester. Miss Chester came to Lakelands from Atlanta, where she worked in a department store. This was the first vacation outing of her life. The wife of the store manager had once spent a summer at the Eagle House. She had taken a fancy to Rose, and had persuaded her to go there for her three weeks' holiday. The manager's wife gave her a letter to Mrs. Rankin, who gladly received her in her own charge and care.

Miss Chester was not very strong. She was about twenty, and pale and delicate from an indoor life. But one week of Lakelands gave her a brightness and spirit that changed her wonderfully. The time was early September when the Cumberlands are at their greatest beauty. The mountain foliage was growing brilliant with autumnal colors; one breathed aerial champagne, the nights were deliciously cool, causing one to snuggle cosily under the warm blankets of the Eagle House.

Father Abram and Miss Chester became great friends. The old miller learned her story from Mrs. Rankin, and his interest went out quickly to the slender lonely girl who was making her own way in the world.

The mountain country was new to Miss Chester. She had lived many years in the warm, flat town of Atlanta; and the grandeur and variety of the Cumberlands delighted her. She was determined to enjoy every moment of her stay. Her little hoard of savings had been estimated so carefully in connection with her expenses that she knew almost to a penny what her very small surplus would be when she returned to work.

Miss Chester was fortunate in gaining Father Abram for a friend and companion. He knew every road and peak and slope of the mountains near Lakelands. Through him she became acquainted with the solemn delight of the shadowy, tilted aisles of the pine forests, the dignity of the bare crags, the crystal, tonic mornings, the dreamy, golden afternoons full of mysterious sadness. So her health improved, and her spirits grew light. She had a laugh as genial and hearty in its feminine way as the famous laugh of Father Abram. Both of them were natural optimists; and both knew how to present a serene and cheerful face to the world.

One day Miss Chester learned from one of the guests the history of Father Abram's lost child. Quickly she hurried away and found the miller seated on his favorite rustic bench near the chalybeate spring. He was surprised when his little friend slipped her hand into his, and looked at him with tears in her eyes.

"Oh, Father Abram," she said, "I'm so sorry! I didn't know until to-day about your little daughter. You will find her yet some day—Oh, I hope you will."

The miller looked down at her with his strong, ready smile.

"Thank you, Miss Rose," he said, in his usual cheery tones. "But I do not expect to find Aglaia. For a few years I hoped that she had been stolen by vagrants, and that she still lived; but I have lost that hope. I believe that she was drowned."

"I can understand," said Miss Chester, "how the doubt must have made it so hard to bear. And yet you are so cheerful and so ready to make other people's burdens light. Good Father Abram!"

"Good Miss Rose!" mimicked the miller, smiling. "Who thinks of others more than you do?"

A whimsical mood seemed to strike Miss Chester.

"Oh, Father Abram," she cried, "wouldn't it be grand if I should prove to be your daughter? Wouldn't it be romantic? And wouldn't you like to have me for a daughter?"

"Indeed, I would," said the miller, heartily. "If Aglaia had lived I could wish for nothing better than for her to have grown up to be just such a little woman as you are. Maybe you are Aglaia," he continued, falling in with her playful mood; "can't you remember when we lived at the mill?"

Miss Chester fell swiftly into serious meditation. Her large eyes were fixed vaguely upon something in the distance. Father Abram was amused at her quick return to seriousness. She sat thus for a long time before she spoke.

"No," she said at length, with a long sigh, "I can't remember anything at all about a mill. I don't think that I ever saw a flour mill in my life until I saw your funny little church. And if I were your little girl I would remember it, wouldn't I? I'm so sorry, Father Abram."

"So am I," said Father Abram, humoring her. "But if you cannot remember that you are my little girl, Miss Rose, surely you can recollect being some one else's. You remember your own parents, of course."

"Oh, yes; I remember them very well—especially my father. He wasn't a bit like you, Father Abram. Oh, I was only making believe: Come, now, you've rested long enough. You promised to show me the pool where you can see the trout playing, this afternoon. I never saw a trout."

Late one afternoon Father Abram set out for the old mill alone. He often went to sit and think of the old days when he lived in the cottage across the road. Time had smoothed away the sharpness of his grief until he no longer found the memory of those times painful. But whenever Abram Strong sat in the melancholy September afternoons on the spot where "Dums" used to run in every day with her yellow curls flying, the smile that Lakelands always saw upon his face was not there. The miller made his way slowly up the winding, steep road. The trees crowded so close to the edge of it that he walked in their shade, with his hat in his hand. Squirrels ran playfully upon the old rail fence at his right. Quails were calling to their young broods in the wheat stubble. The low sun sent a torrent of pale gold up the ravine that opened to the west. Early September!—it was within a few days only of the anniversary of Aglaia's disappearance.

The old overshot-wheel, half covered with mountain ivy, caught patches of the warm sunlight filtering through the trees. The cottage across the road was still standing, but it would doubtless go down before the next winter's mountain blasts. It was overrun with morning glory and wild gourd vines, and the door hung by one hinge.

Father Abram pushed open the mill door, and entered softly. And then he stood still, wondering. He heard the sound of some one within, weeping inconsolably. He looked, and saw Miss Chester sitting in a dim pew, with her head bowed upon an open letter that her hands held.

Father Abram went to her, and laid one of his strong hands firmly upon hers. She looked up, breathed his name, and tried to speak further.

"Not yet, Miss Rose," said the miller, kindly. "Don't try to talk yet. There's nothing as good for you as a nice, quiet little cry when you are feeling blue."

It seemed that the old miller, who had known so much sorrow himself, was a magician in driving it away from others. Miss Chester's sobs grew easier. Presently she took her little plain-bordered handkerchief and wiped away a drop or two that had fallen from her eyes upon Father Abram's big hand. Then she looked up and smiled through her tears. Miss Chester could always smile before her tears had dried, just as Father Abram could smile through his own grief. In that way the two were very much alike.

The miller asked her no questions; but by and by Miss Chester began to tell him.

It was the old story that always seems so big and important to the young, and that brings reminiscent smiles to their elders. Love was the theme, as may be supposed. There was a young man in Atlanta, full of all goodness and the graces, who had discovered that Miss Chester also possessed these qualities above all other people in Atlanta or anywhere else from Greenland to Patagonia. She showed Father Abram the letter over which she had been weeping. It was a manly, tender letter, a little superlative and urgent, after the style of love letters written by young men full of goodness and the graces. He proposed for Miss Chester's hand in marriage at once. Life, he said, since her departure for a three-weeks' visit, was not to be endured. He begged for an immediate answer; and if it were favorable he promised to fly, ignoring the narrow-gauge railroad, at once to Lakelands.

"And now where does the trouble come in?" asked the miller when he had read the letter.

"I cannot marry him," said Miss Chester.

"Do you want to marry him?" asked Father Abram.

"Oh, I love him," she answered, "but—" Down went her head and she sobbed again.

"Come, Miss Rose," said the miller; "you can give me your confidence. I do not question you, but I think you can trust me."

"I do trust you," said the girl. "I will tell you why I must refuse Ralph. I am nobody; I haven't even a name; the name I call myself is a lie. Ralph is a noble man. I love him with all my heart, but I can never be his."

"What talk is this?" said Father Abram. "You said that you remember your parents. Why do you say you have no name? I do not understand."

"I do remember them," said Miss Chester. "I remember them too well. My first recollections are of our life somewhere in the far South. We moved many times to different towns and states. I have picked cotton, and worked in factories, and have often gone without enough food and clothes. My mother was sometimes good to me; my father was always cruel, and beat me. I think they were both idle and unsettled.

"One night when we were living in a little town on a river near Atlanta they had a great quarrel. It was while they were abusing and taunting each other that I learned—oh, Father

Abram, I learned that I didn't even have the right to be—don't you understand? I had no right even to a name; I was nobody.

"I ran away that night. I walked to Atlanta and found work. I gave myself the name of Rose Chester, and have earned my own living ever since. Now you know why I cannot marry Ralph—and, oh, I can never tell him why."

Better than any sympathy, more helpful than pity, was Father Abram's depreciation of her woes.

"Why, dear, dear! is that all?" he said. "Fie, fie! I thought something was in the way. If this perfect young man is a man at all he will not care a pinch of bran for your family tree. Dear Miss Rose, take my word for it, it is yourself he cares for. Tell him frankly, just as you have told me, and I'll warrant that he will laugh at your story, and think all the more of you for it."

"I shall never tell him," said Miss Chester, sadly. "And I shall never marry him nor any one else. I have not the right."

But they saw a long shadow come bobbing up the sunlit road. And then came a shorter one bobbing by its side; and presently two strange figures approached the church. The long shadow was made by Miss Phœbe Summers, the organist, come to practise. Tommy Teague, aged twelve, was responsible for the shorter shadow. It was Tommy's day to pump the organ for Miss Phœbe, and his bare toes proudly spurned the dust of the road.

Miss Phœbe, in her lilac-spray chintz dress, with her accurate little curls hanging over each ear, courtesied low to Father Abram, and shook her curls ceremoniously at Miss Chester. Then she and her assistant climbed the steep stairway to the organ loft.

In the gathering shadows below, Father Abram and Miss Chester lingered. They were silent; and it is likely that they were busy with their memories. Miss Chester sat, leaning her head on her hand, with her eyes fixed far away. Father Abram stood in the next pew, looking thoughtfully out of the door at the road and the ruined cottage.

Suddenly the scene was transformed for him back almost a score of years into the past. For, as Tommy pumped away, Miss Phœbe struck a low bass note on the organ and held it to test the volume of air that it contained. The church ceased to exist, so far as Father Abram was concerned. The deep, booming vibration that shook the little frame building was no note from an organ, but the humming of the mill machinery. He felt sure that the old overshot-wheel was turning; that he was back again, a dusty, merry miller in the old mountain mill. And now evening was come, and soon would come Aglaia with flying colors, toddling across the road to take him home to supper. Father Abram's eyes were fixed upon the broken door of the cottage.

And then came another wonder. In the gallery overhead the sacks of flour were stacked in long rows. Perhaps a mouse had been at one of them; anyway the jar of the deep organ note shook down between the cracks of the gallery floor a stream of flour, covering Father Abram from head to foot with the white dust. And then the old miller stepped into the aisle, and waved his arms and began to sing the miller's song:

> "The wheel goes round,
> The grist is ground,
> The dusty miller's merry—"

And then the rest of the miracle happened. Miss Chester was leaning forward from her pew, as pale as the flour itself, her wide-open eyes staring at Father Abram like one in a waking dream. When he began the song she stretched out her arms to him; her lips moved; she called to him in dreamy tones: "Da-da, come take Dums home!"

Miss Phœbe released the low key of the organ. But her work had been well done. The note that she struck had beaten down the doors of a closed memory; and Father Abram held his lost Aglaia close in his arms.

When you visit Lakelands they will tell you more of this story. They will tell you how the lines of it were afterward traced, and the history of the miller's daughter revealed after the gipsy wanderers had stolen her on that September day, attracted by her childish beauty. But you should wait until you sit comfortably on the shaded porch of the Eagle House, and then you can have the story at your ease. It seems best that our part of it should close while Miss Phœbe's deep bass note was yet reverberating softly.

And yet, to my mind, the finest thing of it all happened while Father Abram and his daughter were walking back to the Eagle House in the long twilight, almost too glad to speak.

"Father," she said, somewhat timidly and doubtfully, "have you a great deal of money?"

"A great deal?" said the miller. "Well, that depends. There is plenty unless you want to buy the moon or something equally expensive."

"Would it cost very, very much," asked Aglaia, who had always counted her dimes so carefully, "to send a telegram to Atlanta?"

"Ah," said Father Abram, with a little sigh, "I see. You want to ask Ralph to come."

Aglaia looked up at him with a tender smile.

"I want to ask him to wait," she said. "I have just found my father, and I want it to be just we two for a while. I want to tell him he will have to wait."

Juneteenth

June 19th

"Abraham Lincoln and his Emancipation Proclamation"

The Strobridge Lith. Co., Cincinnati, ca. 1888.

A Municipal Report

The Cities are full of pride,
Challenging each to each—
This from her mountainside,
That from her burthened beach.

—Rudyard Kipling

Fancy a novel about Chicago or
Buffalo, let us say, or Nashville,
Tennessee! There are just three
big cities in the United States
that are "story cities"—New
York, of course, New Orleans,
and, best of the lot, San
Francisco.

—Frank Norris

East is East, and West is San Francisco, according to Californians. Californians are a race of people; they are not merely inhabitants of a State. They are the Southerners of the West. Now, Chicagoans are no less loyal to their city; but when you ask them why, they stammer and speak of lake fish and the new Odd Fellows Building. But Californians go into detail.

Of course they have, in the climate, an argument that is good for half an hour while you are thinking of your coal bills and heavy underwear. But as soon as they come to mistake your silence for conviction, madness comes upon them, and they picture the city of the Golden Gate as the Bagdad of the New World. So far, as a matter of opinion, no refutation is necessary. But, dear cousins all (from Adam and Eve descended), it is a rash one who will lay his finger on the map and say: "In this town there can be no romance—what could happen here?" Yes, it is a bold and a rash deed to challenge in one sentence history, romance, and Rand and McNally.

> NASHVILLE—*A city, port of delivery, and the capital of the State of Tennessee, is on the Cumberland River and on the N. C. & St. L. and the L. & N. railroads. This city is regarded as the most important educational center in the South.*

I stepped off the train at 8 P.M. Having searched the thesaurus in vain for adjectives, I must, as a substitution, hie me to comparison in the form of a recipe.

Take a London fog 30 parts; malaria 10 parts; gas leaks 20 parts; dewdrops gathered in a brick yard at sunrise, 25 parts; odor of honeysuckle 15 parts. Mix.

The mixture will give you an approximate conception of a Nashville drizzle. It is not so fragrant as a moth-ball nor as thick as pea-soup; but 'tis enough—'twill serve.

I went to a hotel in a tumbril. It required strong self-suppression for me to keep from climbing to the top of it and giving an imitation of Sidney Carton. The vehicle was drawn by beasts of a bygone era and driven by someone dark and emancipated.

I was sleepy and tired, so when I got to the hotel I hurriedly

paid him the fifty cents he demanded (with approximate la-
gniappe, I assure you). I knew his habits; and I did not want to
hear him prate about his old "marster" or anything that happened "befo' de wah."

The hotel was one of the kind described as "renovated."
That means $20,000 worth of new marble pillars, tiling, electric
lights and brass cuspidors in the lobby, and a new L. & N. time
table and a lithograph of Lookout Mountain in each one of the
great rooms above. The management was without reproach, the
attention full of exquisite Southern courtesy, the service as slow
as the progress of a snail and as good-humored as Rip Van Win-
kle. The food was worth traveling a thousand miles for. There
is no other hotel in the world where you can get such chicken
livers *en brochette.*

At dinner I asked a waiter if there was anything doing in
town. He pondered gravely for a minute, and then replied:
"Well, boss, I don't really reckon there's anything at all doin' after sundown."

Sundown had been accomplished; it had been drowned in
the drizzle long before. So that spectacle was denied me. But I
went forth upon the streets in the drizzle to see what might be
there.

*It is built on undulating grounds; and the streets are lighted
by electricity at a cost of $32,470 per annum.*

As I left the hotel there was a race riot. Down upon me charged
a company of freedmen, or Arabs, or Zulus, armed with—no,
I saw with relief that they were not rifles, but whips. And I saw
dimly a caravan of black, clumsy vehicles; and at the reassuring
shouts, "Kyar you anywhere in the town, boss, fuh fifty cents," I
reasoned that I was merely a "fare" instead of a victim.

I walked through long streets, all leading uphill. I wondered how those streets ever came down again. Perhaps they didn't until they were "graded." On a few of the "main streets" I saw lights in stores here and there; saw street cars go by conveying worthy burghers hither and yon; saw people pass engaged in the art of conversation, and heard a burst of semi-lively laughter issuing from a soda-water and ice-cream parlor. The streets other than "main" seemed to have enticed upon their borders houses consecrated to peace and domesticity. In many of them lights shone behind discreetly drawn window shades; in a few pianos tinkled orderly and irreproachable music. There was, indeed, little "doing." I wished I had come before sundown. So I returned to my hotel.

In November, 1864, the Confederate General Hood advanced against Nashville, where he shut up a National force under General Thomas. The latter then sallied forth and defeated the Confederates in a terrible conflict.

All my life I have heard of, admired, and witnessed the fine marksmanship of the South in its peaceful conflicts in the tobacco-chewing regions. But in my hotel a surprise awaited me. There were twelve bright, new, imposing, capacious brass cuspidors in the great lobby, tall enough to be called urns and so wide-mouthed that the crack pitcher of a lady baseball team should have been able to throw a ball into one of them at five paces distant. But, although a terrible battle had raged and was still raging, the enemy had not suffered. Bright, new, imposing, capacious, untouched, they stood. But, shades of Jefferson Brick! the tile floor—the beautiful tile floor! I could not avoid thinking of the battle of Nashville, and trying to draw, as is my foolish habit, some deductions about hereditary marksmanship.

Here I first saw Major (by misplaced courtesy) Wentworth Caswell. I knew him for a type the moment my eyes suffered from the sight of him. A rat has no geographical habitat. My old friend, Alfred Tennyson, said, as he so well said almost everything:

> Prophet, curse me the blabbing lip,
> And curse me the British vermin, the rat.

Let us regard the word "British" as interchangeable *ad lib*. A rat is a rat.

This man was hunting about the hotel lobby like a starved dog that had forgotten where he had buried a bone. He had a face of great acreage, red, pulpy, and with a kind of sleepy massiveness like that of Buddha. He possessed one single virtue—he was very smoothly shaven. The mark of the beast is not indelible upon a man until he goes about with a stubble. I think that if he had not used his razor that day I would have repulsed his advances, and the criminal calendar of the world would have been spared the addition of one murder.

I happened to be standing within five feet of a cuspidor when Major Caswell opened fire upon it. I had been observant enough to perceive that the attacking force was using Gatlings instead of squirrel rifles; so I side-stepped so promptly that the major seized the opportunity to apologize to a noncombatant. He had the blabbing lip. In four minutes he had become my friend and had dragged me to the bar.

I desire to interpolate here that I am a Southerner. But I am not one by profession or trade. I eschew the string tie, the slouch hat, the Prince Albert, the number of bales of cotton destroyed by Sherman, and plug chewing. When the orchestra plays Dixie I do not cheer. I slide a little lower on the leather-cornered seat and, well, order another Würzburger and wish that Longstreet had—but what's the use?

Major Caswell banged the bar with his fist, and the first gun at Fort Sumter re-echoed. When he fired the last one at

Appomattox I began to hope. But then he began on family trees, and demonstrated that Adam was only a third cousin of a collateral branch of the Caswell family. Genealogy disposed of, he took up, to my distaste, his private family matters. He spoke of his wife, traced her descent back to Eve, and profanely denied any possible rumor that she may have had relations in the land of Nod.

By this time I was beginning to suspect that he was trying to obscure by noise the fact that he had ordered the drinks, on the chance that I would be bewildered into paying for them. But when they were down he crashed a silver dollar loudly upon the bar. Then, of course, another serving was obligatory. And when I had paid for that I took leave of him brusquely; for I wanted no more of him. But before I had obtained my release he had prated loudly of an income that his wife received, and showed a handful of silver money.

When I got my key at the desk the clerk said to me courteously: "If that man Caswell has annoyed you, and if you would like to make a complaint, we will have him ejected. He is a nuisance, a loafer, and without any known means of support, although he seems to have some money most of the time. But we don't seem to be able to hit upon any means of throwing him out legally."

"Why, no," said I, after some reflection; "I don't see my way clear to making a complaint. But I would like to place myself on record as asserting that I do not care for his company. Your town," I continued, "seems to be a quiet one. What manner of entertainment, adventure, or excitement have you to offer to the stranger within your gates?"

"Well, sir," said the clerk, "there will be a show here next Thursday. It is—I'll look it up and have the announcement sent up to your room with the ice water. Good night."

After I went up to my room I looked out the window. It was

only about ten o'clock, but I looked upon a silent town. The drizzle continued, spangled with dim lights, as far apart as currants in a cake sold at the Ladies' Exchange.

"A quiet place," I said to myself, as my first shoe struck the ceiling of the occupant of the room beneath mine. "Nothing of the life here that gives color and variety to the cities in the East and West. Just a good, ordinary, humdrum, business town."

Nashville occupies a foremost place among the manufacturing centers of the country. It is the fifth boot and shoe market in the United States, the largest candy and cracker manufacturing city in the South, and does an enormous wholesale drygoods, grocery, and drug business.

I must tell you how I came to be in Nashville, and I assure you the digression brings as much tedium to me as it does to you. I was traveling elsewhere on my own business, but I had a commission from a Northern literary magazine to stop over there and establish a personal connection between the publication and one of its contributors, Azalea Adair.

Adair (there was no clue to the personality except the handwriting) had sent in some essays (lost art!) and poems that had made the editors swear approvingly over their one o'clock luncheon. So they had commissioned me to round up said Adair and corner by contract his or her output at two cents a word before some other publisher offered her ten or twenty.

At nine o'clock the next morning, after my chicken livers *en brochette* (try them if you can find that hotel), I strayed out into the drizzle, which was still on for an unlimited run. At the first corner, I came upon Uncle Caesar. He was a stalwart southerner, older than the pyramids, with gray hair and a face that reminded me of Brutus, and a second afterwards of the late King Cetshwayo. He wore the most remarkable coat that I ever had seen or expect to see. It reached to his ankles and had once been a Confederate gray in colors. But rain and sun and age had so variegated it that Joseph's coat, beside it, would have faded to a pale monochrome. I must linger with that coat, for it has to do with the story—the story that is so long in coming, because you can hardly expect anything to happen in Nashville.

Once it must have been the military coat of an officer. The cape of it had vanished, but all adown its front it had been frogged and tasseled magnificently. But now the frogs and tassels were gone. In their stead had been patiently stitched (I surmised by some surviving "black mammy") new frogs made of cunningly twisted common hempen twine. This twine was frayed and disheveled. It must have been added to the coat as a substitute for vanished splendors, with tasteless but painstaking devotion, for it followed faithfully the curves of the long-missing frogs. And, to complete the comedy and pathos of the garment, all its buttons were gone save one. The second button from the top alone remained. The coat was fastened by other twine strings tied through the buttonholes and other holes rudely pierced in the opposite side. There was never such a weird garment so fantastically bedecked and of so many mottled hues. The lone button was the size of a half-dollar, made of yellow horn and sewed on with coarse twine.

Uncle Caesar stood by a carriage so old that Ham himself might have started a hack line with it after he left the ark with the two animals hitched to it. As I approached he threw open the door, drew out a feather duster, waved it without using it, and said in deep, rumbling tones:

"Step right in, suh; ain't a speck of dust in it—jus' got back from a funeral, suh."

I inferred that on such gala occasions carriages were given an extra cleaning. I looked up and down the street and perceived that there was little choice among the vehicles for hire that lined the curb. I looked in my memorandum book for the address of Azalea Adair.

"I want to go to 861 Jessamine Street," I said, and was about to step into the hack. But for an instant the thick, long, imposing arm of Uncle Caesar barred me. On his massive and saturnine face a look of sudden suspicion and enmity flashed for a moment. Then, with quickly returning conviction, he asked blandishingly: "What are you gwine there for, boss?"

"What is it to you?" I asked, a little sharply.

"Nothin', suh, jus' nothin'. Only it's a lonesome kind of part of town and few folks ever has business out there. Step right in. The seats is clean—jes' got back from a funeral, suh."

A mile and a half it must have been to our journey's end. I could hear nothing but the fearful rattle of the ancient hack over the uneven brick paving; I could smell nothing but the drizzle, now further flavored with coal smoke and something like a mixture of tar and oleander blossoms. All I could see through the streaming windows were two rows of dim houses.

The city has an area of 10 square miles; 181 miles of streets, of which 137 miles are paved; a system of waterworks that cost $2,000,000, with 77 miles of mains.

Eight-sixty-one Jessamine Street was a decayed mansion. Thirty yards back from the street it stood, outmerged in a splendid grove of trees and untrimmed shrubbery. A row of box bushes overflowed and almost hid the paling fence from sight; the gate was kept closed by a rope noose that encircled the gate post and the first paling of the gate. But when you got inside you saw that 861 was a shell, a shadow, a ghost of former grandeur and excellence. But in the story, I have not yet got inside.

When the hack had ceased from rattling and the weary

quadrupeds came to a rest I handed my jehu his fifty cents with an additional quarter, feeling a glow of conscious generosity, as I did so. He refused it.

"It's two dollars, suh," he said.

"How's that?" I asked. "I plainly heard you call out at the hotel: 'Fifty cents to any part of the town.'"

"It's two dollars, suh," he repeated obstinately. "It's a long ways from the hotel."

"It is within the city limits and well within them," I argued. "Don't think that you have picked up a greenhorn Yankee. Do you see those hills over there?" I went on, pointing toward the east(I could not see them, myself, for the drizzle); "well, I was born and raised on their other side. You old fool, can't you tell people from other people when you see 'em?"

The grim face of King Cetshwayo softened. "Is you from the South, suh? I reckon it was them shoes of yourn fooled me. They is somethin' sharp in the toes for a Southern gen'lman to wear."

"Then the charge is fifty cents, I suppose?" said I inexorably.

His former expression, a mingling of cupidity and hostility, returned, remained ten seconds, and vanished.

"Boss," he said, "fifty cents is right; but I *needs* two dollars, suh; I'm *obleeged* to have two dollars. I ain't *demandin'* it now, suh; after I know whar you's from; I'm jus' sayin' that I *has* to have two dollars to-night, and business mighty po'."

Peace and confidence settled upon his heavy features. He had been luckier than he had hoped. Instead of having picked up a greenhorn, ignorant of rates, he had come upon an inheritance.

"You confounded old rascal," I said, reaching down to my pocket, "you ought to be turned over to the police."

For the first time I saw him smile. He knew; *he knew*. HE KNEW.

I gave him two one-dollar bills. As I handed them over I

noticed that one of them had seen parlous times. Its upper right-hand corner was missing, and it had been torn through the middle, but joined again. A strip of blue tissue paper, pasted over the split, preserved its negotiability.

Enough of the jehu bandit for the present: I left him happy, lifted the rope and opened a creaky gate.

The house, as I said, was a shell. A paint brush had not touched it in twenty years. I could not see why a strong wind should not have bowled it over like a house of cards until I looked again at the trees that hugged it close—the trees that saw the battle of Nashville and still drew their protecting branches around it against storm and enemy and cold.

Azalea Adair, fifty years old, white-haired, a descendant of the cavaliers, as thin and frail as the house she lived in, robed in the cheapest and cleanest dress I ever saw, with an air as simple as a queen's, received me.

The reception room seemed a mile square, because there was nothing in it except some rows of books, on unpainted white-pine bookshelves, a cracked marble-top table, a rag rug, a hairless horsehair sofa and two or three chairs. Yes, there was a picture on the wall, a colored crayon drawing of a cluster of pansies. I looked around for the portrait of Andrew Jackson and the pinecone hanging basket but they were not there.

Azalea Adair and I had conversation, a little of which will be repeated to you. She was a product of the old South, gently nurtured in the sheltered life. Her learning was not broad, but was deep and of splendid originality in its somewhat narrow scope. She had been educated at home, and her knowledge of the world was derived from inference and by inspiration. Of such is the precious, small group of essayists made. While she talked to me I kept brushing my fingers, trying, unconsciously, to rid them guiltily of the absent dust from the half-calf backs of Lamb, Chaucer, Hazlitt, Marcus Aurelius, Montaigne and Hood. She was exquisite, she was a valuable discovery. Nearly everybody nowadays knows too much—oh, so much too much—of real life.

I could perceive clearly that Azalea Adair was very poor. A house and a dress she had, not much else, I fancied. So, divided between my duty to the magazine and my loyalty to the poets and essayists who fought Thomas in the valley of the Cumberland, I listened to her voice, which was like a harpsichord's, and found that I could not speak of contracts. In the presence of the nine Muses and the three Graces one hesitated to lower the topic to two cents. There would have to be another colloquy after I had regained my commercialism. But I spoke of my mission, and three o'clock of the next afternoon was set for the discussion of the business proposition.

"Your town," I said, as I began to make ready to depart (which is the time for smooth generalities), "seems to be a quiet, sedate place. A home town, I should say, where few things out of the ordinary ever happen."

> It carries on an extensive trade in stoves and hollow ware with the West and South, and its flouring mills have a daily capacity of more than 2,000 barrels.

Azalea Adair seemed to reflect.

"I have never thought of it that way," she said, with a kind of sincere intensity that seemed to belong to her. "Isn't it in the still, quiet places that things do happen? I fancy that when God began to create the earth on the first Monday morning one could have leaned out one's window and heard the drops of mud splashing from His trowel as He built up the everlasting hills. What did the noisiest project in the world—I mean the building of the Tower of Babel—result in finally? A page and a half of Esperanto in the *North American Review*."

"Of course," said I platitudinously, "human nature is the same everywhere; but there is more color—er—more drama and movement and—er—romance in some cities than in others."

"On the surface," said Azalea Adair. "I have traveled many times around the world in a golden airship wafted on two wings—print and dreams. I have seen (on one of my imaginary tours) the Sultan of Turkey bowstring with his own hands one of his wives who had uncovered her face in public. I have seen a man in Nashville tear up his theater tickets because his wife was going out with her face covered—with rice powder. In San Francisco's Chinatown I saw the slave girl Sing Yee dipped slowly, inch by inch, in boiling almond oil to make her swear she would never see her American lover again. She gave in when the boiling oil had reached three inches above her knee. At a euchre party in East Nashville the other night I saw Kitty Morgan cut dead by seven of her schoolmates and lifelong friends because she had married a house painter. The boiling oil was sizzling as high as her heart; but I wish you could have seen the fine little smile that she carried from table to table. Oh, yes, it is a humdrum town. Just a few miles of red brick houses and mud and lumber yards."

Some one knocked hollowly at the back of the house. Azalea Adair breathed a soft apology and went to investigate the sound. She came back in three minutes with brightened eyes, a faint flush on her cheeks, and ten years lifted from her shoulders.

"You must have a cup of tea before you go," she said, "and a sugar cake."

She reached and shook a little iron bell. In shuffled a small black girl about twelve, barefoot, not very tidy, glowering at me with thumb in mouth and bulging eyes.

Azlea Adair opened a tiny, worn purse and drew out a dollar bill, a dollar bill with the upper right-hand corner missing, torn in two pieces, and pasted together again with a strip of blue tissue paper. It was one of the bills I had given the piratical Caesar—there was no doubt about it.

"Go up to Mr. Baker's store on the corner, Impy," she said, handing the girl the dollar bill, "and get a quarter of a pound of tea—the kind he always sends me—and ten cents worth of sugar cakes. Now, hurry. The supply of tea in the house happens to be exhausted," she explained to me.

Impy left by the back way. Before the scrape of her hard, bare feet had died away on the back porch, a wild shriek—I was sure it was hers—filled the hollow house. Then the deep, gruff tones of an angry man's voice mingled with the girl's further squeals and unintelligible words.

Azalea Adair rose without surprise or emotion and disappeared. For two minutes I heard the hoarse rumble of the man's voice; then something like an oath and a slight scuffle, and she returned calmly to her chair.

"This is a roomy house," she said, "and I have a tenant for part of it. I am sorry to have to rescind my invitation to tea. It was impossible to get the kind I always use at the store. Perhaps tomorrow, Mr. Baker will be able to supply me."

I was sure that Impy had not had time to leave the house. I inquired concerning street-car lines and took my leave. After I was well on my way I remembered that I had not learned Azalea Adair's name. But to-morrow would do.

That same day I started in on the course of iniquity that this uneventful city forced upon me. I was in the town only two days, but in that time I managed to lie shamelessly by telegraph, and to be an accomplice—after the fact, if that is the correct legal term—to a murder.

As I rounded the corner nearest my hotel the jehu coachman of the polychromatic, nonpareil coat seized me, swung open the dungeony door of his peripatetic sarcophagus, flirted his feather duster and began his ritual: "Step right in, boss. Carriage is clean—jus' got back from a funeral. Fifty cents to any—"

And then he knew me and grinned broadly. "'Scuse me, boss; you is de gen'l'man what rid out with me dis mawnin'. Thank you kindly, suh."

"I am going out to 861 again to-morrow afternoon at three," said I, "and if you will be here, I'll let you drive me. So you know Miss Adair?" I concluded, thinking of my dollar bill.

"I belonged to her father, Judge Adair, suh," he replied.

"I judge that she is pretty poor," I said. "She hasn't much money to speak of, has she?"

For an instant I looked again at the fierce countenance of King Cetshwayo, and then he changed back to an extortionate old hack driver.

"She ain't gwine to starve, suh," he said slowly. "She has reso'ces, suh; she has reso'ces."

"I shall pay you fifty cents for the trip," said I.

"Dat is puffeckly correct, suh," he answered humbly. "I jus' *had* to have dat two dollars dis mawnin', boss."

I went to the hotel and lied by electricity. I wired the magazine: "A. Adair holds out for eight cents a word."

The answer that came back was: "Give it to her quick, you duffer."

Just before dinner "Major" Wentworth Caswell bore down upon me with the greetings of a long-lost friend. I have seen few men whom I have so instantaneously hated, and of whom it was so difficult to be rid. I was standing at the bar when he invaded me; therefore I could not wave the white ribbon in his face. I would have paid gladly for the drinks, hoping, thereby,

225

to escape another; but he was one of those despicable, roaring, advertising bibbers who must have brass bands and fireworks attend upon every cent that they waste in their follies.

With an air of producing millions he drew two one-dollar bills from a pocket and dashed one of them upon the bar. I looked once more at the dollar bill with the upper right-hand corner missing, torn through the middle, and patched with a strip of blue tissue paper. It was my dollar bill again. It could have been no other.

I went up to my room. The drizzle and the monotony of a dreary, eventless Southern town had made me tired and listless. I remember that just before I went to bed I mentally disposed of the mysterious dollar bill (which might have formed the clue to a tremendously fine detective story of San Francisco) by saying to myself sleepily: "Seems as if a lot of people here own stock in the Hack-Driver's Trust. Pays dividends promptly, too. Wonder if—" Then I fell asleep.

King Cetshwayo was at his post the next day, and rattled my bones over the stones out to 861. He was to wait and rattle me back again when I was ready.

Azalea Adair looked paler and cleaner and frailer than she had looked on the day before. After she had signed the contract at eight cents per word she grew still paler and began to slip out of her chair. Without much trouble I managed to get her up on the antediluvian horsehair sofa and then I ran out to the sidewalk and yelled to the hackney driver to bring a doctor. With a wisdom that I had not expected in him, he abandoned his team and struck off up the street afoot, realizing the value of speed. In ten minutes he returned with a grave, gray-haired and capable man of medicine. In a few words (worth much less than eight cents each) I explained to him my presence in the hollow house of mystery. He bowed with stately understanding, and turned to King Cetshwayo.

"Uncle Caesar," he said calmly, "Run up to my house and ask Miss Lucy to give you a cream pitcher full of fresh milk and half a tumbler of port wine. And hurry back. Don't drive—run. I want you to get back sometime this week."

It occurred to me that Dr. Merriman also felt a distrust as to the speeding powers of the land-pirate's steeds. After Uncle Caesar was gone, lumberingly, but swiftly, up the street, the doctor looked me over with great politeness and as much careful calculation until he had decided that I might do.

"It is only a case of insufficient nutrition," he said. "In other words, the result of poverty, pride, and starvation. Mrs. Caswell has many devoted friends who would be glad to aid her, but she will accept nothing except from Uncle Caesar, who was once owned by her family."

"Mrs. Caswell!" said I, in surprise. And then I looked at the contract and saw that she had signed it "Azalea Adair Caswell."

"I thought she was Miss Adair," I said.

"Married to a drunken, worthless loafer, sir," said the doctor. "It is said that he robs her even of the small sums that her old servant contributes toward her support."

When the milk and wine had been brought the doctor soon revived Azalea Adair. She sat up and talked of the beauty of the autumn leaves that were then in season, and their height of color. She referred lightly to her fainting seizure as the outcome of an old palpitation of the heart. Impy fanned her as she lay on the sofa. The doctor was due elsewhere, and I followed him to the door. I told him that it was within my power and intentions to make a reasonable advance of money to Azalea Adair on future contributions to the magazine, and he seemed pleased.

"By the way," he said, "perhaps you would like to know that you have had royalty for a coachman. Old Caesar's grandfather was a king in Congo. Caesar himself has royal ways, as you may have observed."

As the doctor was moving off I heard Uncle Caesar's voice inside: "Did he get bofe of dem two dollars from you, Mis' Zalea?"

"Yes, Caesar," I heard Azalea Adair answer weakly. And then I went in and concluded business negotiations with our contributor. I assumed the responsibility of advancing fifty dollars, putting it as a necessary formality in binding our bargain. And then Uncle Caesar drove me back to the hotel.

Here ends all of the story as far as I can testify as a witness. The rest must be only bare statements of facts.

At about six o'clock I went out for a stroll. Uncle Caesar was at his corner. He threw open the door of his carriage, flourished his duster and began his depressing formula: "Step right in, suh. Fifty cents to anywhere in the city—hack's puffickly clean, suh—jus' got back from a funeral—"

And then he recognized me. I think his eyesight was getting bad. His coat had taken on a few more faded shades of color, the twine strings were more frayed and ragged, the last remaining button—the button of yellow horn—was gone. A motley descendant of kings was Uncle Caesar!

About two hours later I saw an excited crowd besieging the front of a drug store. In a desert where nothing happens this was manna; so I edged my way inside. On an extemporized couch of empty boxes and chairs was stretched the mortal corporeality of Major Wentworth Caswell. A doctor was testing him for the immortal ingredient. His decision was that it was conspicuous by its absence.

The erstwhile Major had been found dead on a dark street and brought by curious and ennuied citizens to the drug store.

The late human being had been engaged in terrific battle—the details showed that. Loafer and reprobate though he had been, he had been also a warrior. But he had lost. His hands were yet clinched so tightly that his fingers would not be opened. The gentle citizens who had known him stood about and searched their vocabularies to find some good words, if it were possible, to speak of him. One kind-looking man said, after much thought: "When 'Cas' was about fo'teen he was one of the best spellers in school."

While I stood there the fingers of the right hand of "the man that was" which hung down the side of a white pine box, relaxed, and dropped something at my feet. I covered it with one foot quietly, and a little later on I picked it up and pocketed it. I reasoned that in his last struggle his hand must have seized that object unwittingly and held it in a death grip.

At the hotel that night the main topic of conversation, with the possible exceptions of politics and prohibition, was the demise of Major Caswell. I heard one man say to a group of listeners:

"In my opinion, gentlemen, Caswell was murdered by some ne'er-do-well for his money. He had fifty dollars this afternoon which he showed to several gentlemen in the hotel. When he was found the money was not on his person."

I left the city the next morning at nine, and as the train was crossing the bridge over the Cumberland River I took out of my pocket a yellow horn overcoat button the size of a fifty-cent piece, with frayed ends of coarse twine hanging from it, and cast it out of the window into the slow, muddy waters below.

I wonder what's doing in Buffalo!

Independence Day

July 4th

The Spirit of '76

Archibald Willard, 1875

Archibald MacNeal Willard (August 22, 1836 – October 11, 1918)

The Day We Celebrate

"In the tropics" ("Hop-along" Bibb, the bird fancier, was saying to me) "the seasons, months, fortnights, week-ends, holidays, dog-days, Sundays, and yesterdays get so jumbled together in the shuffle that you never know when a year has gone by until you're in the middle of the next one."

"Hop-along" Bibb kept his bird store on lower Fourth Avenue. He was an ex-seaman and beachcomber who made regular voyages to southern ports and imported personally conducted invoices of talking parrots and dialectic paroquets. He had a stiff knee, neck, and nerve. I had gone to him to buy a parrot to present, at Christmas, to my Aunt Joanna.

"This one," said I, disregarding his homily on the subdivisions of time—"this one that seems all red, white, and blue—to what genus of beasts does he belong? He appeals at once to my patriotism and to my love of discord in color schemes."

"That's a cockatoo from Ecuador," said Bibb. "All he has been taught to say is 'Merry Christmas.' A seasonable bird. He's only seven dollars; and I'll bet many a human has stuck you for more money by making the same speech to you."

And then Bibb laughed suddenly and loudly.

"That bird," he explained, "reminds me. He's got his dates mixed. He ought to be saying '*E pluribus unum*,' to match his feathers, instead of trying to work the Santa Claus graft. It reminds me of the time me and Liverpool Sam got our ideas of things tangled up on the coast of Costa Rica on account of the weather and other phenomena to be met with in the tropics.

"We were, as it were, stranded on that section of the Spanish main with no money to speak of and no friends that should be talked about either. We had stoked and second-cooked ourselves down there on a fruit steamer from New Orleans to try our luck, which was discharged, after we got there, for lack of evidence. There was no work suitable to our instincts; so me and Liverpool began to subsist on the red rum of the country and such fruit as we could reap where we had not sown. It was an alluvial town, called Soledad, where there was no harbor or future or recourse. Between steamers the town slept and drank rum. It only woke up when there were bananas to ship. It was like a man sleeping through dinner until the dessert.

"When me and Liverpool got so low down that the American consul wouldn't speak to us we knew we'd struck bed rock.

"We boarded with a snuff-brown lady named Chica, who kept a rum-shop and a ladies' and gents' restaurant in a street called the *calle de los* Forty-seven Inconsolable Saints. When our credit played out there, Liverpool, whose stomach overshadowed his sensations of *noblesse oblige*, married Chica. This kept us in rice and fried plantain for a month; and then Chica pounded Liverpool one morning sadly and earnestly for fifteen minutes with a casserole handed down from the stone age, and we knew that we had out-welcomed our liver. That night we signed an engagement with Don Jaime McSpinosa, a hybrid banana fancier of the place, to work on his fruit preserves nine miles out of town. We had to do it or be reduced to sea water and broken doses of feed and slumber.

"Now, speaking of Liverpool Sam, I don't malign or inexculpate him to you any more than I would to his face. But in my

234

opinion, when an Englishman gets as low as he can he's got to dodge so that the dregs of other nations don't drop ballast on him out of their balloons. And if he's a Liverpool Englishman, why, fire-damp is what he's got to look out for. Being a natural American, that's my personal view. But Liverpool and me had much in common. We were without decorous clothes or ways and means of existence; and, as the saying goes, misery certainly does enjoy the society of accomplices.

"Our job on old McSpinosa's plantation was chopping down banana stalks and loading the bunches of fruit on the backs of horses. Then a native dressed up in an alligator hide belt, a machete, and a pair of AA sheeting pajamas, drives 'em over to the coast and piles 'em up on the beach.

"You ever been in a banana grove? It's as solemn as a rathskeller at seven a. m. It's like being lost behind the scenes at one of these mushroom musical shows. You can't see the sky for the foliage above you; and the ground is knee deep in rotten leaves; and it's so still that you can hear the stalks growing again after you chop 'em down.

"At night me and Liverpool herded in a lot of grass huts on the edge of a lagoon with the red, yellow, and black employees of Don Jaime. There we lay fighting mosquitoes and listening to the monkeys squalling and the alligators grunting and splashing in the lagoon until daylight with only snatches of sleep between times.

"We soon lost all idea of what time of the year it was. It's just about eighty degrees there in December and June and on Fridays and at midnight and election day and any other old time. Sometimes it rains more than at others, and that's all the difference you notice. A man is liable to live along there without noticing any fugiting of tempus until some day the undertaker calls in for him just when he's beginning to think about cutting out the gang and saving up a little to invest in real estate.

"I don't know how long we worked for Don Jaime; but it was through two or three rainy spells, eight or ten hair cuts, and the life of three pairs of sail-cloth trousers. All the money we earned went for rum and tobacco; but we ate, and that was something.

"All of a sudden one day me and Liverpool find the trade of committing surgical operations on banana stalks turning to aloes and quinine in our mouths. It's a seizure that often comes upon white men in Latin and geographical countries. We wanted to be addressed again in language and see the smoke of a steamer and read the real estate transfers and gents' outfitting ads in an old newspaper. Even Soledad seemed like a center of civilization to us, so that evening we put our thumbs on our nose at Don Jaime's fruit stand and shook his grass burrs off our feet.

"It was only twelve miles to Soledad, but it took me and Liverpool two days to get there. It was banana grove nearly all the way; and we got twisted time and again. It was like paging the palm room of a New York hotel for a man named Smith.

"When we saw the houses of Soledad between the trees all my disinclination toward this Liverpool Sam rose up in me. I stood him while we were two white men against the banana brindles; but now, when there were prospects of my exchanging even cuss words with an American citizen, I put him back in his proper place. And he was a sight, too, with his rum-painted nose and his red whiskers and elephant feet with leather sandals strapped to them. I suppose I looked about the same.

"'It looks to me,' says I, 'like Great Britain ought to be made to keep such gin-swilling, scurvy, unbecoming mud larks as you at home instead of sending 'em over here to degrade and taint foreign lands. We kicked you out of America once and we ought to put on rubber boots and do it again.'

"'Oh, you go to 'ell,' says Liverpool, which was about all the repartee he ever had.

"Well, Soledad, looked fine to me after Don Jaime's plantation. Liverpool and me walked into it side by side, from force of habit, past the calabosa and the Hotel Grande, down across the plaza toward Chica's hut, where we hoped that Liverpool, being a husband of hers, might work his luck for a meal.

"As we passed the two-story little frame house occupied by the American Club, we noticed that the balcony had been decorated all around with wreaths of evergreens and flowers, and the flag was flying from the pole on the roof. Stanzey, the consul, and Arkright, a gold-mine owner, were smoking on the balcony. Me and Liverpool waved our dirty hands toward 'em and smiled real society smiles; but they turned their backs to us and went on talking. And we had played whist once with the two of 'em up to the time when Liverpool held all thirteen trumps for four hands in succession. It was some holiday, we knew; but we didn't know the day nor the year.

"A little further along we saw a reverend man named Pendergast, who had come to Soledad to build a church, standing under a cocoanut palm with his little black alpaca coat and green umbrella.

"'Boys, boys!' says he, through his blue spectacles, 'is it as bad as this? Are you so far reduced?'

"'We're reduced,' says I, 'to very vulgar fractions.'

"'It is indeed sad,' says Pendergast, 'to see my countrymen in such circumstances.'

"'Cut 'arf of that out, old party,' says Liverpool. 'Cawn't you tell a member of the British upper classes when you see one?'

"'Shut up,' I told Liverpool. 'You're on foreign soil now, or that portion of it that's not on you.'

"'And on this day, too!' goes on Pendergast, grievous—'on this most glorious day of the year when we should all be celebrating the dawn of Christian civilization and the downfall of the wicked.'

"'I did notice bunting and bouquets decorating the town, reverend,' says I, 'but I didn't know what it was for. We've been so long out of touch with calendars that we didn't know whether it was summer time or Saturday afternoon.'

"'Here is two dollars,' says Pendergast digging up two Chili silver wheels and handing 'em to me. 'Go, my men, and observe the rest of the day in a befitting manner.'

"Me and Liverpool thanked him kindly, and walked away.

"'Shall we eat?' I asks.

"'Oh, 'ell!' says Liverpool. 'What's money for?'

"'Very well, then,' I says, 'since you insist upon it, we'll drink.'

"So we pull up in a rum shop and get a quart of it and go down on the beach under a cocoanut tree and celebrate.

"Not having eaten anything but oranges in two days, the rum has immediate effect; and once more I conjure up great repugnance toward the British nation.

"'Stand up here,' I says to Liverpool, 'you scum of a despot limited monarchy, and have another dose of Bunker Hill. That good man, Mr. Pendergast,' says I, 'said we were to observe the day in a befitting manner, and I'm not going to see his money misapplied.'

"'Oh, you go to 'ell!' says Liverpool, and I started in with a fine left-hander on his right eye.

"Liverpool had been a fighter once, but dissipation and bad company had taken the nerve out of him. In ten minutes I had him lying on the sand waving the white flag.

"'Get up,' says I, kicking him in the ribs, 'and come along with me.'

"Liverpool got up and followed behind me because it was his habit, wiping the red off his face and nose. I led him to Reverend Pendergast's shack and called him out.

"'Look at this, sir,' says I—'look at this thing that was once a proud Britisher. You gave us two dollars and told us to celebrate the day. The star-spangled banner still waves. Hurrah for the stars and eagles!'

"'Dear me,' says Pendergast, holding up his hands. 'Fighting on this day of all days! On Christmas day, when peace on—'

"'Christmas, hell!' says I. 'I thought it was the Fourth of July.'"

"Merry Christmas!" said the red, white, and blue cockatoo.

"Take him for six dollars," said Hop-along Bibb. "He's got his dates and colors mixed."

Labor Day

First Monday in September

1894 Labor Day Parade on Pennsylvania Avenue, Washington D.C. in the vicinity of Kernan's Lyceum theater and unfinished post office building.

Courtesy Library of Congress

Vanity And Some Sables

When "Kid" Brady was sent to the rope by Molly McKeever's blue-black eyes he withdrew from the Stovepipe Gang. So much for the power of a colleen's blanderin' tongue and stubborn true-heartedness. If you are a man who read this, may such an influence be sent you before 2 o'clock to-morrow; if you are a woman, may your Pomeranian greet you this morning with a cold nose—a sign of doghealth and your happiness.

The Stovepipe Gang borrowed its name from a sub-district of the city called the "Stovepipe," which is a narrow and natural extension of the familiar district known as "Hell's Kitchen." The "Stovepipe" strip of town runs along Eleventh and Twelfth avenues on the river, and bends a hard and sooty elbow around little, lost homeless DeWitt Clinton park. Consider that a stovepipe is an important factor in any kitchen and the situation is analyzed. The chefs in "Hell's Kitchen" are many, and the "Stovepipe" gang, wears the cordon blue.

The members of this unchartered but widely known brotherhood appeared to pass their time on street corners arrayed like the lilies of the conservatory and busy with nail files and penknives. Thus displayed as a guarantee of good faith, they carried on an innocuous conversation in a 200-word vocabulary, to the casual observer as innocent and immaterial as that heard in clubs seven blocks to the east.

But off exhibition the "Stovepipes" were not mere street corner ornaments addicted to posing and manicuring. Their serious occupation was the separating of citizens from their coin and valuables. Preferably this was done by weird and singular tricks without noise or bloodshed; but whenever the citizen honored by their attentions refused to impoverish himself gracefully his objections came to be spread finally upon some police station blotter or hospital register.

The police held the "Stovepipe" gang in perpetual suspicion and respect. As the nightingale's liquid note is heard in the deepest shadows, so along the "Stovepipe's" dark and narrow confines the whistle for reserves punctures the dull ear of night. Whenever there was smoke in the "stovepipe" the tasseled men in blue knew there was fire in "Hell's Kitchen."

"Kid" Brady promised Molly to be good. "Kid" was the vainest, the strongest, the wariest and the most successful plotter in the gang. Therefore, the boys were sorry to give him up.

But they witnessed his fall to a virtuous life without protest. For, in the Kitchen it is considered neither unmanly nor improper for a guy to do as his girl advises.

Black her eye for love's sake, if you will; but it is all-to-the-good business to do a thing when she wants you to do it.

"Turn off the hydrant," said the Kid, one night when Molly, tearful, besought him to amend his ways. "I'm going to cut out the gang. You for mine, and the simple life on the side. I'll tell you, Moll—I'll get work; and in a year we'll get married. I'll do it for you. We'll get a flat and a flute, and a sewing machine and a rubber plant and live as honest as we can."

"Oh, Kid," sighed Molly, wiping the powder off his shoulder with her handkerchief, "I'd rather hear you say that than to own all of New York. And we can be happy on so little!"

The Kid looked down at his speckless cuffs and shining patent leathers with a suspicion of melancholy.

"It'll hurt hardest in the rags department," said he. "I've kind of always liked to rig out swell when I could. You know how I hate cheap things, Moll. This suit set me back sixty-five. Anything in the wearing apparel line has got to be just so, or it's to the misfit parlors for it, for mine. If I work I won't have so much coin to hand over to the little man with the big shears."

"Never mind, Kid. I'll like you just as much in a blue jumper as I would in a red automobile."

Before the Kid had grown large enough to knock out his father he had been compelled to learn the plumber's art. So now back to this honorable and useful profession he returned. But it was as an assistant that he engaged himself; and it is the master plumber and not the assistant, who wears diamonds as large as hailstones and looks contemptuously upon the marble colonnades of Senator Clark's mansion.

Eight months went by as smoothly and surely as though they had "elapsed" on a theater program. The Kid worked away at his pipes and solder with no symptoms of backsliding. The Stovepipe gang continued its piracy on the high avenues, cracked policemen's heads, held up late travelers, invented new methods of peaceful plundering, copied Fifth avenue's cut of clothes and neckwear fancies and comported itself according to its lawless bylaws. But the Kid stood firm and faithful to his Molly, even though the polish was gone from his fingernails and it took him 15 minutes to tie his purple silk ascot so that the worn places would not show.

One evening he brought a mysterious bundle with him to Molly's house.

"Open that, Moll!" he said in his large, quiet way. "It's for you."

Molly's eager fingers tore off the wrappings. She shrieked aloud, and in rushed a sprinkling of little McKeevers, and Ma McKeever, dishwashy, but an undeniable relative of the late Mrs. Eve.

Again Molly shrieked, and something dark and long and sinuous flew and enveloped her neck like an anaconda.

"Russian sables," said the Kid, pridefully, enjoying the sight of Molly's round cheek against the clinging fur. "The real thing. They don't grow anything in Russia too good for you, Moll."

Molly plunged her hands into the muff, overturned a row of the family infants and flew to the mirror. Hint for the beauty column. To make bright eyes, rosy checks and a bewitching smile: Recipe—one set Russian sables. Apply.

When they were alone Molly became aware of a small cake of the ice of common sense floating down the full tide of her happiness.

"You're a bird, all right, Kid," she admitted gratefully. "I never had any furs on before in my life. But ain't Russian sables awful expensive? Seems to me I've heard they were."

"Have I ever chucked any bargain-sale stuff at you, Moll?" asked the Kid, with calm dignity. "Did you ever notice me leaning on the remnant counter or peering in the window of the five-and-ten? Call that scarf $250 and the muff $175 and you won't make any mistake about the price of Russian sables. The swell goods for me. Say, they look fine on you, Moll."

Molly hugged the sables to her bosom in rapture. And then her smile went away little by little, and she looked the Kid straight in the eye sadly and steadily. He knew what every look of hers meant; and he laughed with a faint flush upon his face.

"Cut it out," he said, with affectionate roughness. "I told you I was done with that. I bought 'em and paid for 'em, all right, with my own money."

"Out of the money you worked for, Kid? Out of $75 a month?"

"Sure. I been saving up."

"Let's see—saved $425 in eight months, Kid?"

"Ah, let up," said the Kid, with some heat. "I had some money when I went to work. Do you think I've been holding 'em up again? I told you I'd quit. They're paid for on the square. Put 'em on and come out for a walk."

Molly calmed her doubts. Sables are soothing. Proud as a queen she went forth in the streets at the Kid's side. In all that region of low-lying streets Russian sables had never been seen before. The word sped, and doors and windows blossomed with heads eager to see the swell furs Kid Brady had given his girl. All down the street there were "Oh's" and "Ah's" and the reported fabulous sum paid for the sables was passed from lip to lip, increasing as it went. At her right elbow sauntered the Kid with the air of princes. Work had not diminished his love of pomp and show and his passion for the costly and genuine. On a corner they saw a group of the Stovepipe Gang loafing, immaculate. They raised their hats to the Kid's girl and went on with their calm, unaccented palaver.

Three blocks behind the admired couple strolled Detective Ransom, of the Central office. Ransom was the only detective on the force who could walk abroad with safety in the Stovepipe district. He was fair dealing and unafraid and went there with the hypothesis that the inhabitants were human. Many liked him, and now and then one would tip off to him something that he was looking for.

"What's the excitement down the street?" asked Ransom of a pale youth in a red sweater.

"Dey're out rubberin' at a set of buffalo robes Kid Brady staked his girl to," answered the youth. "Some say he paid $900 for de skins. Dey're swell all right enough."

"I hear Brady has been working at his old trade for nearly a year," said the detective. "He doesn't travel with the gang any more, does he?"

"He's workin', all right," said the red sweater, "but—say, sport, are you trailin' anything in the fur line? A job in a plumbin' shop don' match wid dem skins de Kid's girl's got on."

Ransom overtook the strolling couple on an empty street near the river bank. He touched the Kid's arm from behind.

"Let me see you a moment, Brady," he said, quietly. His eye rested for a second on the long fur scarf thrown stylishly back over Molly's left shoulder. The Kid, with his old-time police hating frown on his face, stepped a yard or two aside with the detective.

"Did you go to Mrs. Hethcote's on West 7—th street yesterday to fix a leaky water pipe?" asked Ransom.

"I did," said the Kid. "What of it?"

"The lady's $1,000 set of Russian sables went out of the house about the same time you did. The description fits the ones this lady has on."

"To hell Harlem with you," cried the Kid, angrily. "You know I've cut out that sort of thing, Ransom. I bought them sables yesterday at—"

The Kid stopped short.

"I know you've been working straight lately," said Ransom. "I'll give you every chance. I'll go with you where you say you bought the furs and investigate. The lady can wear 'em along with us and nobody'll be on. That's fair, Brady."

"Come on," agreed the Kid, hotly. And then he stopped suddenly in his tracks and looked with an odd smile at Molly's distressed and anxious face.

"No use," he said, grimly. "They're the Hethcote sables, all right. You'll have to turn 'em over, Moll, but they ain't too good for you if they cost a million."

Molly, with anguish in her face, hung upon the Kid's arm.

"Oh, Kiddy, you've broke my heart," she said. "I was so proud of you—and now they'll do you—and where's our happiness gone?"

"Go home," said the Kid, wildly. "Come on, Ransom—take the furs. Let's get away from here. Wait a minute—I've a good mind to—no, I'll be damned if I can do it—run along, Moll—I'm ready, Ransom."

Around the corner of a lumber-yard came Policeman Kohen on his way to his beat along the river. The detective signed to him for assistance. Kohen joined the group. Ransom explained.

"Sure," said Kohen. "I hear about those saples dat vas stole. You say you have dem here?" Policeman Kohen took the end of Molly's late scarf in his hands and looked at it closely.

"Once," he said, "I sold furs in Sixth avenue. Yes, dese are saples. Dey come from Alaska. Dis scarf is vort $12 and dis muff—"

"Biff!" came the palm of the Kid's powerful hand upon the policeman's mouth. Kohen staggered and rallied. Molly screamed. The detective threw himself upon Brady and with Kohen's aid got the nippers on his wrist.

"The scarf is vort $12 and the muff is vort $9," persisted the policeman. "Vot is dis talk about $1,000 saples?"

The Kid sat upon a pile of lumber and his face turned dark red.

"Correct, Solomonski!" he declared, viciously. "I paid $21.50 for the set. I'd rather have got six months and not have told it. Me, the swell guy that wouldn't look at anything cheap! I'm a plain bluffer. Moll—my salary couldn't spell sables in Russian."

Molly cast herself upon his neck.

"What do I care for all the sables and money in the world," she cried. "It's my Kiddy I want. Oh, you dear, stuck-up, crazy blockhead!"

"You can take dose nippers off," said Kohen to the detective. "Before I leaf de station de report come in dat de lady vind her saples—hanging in her wardrobe. Young man, I excuse you dat punch in my vace—dis von time."

Ransom handed Molly her furs. Her eyes were smiling upon the Kid. She wound the scarf and threw the end over her left shoulder with a duchess' grace.

"A gouple of young vools," said Policeman Kohen to Ransom; "come on away."

Columbus Day

Second Monday in October

Landing of Columbus (1847)

John Vanderlyn (October 18, 1775 – September 23, 1852)

Christopher Columbus and members of his crew on a beach in the West
Indies, newly landed from his flagship Santa Maria on October 12, 1492.

Location: Capitol Rotunda

The Ransom of Red Chief

It looked like a good thing: but wait till I tell you. We were down South, in Alabama—Bill Driscoll and myself—when this kidnapping idea struck us. It was, as Bill afterward expressed it, "during a moment of temporary mental apparition"; but we didn't find that out till later.

There was a town down there, as flat as a flannel-cake, and called Summit, of course. It contained inhabitants of as undeleterious and self-satisfied a class of peasantry as ever clustered around a Maypole.

Bill and me had a joint capital of about six hundred dollars, and we needed just two thousand dollars more to pull off a fraudulent town-lot scheme in Western Illinois with. We talked it over on the front steps of the hotel. Philoprogenitiveness, says we, is strong in semi-rural communities; therefore and for other reasons, a kidnapping project ought to do better there than in the radius of newspapers that send reporters out in plain clothes to stir up talk about such things. We knew that Summit couldn't get after us with anything stronger than constables and maybe some lackadaisical bloodhounds and a diatribe or two in the *Weekly Farmers' Budget*. So, it looked good.

We selected for our victim the only child of a prominent citizen named Ebenezer Dorset. The father was respectable and tight, a mortgage fancier and a stern, upright collection-plate passer and forecloser. The kid was a boy of ten, with bas-relief freckles, and hair the color of the cover of the magazine you buy at the news-stand when you want to catch a train. Bill and me figured that Ebenezer would melt down for a ransom of two thousand dollars to a cent. But wait till I tell you.

About two miles from Summit was a little mountain, covered with a dense cedar brake. On the rear elevation of this mountain was a cave. There we stored provisions. One evening after sundown, we drove in a buggy past old Dorset's house. The kid was in the street, throwing rocks at a kitten on the opposite fence.

"Hey, little boy!" says Bill, "would you like to have a bag of candy and a nice ride?"

The boy catches Bill neatly in the eye with a piece of brick.

"That will cost the old man an extra five hundred dollars," says Bill, climbing over the wheel.

That boy put up a fight like a welter-weight cinnamon bear; but, at last, we got him down in the bottom of the buggy and drove away. We took him up to the cave and I hitched the horse in the cedar brake. After dark I drove the buggy to the little village, three miles away, where we had hired it, and walked back to the mountain.

Bill was pasting court-plaster over the scratches and bruises on his features. There was a fire burning behind the big rock at the entrance of the cave, and the boy was watching a pot of boiling coffee, with two buzzard tail-feathers stuck in his red hair. He points a stick at me when I come up, and says:

"Ha! cursed paleface, do you dare to enter the camp of Red Chief, the terror of the plains?

"He's all right now," says Bill, rolling up his trousers and examining some bruises on his shins. "We're playing Indian. We're making Buffalo Bill's show look like magic-lantern views of Palestine in the town hall. I'm Old Hank, the Trapper, Red Chief's captive, and I'm to be scalped at daybreak. By Geronimo! that kid can kick hard."

Yes, sir, that boy seemed to be having the time of his life. The fun of camping out in a cave had made him forget that he was a captive himself. He immediately christened me Snake-eye, the Spy, and announced that, when his braves returned from the warpath, I was to be broiled at the stake at the rising of the sun.

Then we had supper; and he filled his mouth full of bacon and bread and gravy, and began to talk. He made a during-dinner speech something like this:

"I like this fine. I never camped out before; but I had a pet 'possum once, and I was nine last birthday. I hate to go to school. Rats ate up sixteen of Jimmy Talbot's aunt's speckled hen's eggs. Are there any real Indians in these woods? I want some more gravy. Does the trees moving make the wind blow? We had five puppies. What makes your nose so red, Hank? My father has lots of money. Are the stars hot? I whipped Ed Walker twice, Saturday. I don't like girls. You dassent catch toads unless with a string. Do oxen make any noise? Why are oranges round? Have you got beds to sleep on in this cave? Amos Murray has got six toes. A parrot can talk, but a monkey or a fish can't. How many does it take to make twelve?"

Every few minutes he would remember that he was a pesky redskin, and pick up his stick rifle and tiptoe to the mouth of the cave to rubber for the scouts of the hated paleface. Now and then he would let out a war-whoop that made Old Hank the Trapper shiver. That boy had Bill terrorized from the start.

"Red Chief," says I to the kid, "would you like to go home?"

"Aw, what for?" says he. "I don't have any fun at home. I hate to go to school. I like to camp out. You won't take me back home again, Snake-eye, will you?"

"Not right away," says I. "We'll stay here in the cave a while."

"All right!" says he. "That'll be fine. I never had such fun in all my life."

We went to bed about eleven o'clock. We spread down some wide blankets and quilts and put Red Chief between us. We weren't afraid he'd run away. He kept us awake for three hours, jumping up and reaching for his rifle and screeching: "Hist! pard," in mine and Bill's ears, as the fancied crackle of a twig or the rustle of a leaf revealed to his young imagination the stealthy approach of the outlaw band. At last, I fell into a troubled sleep, and dreamed that I had been kidnapped and chained to a tree by a ferocious pirate with red hair.

Just at daybreak, I was awakened by a series of awful screams from Bill. They weren't yells, or howls, or shouts, or whoops, or yawps, such as you'd expect from a manly set of vocal organs— they were simply indecent, terrifying, humiliating screams, such as women emit when they see ghosts or caterpillars. It's an awful thing to hear a strong, desperate, fat man scream incontinently in a cave at daybreak.

I jumped up to see what the matter was. Red Chief was sitting on Bill's chest, with one hand twined in Bill's hair. In the other he had the sharp case-knife we used for slicing bacon; and he was industriously and realistically trying to take Bill's scalp, according to the sentence that had been pronounced upon him the evening before.

I got the knife away from the kid and made him lie down again. But, from that moment, Bill's spirit was broken. He laid down on his side of the bed, but he never closed an eye again in sleep as long as that boy was with us. I dozed off for a while, but along toward sun-up I remembered that Red Chief had said I was to be burned at the stake at the rising of the sun. I wasn't nervous or afraid; but I sat up and lit my pipe and leaned against a rock.

"What you getting up so soon for, Sam?" asked Bill.

"Me?" says I. "Oh, I got a kind of a pain in my shoulder. I thought sitting up would rest it."

"You're a liar!" says Bill. "You're afraid. You was to be burned at sunrise, and you was afraid he'd do it. And he would, too, if he could find a match. Ain't it awful, Sam? Do you think anybody will pay out money to get a little imp like that back home?"

"Sure," said I. "A rowdy kid like that is just the kind that parents dote on. Now, you and the Chief get up and cook breakfast, while I go up on the top of this mountain and reconnoitre."

I went up on the peak of the little mountain and ran my eye over the contiguous vicinity. Over toward Summit I expected to see the sturdy yeomanry of the village armed with scythes and pitchforks beating the countryside for the dastardly kidnappers. But what I saw was a peaceful landscape dotted with one man ploughing with a dun mule. Nobody was dragging the creek; no couriers dashed hither and yon, bringing tidings of no news to the distracted parents. There was a sylvan attitude of somnolent sleepiness pervading that section of the external outward surface of Alabama that lay exposed to my view. "Perhaps," says I to myself, "it has not yet been discovered that the wolves have borne away the tender lambkin from the fold. Heaven help the wolves!" says I, and I went down the mountain to breakfast.

When I got to the cave I found Bill backed up against the side of it, breathing hard, and the boy threatening to smash him with a rock half as big as a cocoanut.

"He put a red-hot boiled potato down my back," explained Bill, "and then mashed it with his foot; and I boxed his ears. Have you got a gun about you, Sam?"

I took the rock away from the boy and kind of patched up the argument. "I'll fix you," says the kid to Bill. "No man ever yet struck the Red Chief but what he got paid for it. You better beware!"

After breakfast the kid takes a piece of leather with strings wrapped around it out of his pocket and goes outside the cave unwinding it.

"What's he up to now?" says Bill, anxiously. "You don't think he'll run away, do you, Sam?"

"No fear of it," says I. "He don't seem to be much of a home body. But we've got to fix up some plan about the ransom. There don't seem to be much excitement around Summit on account of his disappearance; but maybe they haven't realized yet that he's gone. His folks may think he's spending the night with Aunt Jane or one of the neighbors. Anyhow, he'll be missed to-day. To-night we must get a message to his father demanding the two thousand dollars for his return."

Just then we heard a kind of war-whoop, such as David might have emitted when he knocked out the champion Goliath. It was a sling that Red Chief had pulled out of his pocket, and he was whirling it around his head.

I dodged, and heard a heavy thud and a kind of a sigh from Bill, like a horse gives out when you take his saddle off. A rock the size of an egg had caught Bill just behind his left ear. He loosened himself all over and fell in the fire across the frying pan of hot water for washing the dishes. I dragged him out and poured cold water on his head for half an hour.

By and by, Bill sits up and feels behind his ear and says: "Sam, do you know who my favorite Biblical character is?"

"Take it easy," says I. "You'll come to your senses presently."

"King Herod," says he. "You won't go away and leave me here alone, will you, Sam?"

I went out and caught that boy and shook him until his freckles rattled.

"If you don't behave," says I, "I'll take you straight home. Now, are you going to be good, or not?"

"I was only funning," says he sullenly. "I didn't mean to hurt Old Hank. But what did he hit me for? I'll behave, Snake-eye, if you won't send me home, and if you'll let me play the Black Scout to-day."

"I don't know the game," says I. "That's for you and Mr. Bill to decide. He's your playmate for the day. I'm going away for a while, on business. Now, you come in and make friends with him and say you are sorry for hurting him, or home you go, at once."

I made him and Bill shake hands, and then I took Bill aside and told him I was going to Poplar Cove, a little village three miles from the cave, and find out what I could about how the kidnapping had been regarded in Summit. Also, I thought it best to send a peremptory letter to old man Dorset that day, demanding the ransom and dictating how it should be paid.

"You know, Sam," says Bill, "I've stood by you without batting an eye in earthquakes, fire and flood—in poker games, dynamite outrages, police raids, train robberies and cyclones. I never lost my nerve yet till we kidnapped that two-legged skyrocket of a kid. He's got me going. You won't leave me long with him, will you, Sam?"

"I'll be back some time this afternoon," says I. "You must keep the boy amused and quiet till I return. And now we'll write the letter to old Dorset."

Bill and I got paper and pencil and worked on the letter while Red Chief, with a blanket wrapped around him, strutted up and down, guarding the mouth of the cave. Bill begged me tearfully to make the ransom fifteen hundred dollars instead of two thousand. "I ain't attempting," says he, "to decry the celebrated moral aspect of parental affection, but we're dealing with humans, and it

259

ain't human for anybody to give up two thousand dollars for that forty-pound chunk of freckled wildcat. I'm willing to take a chance at fifteen hundred dollars. You can charge the difference up to me."

So, to relieve Bill, I acceded, and we collaborated a letter that ran this way:

Ebenezer Dorset, Esq.:

We have your boy concealed in a place far from Summit. It is useless for you or the most skillful detectives to attempt to find him. Absolutely, the only terms on which you can have him restored to you are these: We demand fifteen hundred dollars in large bills for his return; the money to be left at midnight to-night at the same spot and in the same box as your reply—as hereinafter described. If you agree to these terms, send your answer in writing by a solitary messenger to-night at half-past eight o'clock. After crossing Owl Creek, on the road to Poplar Cove, there are three large trees about a hundred yards apart, close to the fence of the wheat field on the right-hand side. At the bottom of the fence-post, opposite the third tree, will be found a small pasteboard box.

The messenger will place the answer in this box and return immediately to Summit.

If you attempt any treachery or fail to comply with our demand as stated, you will never see your boy again.

If you pay the money as demanded, he will be returned to you safe and well within three hours. These terms are final, and if you do not accede to them no further communication will be attempted.

TWO DESPERATE MEN.

I addressed this letter to Dorset, and put it in my pocket. As I was about to start, the kid comes up to me and says:

"Aw, Snake-eye, you said I could play the Black Scout while you was gone."

"Play it, of course," says I. "Mr. Bill will play with you. What kind of a game is it?"

"I'm the Black Scout," says Red Chief, "and I have to ride to the stockade to warn the settlers that the Indians are coming. I'm tired of playing Indian myself. I want to be the Black Scout."

"All right," says I. "It sounds harmless to me. I guess Mr. Bill will help you foil the pesky savages."

"What am I to do?" asks Bill, looking at the kid suspiciously.

"You are the hoss," says Black Scout. "Get down on your hands and knees. How can I ride to the stockade without a hoss?"

"You'd better keep him interested," said I, "till we get the scheme going. Loosen up."

Bill gets down on his all fours, and a look comes in his eye like a rabbit's when you catch it in a trap.

"How far is it to the stockade, kid?" he asks, in a husky manner of voice.

"Ninety miles," says the Black Scout. "And you have to hump yourself to get there on time. Whoa, now!"

The Black Scout jumps on Bill's back and digs his heels in his side.

"For Heaven's sake," says Bill, "hurry back, Sam, as soon as you can. I wish we hadn't made the ransom more than a thousand. Say, you quit kicking me or I'll get up and warm you good."

I walked over to Poplar Cove and sat around the post-office and store, talking with the chawbacons that came in to trade. One whiskerando says that he hears Summit is all upset on account of Elder Ebenezer Dorset's boy having been lost or stolen. That was all I wanted to know. I bought some smoking tobacco, referred casually to the price of black-eyed peas, posted my letter surreptitiously and came away. The postmaster said the mail-carrier would come by in an hour to take the mail on to Summit.

When I got back to the cave Bill and the boy were not to be found. I explored the vicinity of the cave, and risked a yodel or two, but there was no response.

So I lighted my pipe and sat down on a mossy bank to await developments.

In about half an hour I heard the bushes rustle, and Bill wabbled out into the little glade in front of the cave. Behind him was the kid, stepping softly like a scout, with a broad grin on his face. Bill stopped, took off his hat and wiped his face with a red handkerchief. The kid stopped about eight feet behind him.

"Sam," says Bill, "I suppose you'll think I'm a renegade, but I couldn't help it. I'm a grown person with masculine proclivities

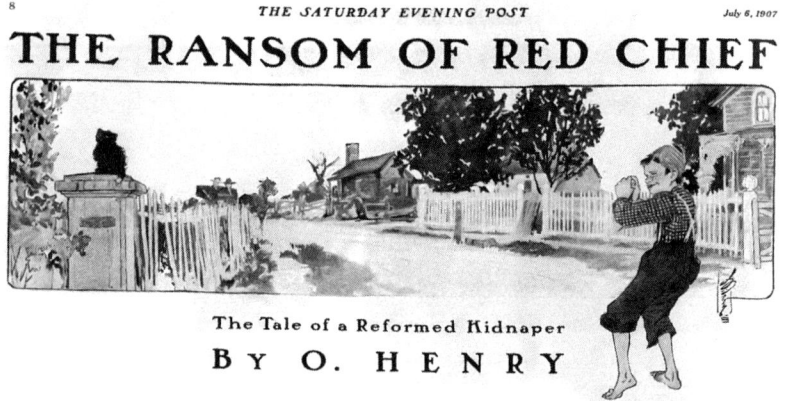

The Ransom of Red Chief
The Saturday Evening Post
July 6, 1907

Austin History Center, Austin Public Library
via University of North Texas Libraries, The Portal to Texas History

and habits of self-defense, but there is a time when all systems of egotism and predominance fail. The boy is gone. I have sent him home. All is off. There was martyrs in old times," goes on Bill, "that suffered death rather than give up the particular graft they enjoyed. None of 'em ever was subjugated to such supernatural tortures as I have been. I tried to be faithful to our articles of depredation; but there came a limit."

"What's the trouble, Bill?" I asks him.

"I was rode," says Bill, "the ninety miles to the stockade, not barring an inch. Then, when the settlers was rescued, I was given oats. Sand ain't a palatable substitute. And then, for an hour I had to try to explain to him why there was nothin' in holes, how a road can run both ways and what makes the grass green. I tell you, Sam, a human can only stand so much. I takes him by the neck of his clothes and drags him down the mountain. On the way he kicks my legs black-and-blue from the knees down; and I've got to have two or three bites on my thumb and hand cauterized.

"But he's gone"—continues Bill—"gone home. I showed him the road to Summit and kicked him about eight feet nearer there at one kick. I'm sorry we lose the ransom; but it was either that or Bill Driscoll to the madhouse."

Bill is puffing and blowing, but there is a look of ineffable peace and growing content on his rose-pink features.

"Bill," says I, "there isn't any heart disease in your family, is there?"

"No," says Bill, "nothing chronic except malaria and accidents. Why?"

"Then you might turn around," says I, "and have a look behind you."

Bill turns and sees the boy, and loses his complexion and sits down plump on the ground and begins to pluck aimlessly at grass and little sticks. For an hour I was afraid for his mind.

And then I told him that my scheme was to put the whole job through immediately and that we would get the ransom and be off with it by midnight if old Dorset fell in with our proposition. So Bill braced up enough to give the kid a weak sort of a smile and a promise to play the Russian in a Japanese war with him as soon as he felt a little better.

I had a scheme for collecting that ransom without danger of being caught by counterplots that ought to commend itself to professional kidnappers. The tree under which the answer was to be left—and the money later on—was close to the road fence with big, bare fields on all sides. If a gang of constables should be watching for any one to come for the note they could see him a long way off crossing the fields or in the road. But no, sirree! At half-past eight I was up in that tree as well hidden as a tree toad, waiting for the messenger to arrive.

Exactly on time, a half-grown boy rides up the road on a bicycle, locates the pasteboard box at the foot of the fence-post, slips a folded piece of paper into it and pedals away again back toward Summit.

I waited an hour and then concluded the thing was square. I slid down the tree, got the note, slipped along the fence till I struck the woods, and was back at the cave in another half an hour. I opened the note, got near the lantern and read it to Bill. It was written with a pen in a crabbed hand, and the sum and substance of it was this:

Two Desperate Men.

Gentlemen: I received your letter to-day by post, in regard to the ransom you ask for the return of my son. I think you are a little high in your demands, and I hereby make you a counter-proposition, which I am inclined to believe you will accept. You bring Johnny home and pay me two hundred and fifty dollars in cash, and I agree to take him off your hands. You had better come at night, for the neighbors believe he is lost, and I couldn't be responsible for what they would do to anybody they saw bringing him back. Very respectfully,

EBENEZER DORSET.

"Great pirates of Penzance!" says I; "of all the impudent—"

But I glanced at Bill, and hesitated. He had the most appealing look in his eyes I ever saw on the face of a dumb or a talking brute.

"Sam," says he, "what's two hundred and fifty dollars, after all? We've got the money. One more night of this kid will send me to a bed in Bedlam. Besides being a thorough gentleman, I think Mr. Dorset is a spendthrift for making us such a liberal offer. You ain't going to let the chance go, are you?"

"Tell you the truth, Bill," says I, "this little he ewe lamb has somewhat got on my nerves too. We'll take him home, pay the ransom and make our get-away."

We took him home that night. We got him to go by telling him that his father had bought a silver-mounted rifle and a pair of moccasins for him, and we were going to hunt bears the next day.

It was just twelve o'clock when we knocked at Ebenezer's front door. Just at the moment when I should have been abstracting the fifteen hundred dollars from the box under the tree, according to the original proposition, Bill was counting out two hundred and fifty dollars into Dorset's hand.

When the kid found out we were going to leave him at home he started up a howl like a calliope and fastened himself as tight as a leech to Bill's leg. His father peeled him away gradually, like a porous plaster.

"How long can you hold him?" asks Bill.

"I'm not as strong as I used to be," says old Dorset, "but I think I can promise you ten minutes."

"Enough," says Bill. "In ten minutes I shall cross the Central, Southern and Middle Western States, and be legging it trippingly for the Canadian border."

And, as dark as it was, and as fat as Bill was, and as good a runner as I am, he was a good mile and a half out of Summit before I could catch up with him.

Halloween

October 31st

Vintage Halloween Postcard (1912)

Courtesy marklawsonantiques.com

The Head-Hunter

When the war between Spain and George Dewey was over, I went to the Philippine Islands. There I remained as bush-whacker correspondent for my paper until its managing editor notified me that an eight-hundred-word cablegram describing the grief of a pet carabao over the death of an infant Moro was not considered by the office to be war news. So I resigned, and came home.

On board the trading-vessel that brought me back I pondered much upon the strange things I had sensed in the weird archipelago of the yellow-brown people. The maneuvers and skirmishings of the petty war interested me not: I was spellbound by the outlandish and unreadable countenance of that race that had turned its expressionless gaze upon us out of an unguessable past.

Particularly during my stay in Mindanao had I been fascinated and attracted by that delightfully original tribe of heathen known as the head-hunters. Those grim, flinty, relentless little men, never seen, but chilling the warmest noonday by the subtle terror of their concealed presence, paralleling the trail of their prey through unmapped forests, across perilous mountain-tops, adown bottomless chasms, into uninhabitable jungles, always near with the invisible hand of death uplifted, betraying their pursuit only by such signs as a beast or a bird or a gliding serpent might make—a twig crackling in the awful, sweat-soaked night, a drench of dew showering from the screening foliage of a giant tree, a whisper at even from the rushes of a water-level—a hint of death for every mile and every hour—they amused me greatly, those little fellows of one idea.

When you think of it, their method is beautifully and almost hilariously effective and simple.

You have your hut in which you live and carry out the destiny that was decreed for you. Spiked to the jamb of your bamboo doorway is a basket made of green withes, plaited. From time to time, as vanity or ennui or love or jealousy or ambition may move you, you creep forth with your snickersnee and take up the silent trail. Back from it you come, triumphant, bearing the severed, gory head of your victim, which you deposit with pardonable pride in the basket at the side of your door. It may be the head of your enemy, your friend, or a stranger, according as competition, jealousy, or simple sportiveness has been your incentive to labor.

In any case, your reward is certain. The village men, in passing, stop to congratulate you, as your neighbor on weaker planes of life stops to admire and praise the begonias in your front yard. Your particular brown maid lingers, with fluttering bosom, casting soft tiger's eyes at the evidence of your love for her. You chew betel-nut and listen, content, to the intermittent soft drip from the ends of the severed neck arteries. And you show your teeth and grunt like a water-buffalo—which is as near as you can come to laughing—at the thought that the cold, acephalous body of your door ornament is being spotted by wheeling vultures in the Mindanaoan wilds.

Truly, the life of the merry head-hunter captivated me. He had reduced art and philosophy to a simple code. To take your adversary's head, to basket it at the portal of your castle, to see it lying there, a dead thing, with its cunning and stratagems and power gone—Is there a better way to foil his plots, to refute his arguments, to establish your superiority over his skill and wisdom?

The ship that brought me home was captained by an erratic Swede, who changed his course and deposited me, with genuine compassion, in a small town on the Pacific coast of one of the Central American republics, a few hundred miles south of the port to which he had engaged to convey me. But I was wearied of movement and exotic fancies; so I leaped contentedly upon the firm sands of the village of Mojada, telling myself I should be sure to find there the rest that I craved. After all, far better to linger there (I thought), lulled by the sedative plash of the waves and the rustling of palm-fronds, than to sit upon the horsehair sofa of my parental home in the East, and there, cast down by currant wine and cake, and scourged by fatuous relatives, drivel into the ears of gaping neighbors sad stories of the death of colonial governors.

When I first saw Chloe Greene she was standing, all in white, in the doorway of her father's tile-roofed 'dobe house. She was polishing a silver cup with a cloth, and she looked like a pearl laid against black velvet. She turned on me a flatteringly protracted but a wiltingly disapproving gaze, and then went inside, humming a light song to indicate the value she placed upon my existence.

Small wonder: for Dr. Stamford (the most disreputable professional man between Juneau and Valparaiso) and I were zig-zagging along the turfy street, tunelessly singing the words of "Auld Lang Syne" to the air of "It's A Long Way to Connemara." We had come from the ice factory, which was Mojada's palace of wickedness, where we had been playing billiards and opening black bottles, white with frost, that we dragged with strings out of old Sandoval's ice-cold vats.

271

I HAD BECOME AWARE THAT WE WERE SWINE CAST BEFORE A PEARL.

The Head-Hunter

Everybody's

May 1908

Illustration by Will Crawford (1869-1944)

Austin History Center, Austin Public Library via University of North Texas
Libraries, The Portal to Texas History

I turned in sudden rage to Dr. Stamford, as sober as the verger of a cathedral. In a moment I had become aware that we were swine cast before a pearl.

"You beast," I said, "this is half your doing. And the other half is the fault of this cursed country. I'd better have gone back to Sleepy-town and died in a wild orgy of currant wine and buns than to have had this happen."

Stamford filled the empty street with his roaring laughter.

"You too!" he cried. "And all as quick as the popping of a cork. Well, she does seem to strike agreeably upon the retina. But don't burn your fingers. All Mojada will tell you that Louis Devoe is the man."

"We will see about that," said I. "And, perhaps, whether he is *a* man as well as *the* man."

I lost no time in meeting Louis Devoe. That was easily accomplished, for the foreign colony in Mojada numbered scarce a dozen; and they gathered daily at a half-decent hotel kept by a Turk, where they managed to patch together the fluttering rags of country and civilization that were left them. I sought Devoe before I did my pearl of the doorway, because I had learned a little of the game of war, and knew better than to strike for a prize before testing the strength of the enemy.

A sort of cold dismay—something akin to fear—filled me when I had estimated him. I found a man so perfectly poised, so charming, so deeply learned in the world's rituals, so full of tact, courtesy, and hospitality, so endowed with grace and ease and a kind of careless, haughty power that I almost overstepped the bounds in probing him, in turning him on the spit to find the weak point that I so craved for him to have. But I left him whole—I had to make bitter acknowledgment to myself that Louis Devoe was a gentleman worthy of my best blows; and I swore to give him them. He was a great merchant of the country, a wealthy importer and exporter. All day he sat in a fastidiously appointed office, surrounded by works of art and evidences of his high culture, directing through glass doors and windows the affairs of his house.

In person he was slender and hardly tall. His small, well-shaped head was covered with thick, brown hair, trimmed short, and he wore a thick, brown beard also cut close and to a fine point. His manners were a pattern.

Before long I had become a regular and a welcome visitor at the Greene home. I shook my wild habits from me like a worn-out cloak. I trained for the conflict with the care of a prize-fighter and the self-denial of a Brahmin.

As for Chloe Greene, I shall weary you with no sonnets to her eyebrow. She was a splendidly feminine girl, as wholesome as a November pippin, and no more mysterious than a window-pane. She had whimsical little theories that she had deduced from life, and that fitted the maxims of Epictetus like princess gowns. I wonder, after all, if that old duffer wasn't rather wise!

Chloe had a father, the Reverend Homer Greene, and an intermittent mother, who sometimes palely presided over a twilight teapot. The Reverend Homer was a burr-like man with a life-work. He was writing a concordance to the Scriptures, and had arrived as far as Kings. Being, presumably, a suitor for his daughter's hand, I was timber for his literary outpourings. I had the family tree of Israel drilled into my head until I used to cry aloud in my sleep: "And Aminadab begat Jay Eye See," and so forth, until he had tackled another book. I once made a calculation that the Reverend Homer's concordance would be worked up as far as the Seven Vials mentioned in Revelations about the third day after they were opened.

Louis Devoe, as well as I, was a visitor and an intimate friend of the Greenes. It was there I met him the oftenest, and a more agreeable man or a more accomplished I have never hated in my life.

Luckily or unfortunately, I came to be accepted as a Boy. My appearance was youthful, and I suppose I had that pleading and homeless air that always draws the motherliness that is in women and the cursed theories and hobbies of paterfamilias.

Chloe called me "Tommy," and made sisterly fun of my attempts to woo her. With Devoe she was vastly more reserved. He was the man of romance, one to stir her imagination and deepest feelings had her fancy leaned toward him. I was closer to her, but standing in no glamour; I had the task before me of winning her in what seems to me the American way of fighting—with cleanness and pluck and everyday devotion to break away the barriers of friendship that divided us, and to take her, if I could, between sunrise and dark, abetted by neither moonlight nor music nor foreign wiles.

Chloe gave no sign of bestowing her blithe affections upon either of us. But one day she let out to me an inkling of what she preferred in a man. It was tremendously interesting to me, but not illuminating as to its application. I had been tormenting her for the dozenth time with the statement and catalogue of my sentiments toward her.

"Tommy," said she, "I don't want a man to show his love for me by leading an army against another country and blowing people off the earth with cannons."

"If you mean that the opposite way," I answered, "as they say women do, I'll see what I can do. The papers are full of this diplomatic row in Russia. My people know some big people in Washington who are right next to the army people, and I could get an artillery commission and—"

"I'm not that way," interrupted Chloe. "I mean what I say. It isn't the big things that are done in the world, Tommy, that count with a woman. When the knights were riding abroad in their armor to slay dragons, many a stay-at-home page won a lonesome lady's hand by being on the spot to pick up her glove and be quick with her cloak when the wind blew. The man I am to like best, whoever he shall be, must show his love in little ways. He must never forget, after hearing it once, that I do not like to have any one walk at my left side; that I detest bright-colored neckties; that I prefer to sit with my back to a light; that I like candied violets; that I must not be talked to when I am looking at the moonlight shining on water, and that I very, very often long for dates stuffed with English walnuts."

"Frivolity," I said, with a frown. "Any well-trained servant would be equal to such details."

"And he must remember," went on Chloe, "to remind me of what I want when I do not know, myself, what I want."

"You're rising in the scale," I said. "What you seem to need is a first-class clairvoyant."

"And if I say that I am dying to hear a Beethoven sonata, and stamp my foot when I say it, he must know by that that what my soul craves is salted almonds; and he will have them ready in his pocket."

"Now," said I, "I am at a loss. I do not know whether your soul's affinity is to be an impresario or a fancy grocer."

Chloe turned her pearly smile upon me.

"Take less than half of what I said as a jest," she went on. "And don't think too lightly of the little things, Boy. Be a paladin if you must, but don't let it show on you. Most women are only very big children, and most men are only very little ones. Please us; don't try to overpower us. When we want a hero we can make one out of even a plain grocer the third time he catches our handkerchief before it falls to the ground."

That evening I was taken down with pernicious fever. That

276

is a kind of coast fever with improvements and high-geared attachments. Your temperature goes up among the threes and fours and remains there, laughing scornfully and feverishly at the cinchona trees and the coal-tar derivatives. Pernicious fever is a case for a simple mathematician instead of a doctor. It is merely this formula: Vitality + the desire to live − the duration of the fever = the result.

I took to my bed in the two-roomed thatched hut where I had been comfortably established, and sent for a gallon of rum. That was not for myself. Drunk, Stamford was the best doctor between the Andes and the Pacific. He came, sat at my bedside, and drank himself into condition.

"My boy," said he, "my lily-white and reformed Romeo, medicine will do you no good. But I will give you quinine, which, being bitter, will arouse in you hatred and anger—two stimulants that will add ten per cent to your chances. You are as strong as a caribou calf, and you will get well if the fever doesn't get in a knockout blow when you're off your guard."

For two weeks I lay on my back feeling like a Hindoo widow on a burning-ghat. Old Atasca, an untrained Indian nurse, sat near the door like a petrified statue of What's-the-Use, attending to her duties, which were, mainly, to see that time went by without slipping a cog. Sometimes I would fancy myself back in the Philippines, or, at worse times, sliding off the horsehair sofa in Sleepytown.

One afternoon I ordered Atasca to vamose, and got up and dressed carefully. I took my temperature, which I was pleased to find 104. I paid almost dainty attention to my dress, choosing so-licitously a necktie of a dull and subdued hue. The mirror showed that I was looking little the worse from my illness. The fever gave brightness to my eyes and color to my face. And while I looked at my reflection my color went and came again as I thought of

Chloe Greene and the millions of eons that had passed since I'd seen her, and of Louis Devoe and the time he had gained on me.

I went straight to her house. I seemed to float rather than walk; I hardly felt the ground under my feet; I thought pernicious fever must be a great boon to make one feel so strong.

I found Chloe and Louis Devoe sitting under the awning in front of the house. She jumped up and met me with a double handshake.

"I'm glad, glad, glad to see you out again!" she cried, every word a pearl strung on the string of her sentence. "You are well, Tommy—or better, of course. I wanted to come to see you, but they wouldn't let me."

"Oh yes," said I, carelessly, "it was nothing. Merely a little fever. I am out again, as you see."

We three sat there and talked for half an hour or so. Then Chloe looked out yearningly and almost piteously across the ocean. I could see in her sea-blue eyes some deep and intense desire. Devoe, curse him! saw it too.

"What is it?" we asked, in unison.

"Cocoanut-pudding," said Chloe, pathetically. "I've wanted some—oh, so badly, for two days. It's got beyond a wish; it's an obsession."

"The cocoanut season is over," said Devoe, in that voice of his that gave thrilling interest to his most commonplace words. "I hardly think one could be found in Mojada. The natives never use them except when they are green and the milk is fresh. They sell all the ripe ones to the fruiterers."

"Wouldn't a broiled lobster or a Welsh rabbit do as well?" I remarked, with the engaging idiocy of a pernicious-fever convalescent.

Chloe came as near to pouting as a sweet disposition and a perfect profile would allow her to come.

The Reverend Homer poked his ermine-lined face through the doorway and added a concordance to the conversation.

"Sometimes," said he, "old Campos keeps the dried nuts in his little store on the hill. But it would be far better, my daughter, to restrain unusual desires, and partake thankfully of the daily dishes that the Lord has set before us."

"Stuff!" said I.

"How was that?" asked the Reverend Homer, sharply.

"I say it's tough," said I, "to drop into the vernacular, that Miss Greene should be deprived of the food she desires—a simple thing like kalsomine-pudding. Perhaps," I continued, solicitously, "some pickled walnuts or a fricassee of Hungarian butternuts would do as well."

Every one looked at me with a slight exhibition of curiosity.

Louis Devoe arose and made his adieus. I watched him until he had sauntered slowly and grandiosely to the corner, around which he turned to reach his great warehouse and store. Chloe made her excuses, and went inside for a few minutes to attend to some detail affecting the seven-o'clock dinner. She was a passed mistress in housekeeping. I had tasted her puddings and bread with beatitude.

When all had gone, I turned casually and saw a basket made of plaited green withes hanging by a nail outside the door-jamb. With a rush that made my hot temples throb there came vividly to my mind recollections of the head-hunters—*those grim, flinty, relentless little men, never seen, but chilling the warmest noonday by the subtle terror of their concealed presence . . . From time to time, as vanity or ennui or love or jealousy or ambition may move him, one creeps forth with his snickersnee and takes up the silent trail . . . Back he comes, triumphant, bearing the severed, gory head of his victim . . . His particular brown or white maid lingers, with fluttering bosom, casting soft tiger's eyes at the evidence of his love for her.*

"OH, TOMMY!" SHE SAID. "IT'S THE LITTLE THINGS THAT COUNT."

The Head-Hunter

Everybody's

May 1908

Illustration by Will Crawford (1869-1944)

I stole softly from the house and returned to my hut. From its supporting nails in the wall I took a machete as heavy as a butcher's cleaver and sharper than a safety-razor. And then I chuckled softly to myself, and set out to the fastidiously appointed private office of Monsieur Louis Devoe, usurper to the hand of the Pearl of the Pacific.

He was never slow at thinking; he gave one look at my face and another at the weapon in my hand as I entered his door, and then he seemed to fade from my sight. I ran to the back door, kicked it open, and saw him running like a deer up the road toward the wood that began two hundred yards away. I was after him, with a shout. I remember hearing children and women screaming, and seeing them flying from the road.

He was fleet, but I was stronger. A mile, and I had almost come up with him. He doubled cunningly and dashed into a brake that extended into a small cañon. I crashed through this after him, and in five minutes had him cornered in an angle of insurmountable cliffs. There his instinct of self-preservation steadied him, as it will steady even animals at bay. He turned to me, quite calm, with a ghastly smile.

"Oh, Rayburn!" he said, with such an awful effort at ease that I was impolite enough to laugh rudely in his face. "Oh, Rayburn!" said he, "come, let's have done with this nonsense. Of course, I know it's the fever and you're not yourself; but collect yourself, man—give me that ridiculous weapon, now, and let's go back and talk it over."

"I will go back," said I, "carrying your head with me. We will see how charmingly it can discourse when it lies in the basket at her door."

"Come," said he, persuasively, "I think better of you than to suppose that you try this sort of thing as a joke. But even the vagaries of a fever-crazed lunatic come some time to a limit.

What is this talk about heads and baskets? Get yourself together and throw away that absurd cane-chopper. What would Miss Greene think of you?" he ended, with the silky cajolery that one would use toward a fretful child.

"Listen," said I. "At last you have struck upon the right note. What would she think of me? Listen," I repeated.

"There are women," I said, "who look upon horsehair sofas and currant wine as dross. To them even the calculated modulation of your well-trimmed talk sounds like the dropping of rotten plums from a tree in the night. They are the maidens who walk back and forth in the villages, scorning the emptiness of the baskets at the doors of the young men who would win them. One such as they," I said, "is waiting. Only a fool would try to win a woman by drooling like a braggart in her doorway or by waiting upon her whims like a footman. They are all daughters of Herodias, and to gain their hearts one must lay the heads of his enemies before them with his own hands. Now, bend your neck, Louis Devoe. Do not be a coward as well as a chatterer at a lady's tea-table."

"There, there!" said Devoe, falteringly. "You know me, don't you, Rayburn?"

"Oh yes," I said, "I know you. I know you. I know you. But the basket is empty. The old men of the village and the young men, and both the dark maidens and the ones who are as fair as pearls walk back and forth and see its emptiness. Will you kneel now, or must we have a scuffle? It is not like you to make things go roughly and with bad form. But the basket is waiting for your head."

With that he went to pieces. I had to catch him as he tried to scamper past me like a scared rabbit. I stretched him out and got a foot on his chest, but he squirmed like a worm, although I appealed repeatedly to his sense of propriety and the duty he owed to himself as a gentleman not to make a row.

But at last he gave me the chance, and I swung the machete.

It was not hard work. He flopped like a chicken during the six or seven blows that it took to sever his head; but finally he lay still, and I tied his head in my handkerchief. The eyes opened and shut thrice while I walked a hundred yards. I was red to my feet with the drip, but what did that matter? With delight I felt under my hands the crisp touch of his short, thick, brown hair and close-trimmed beard.

I reached the house of the Greenes and dumped the head of Louis Devoe into the basket that still hung by the nail in the door-jamb. I sat in a chair under the awning and waited. The sun was within two hours of setting. Chloe came out and looked surprised.

"Where have you been, Tommy?" she asked. "You were gone when I came out."

"Look in the basket," I said, rising to my feet. She looked, and gave a little scream—of delight, I was pleased to note.

"Oh, Tommy!" she said. "It was just what I wanted you to do. It's leaking a little, but that doesn't matter. Wasn't I telling you? It's the little things that count. And you remembered."

Little things! She held the ensanguined head of Louis Devoe in her white apron. Tiny streams of red widened on her apron and dripped upon the floor. Her face was bright and tender.

"Little things, indeed!" I thought again. "The head-hunters are right. These are the things that women like you to do for them."

Chloe came close to me. There was no one in sight. She looked up at me with sea-blue eyes that said things they had never said before.

"You think of me," she said. "You are the man I was describing. You think of the little things, and they are what make the world worth living in. The man for me must consider my little wishes, and make me happy in small ways. He must bring me

283

little red peaches in December if I wish for them, and then I will love him till June. I will have no knight in armor slaying his rival or killing dragons for me. You please me very well, Tommy."

I stooped and kissed her. Then a moisture broke out on my forehead, and I began to feel weak. I saw the red stains vanish from Chloe's apron, and the head of Louis Devoe turn to a brown, dried cocoanut.

"There will be cocoanut-pudding for dinner, Tommy, boy," said Chloe, gayly, "and you must come. I must go in for a little while."

She vanished in a delightful flutter.

Dr. Stamford tramped up hurriedly. He seized my pulse as though it were his own property that I had escaped with.

"You are the biggest fool outside of any asylum!" he said, angrily. "Why did you leave your bed? And the idiotic things you've been doing!—and no wonder, with your pulse going like a sledge-hammer."

"Name some of them," said I.

"Devoe sent for me," said Stamford. "He saw you from his window go to old Campos' store, chase him up the hill with his own yardstick, and then come back and make off with his biggest cocoanut."

"It's the little things that count, after all," said I.

"It's your little bed that counts with you just now," said the doctor. "You come with me at once, or I'll throw up the case. You're as loony as a loon."

So I got no cocoanut-pudding that evening, but I conceived a distrust as to the value of the method of the head-hunters. Perhaps for many centuries the maidens of the villages may have been looking wistfully at the heads in the baskets at the door-ways, longing for other and lesser trophies.

Veterans Day

November 11th

Front Page of N. Y. *Times* on November 11, 1918

The Moment of Victory

Ben Granger is a war veteran aged twenty-nine—which should enable you to guess the war. He is also principal merchant and postmaster of Cadiz, a little town over which the breezes from the Gulf of Mexico perpetually blow.

Ben helped to hurl the Don from his stronghold in the Greater Antilles; and then, hiking across half the world, he marched as a corporal-usher up and down the blazing tropic aisles of the open-air college in which the Filipino was schooled. Now, with his bayonet beaten into a cheese-slicer, he rallies his corporal's guard of cronies in the shade of his well-whittled porch, instead of in the matted jungles of Mindanao. Always have his interest and choice been for deeds rather than for words; but the consideration and digestion of motives is not beyond him, as this story, which is his, will attest.

"What is it," he asked me one moonlit eve, as we sat among his boxes and barrels, "that generally makes men go through dangers, and fire, and trouble, and starvation, and battle, and such recourses? What does a man do it for? Why does he try to outdo his fellow-humans, and be braver and stronger and more daring and showy than even his best friends are? What's his game? What does he expect to get out of it? He don't do it just for the fresh air and exercise. What would you say, now, Bill, that an ordinary man expects, generally speaking, for his efforts along the line of ambition and extraordinary hustling in the marketplaces, forums, shooting-galleries, lyceums, battle-fields, links, cinder-paths, and arenas of the civilized and *vice versa* places of the world?"

"Well, Ben," said I, with judicial seriousness, "I think we might safely limit the number of motives of a man who seeks fame to three—to ambition, which is a desire for popular applause; to avarice, which looks to the material side of success; and to love of some woman whom he either possesses or desires to possess."

Ben pondered over my words while a mocking-bird on the top of a mesquite by the porch trilled a dozen bars.

"I reckon," said he, "that your diagnosis about covers the case according to the rules laid down in the copy-books and historical readers. But what I had in my mind was the case of Willie Robbins, a person I used to know. I'll tell you about him before I close up the store, if you don't mind listening.

"Willie was one of our social set up in San Augustine. I was clerking there then for Brady & Murchison, wholesale dry-goods and ranch supplies. Willie and I belonged to the same german club and athletic association and military company. He played the triangle in our serenading and quartet crowd that used to ring the welkin three nights a week somewhere in town.

"Willie jibed with his name considerable. He weighed about as much as a hundred pounds of veal in his summer suitings, and he had a 'Where-is-Mary?' expression on his features so plain that you could almost see the wool growing on him.

"And yet you couldn't fence him away from the girls with barbed wire. You know that kind of young fellows—a kind of a mixture of fools and angels—they rush in and fear to tread at the same time; but they never fail to tread when they get the chance. He was always on hand when 'a joyful occasion was had,' as the morning paper would say, looking as happy as a king full, and at the same time as uncomfortable as a raw oyster served with sweet pickles. He danced like he had hind hobbles on; and he had a vocabulary of about three hundred and fifty words that he made stretch over four germans a week, and plagiarized from to get him through two ice-cream suppers and a Sunday-night call. He seemed to me to be a sort of a mixture of Maltese kitten, sensitive plant, and a member of a stranded 'Two Orphans' company.

"I'll give you an estimate of his physiological and pictorial make-up, and then I'll stick spurs into the sides of my narrative.

"Willie inclined to the Caucasian in his coloring and manner of style. His hair was opalescent and his conversation fragmentary. His eyes were the same blue shade as the china dog's on the right-hand corner of your Aunt Ellen's mantelpiece. He took things as they came, and I never felt any hostility against him. I let him live, and so did others.

"But what does this Willie do but coax his heart out of his boots and lose it to Myra Allison, the liveliest, brightest, keenest, smartest, and prettiest girl in San Augustine. I tell you, she had the blackest eyes, the shiniest curls, and the most tantalizing— Oh, no, you're off—I wasn't a victim. I might have been, but I knew better. I kept out. Joe Granberry was It from the start. He had everybody else beat a couple of leagues and thence east to a stake and mound. But, anyhow, Myra was a nine-pound, full-merino, fall-clip fleece, sacked and loaded on a four-horse team for San Antone.

"One night there was an ice-cream sociable at Mrs. Colonel Spraggins', in San Augustine. We fellows had a big room up-stairs opened up for us to put our hats and things in, and to comb our hair and put on the clean collars we brought along inside the sweat-bands of our hats—in short, a room to fix up in just like they have everywhere at high-toned doings. A little farther down the hall was the girls' room, which they used to powder up in, and so forth. Downstairs we—that is, the San Augustine Social Cotillion and Merrymakers' Club—had a stretcher put down in the parlor where our dance was going on.

"Willie Robbins and me happened to be up in our—cloak-room, I believe we called it—when Myra Allison skipped through the hall on her way down-stairs from the girls' room. Willie was standing before the mirror, deeply interested in smoothing down the blond grass-plot on his head, which seemed to give him lots of trouble. Myra was always full of life and devilment. She stopped and stuck her head in our door. She certainly was good-looking. But I knew how Joe Granberry stood with her. So did Willie; but he kept on ba-a-a-ing after her and following her around. He had a system of persistence that didn't coincide with pale hair and light eyes.

"'Hello, Willie!' says Myra. 'What are you doing to yourself in the glass?'

"'I'm trying to look fly,' says Willie.

"'Well, you never could *be* fly,' says Myra, with her special laugh, which was the provokingest sound I ever heard except the rattle of an empty canteen against my saddle-horn.

"I looked around at Willie after Myra had gone. He had a kind of a lily-white look on him which seemed to show that her remark had, as you might say, disrupted his soul. I never noticed anything in what she said that sounded particularly destructive to a man's ideas of self-consciousness; but he was set back to an extent you could scarcely imagine.

"After we went down-stairs with our clean collars on, Willie never went near Myra again that night. After all, he seemed to be a diluted kind of a skim-milk sort of a chap, and I never wondered that Joe Granberry beat him out.

"The next day the battleship *Maine* was blown up, and then pretty soon somebody—I reckon it was Joe Bailey, or Ben Tillman, or maybe the Government—declared war against Spain.

"Well, everybody south of Mason & Hamlin's line knew that the North by itself couldn't whip a whole country the size of Spain. So the Yankees commenced to holler for help, and the Johnny Rebs answered the call. 'We're coming, Father William, a hundred thousand strong—and then some,' was the way they sang it. And the old party lines drawn by Sherman's march and nine-cent cotton faded away. We became one undivided country, with no North, very little East, a good-sized chunk of West, and a South that loomed up as big as the first foreign label on a new eight-dollar suit-case.

"Of course the dogs of war weren't a complete pack without a yelp from the San Augustine Rifles, Company D, of the Fourteenth Texas Regiment. Our company was among the first to land in Cuba and strike terror into the hearts of the foe. I'm not going to give you a history of the war, I'm just dragging it in to fill out my story about Willie Robbins, just as the Republican party dragged it in to help out the election in 1898.

"If anybody ever had heroitis, it was that Willie Robbins. From the minute he set foot on the soil of the tyrants of Castile he seemed to engulf danger as a cat laps up cream. He certainly astonished every man in our company, from the captain up. You'd have expected him to gravitate naturally to the job of an orderly to the colonel, or typewriter in the commissary—but not any. He created the part of the flaxen-haired boy hero who lives and gets back home with the goods, instead of dying with an important despatch in his hands at his colonel's feet.

"HELLO, WILLIE! WHAT ARE YOU DOING TO YOURSELF.
IN THE GLASS?"

The Moment of Victory

Munsey's

June 1908

Original illustration by John H. Cassel (April 19, 1874 – January 24, 1960)

"Our company got into a section of Cuban scenery where one of the messiest and most unsung portions of the campaign occurred. We were out every day capering around in the bushes, and having little skirmishes with the Spanish troops that looked more like kind of tired-out feuds than anything else. The war was a joke to us, and of no interest to them. We never could see it any other way than as a howling farce-comedy that the San Augustine Rifles were actually fighting to uphold the Stars and Stripes. And the blamed little señors didn't get enough pay to make them care whether they were patriots or traitors. Now and then somebody would get killed. It seemed like a waste of life to me. I was at Coney Island when I went to New York once, and one of them down-hill skidding apparatuses they call 'roller-coasters' flew the track and killed a man in a brown sack-suit. Whenever the Spaniards shot one of our men, it struck me as just about as unnecessary and regrettable as that was.

"But I'm dropping Willie Robbins out of the conversation.

"He was out for bloodshed, laurels, ambition, medals, recommendations, and all other forms of military glory. And he didn't seem to be afraid of any of the recognized forms of military danger, such as Spaniards, cannon-balls, canned beef, gunpowder, or nepotism. He went forth with his pallid hair and china-blue eyes and ate up Spaniards like you would sardines *à la canopy*. Wars and rumbles of wars never flustered him. He would stand guard-duty, mosquitoes, hardtack, treat, and fire with equally perfect unanimity. No blondes in history ever come in comparison distance of him except the Jack of Diamonds and Queen Catherine of Russia.

"I remember, one time, a little *caballard* of Spanish men sauntered out from behind a patch of sugar-cane and shot Bob Turner, the first sergeant of our company, while we were eating dinner. As required by the army regulations, we fellows went

293

through the usual tactics of falling into line, saluting the enemy, and loading and firing, kneeling.

"That wasn't the Texas way of scrapping; but, being a very important addendum and annex to the regular army, the San Augustine Rifles had to conform to the red-tape system of getting even.

"By the time we had got out our 'Upton's Tactics,' turned to page fifty-seven, said 'one—two—three—one—two—three' a couple of times, and got blank cartridges into our Springfields, the Spanish outfit had smiled repeatedly, rolled and lit cigarettes by squads, and walked away contemptuously.

"I went straight to Captain Floyd, and says to him: 'Sam, I don't think this war is a straight game. You know as well as I do that Bob Turner was one of the whitest fellows that ever threw a leg over a saddle, and now these wirepullers in Washington have fixed his clock. He's politically and ostensibly dead. It ain't fair. Why should they keep this thing up? If they want Spain licked, why don't they turn the San Augustine Rifles and Joe Seely's ranger company and a car-load of West Texas deputy-sheriffs onto these Spaniards, and let us exonerate them from the face of the earth? I never did,' says I, 'care much about fighting by the Lord Chesterfield ring rules. I'm going to hand in my resignation and go home if anybody else I am personally acquainted with gets hurt in this war. If you can get somebody in my place, Sam,' says I, 'I'll quit the first of next week. I don't want to work in an army that don't give its help a chance. Never mind my wages,' says I; 'let the Secretary of the Treasury keep 'em.'

"'Well, Ben,' says the captain to me, 'your allegations and estimations of the tactics of war, government, patriotism, guard-mounting, and democracy are all right. But I've looked into the system of international arbitration and the ethics of justifiable slaughter a little closer, maybe, than you have. Now, you can hand in your resignation the first of next week if you are so minded. But if you do,' says Sam, 'I'll order a corporal's guard to take you over by that limestone bluff on the creek and shoot enough lead into you to ballast a submarine air-ship. I'm captain of this company, and I've swore allegiance to the Amalgamated States regardless of sectional, secessional, and Congressional differences. Have you got any smoking-tobacco?' winds up Sam. 'Mine got wet when I swum the creek this morning.'

"The reason I drag all this *non ex parte* evidence in is because Willie Robbins was standing there listening to us. I was a second sergeant and he was a private then, but among us Texans and Westerners there never was as much tactics and subordination as there was in the regular army. We never called our captain anything but 'Sam' except when there was a lot of major-generals and admirals around, so as to preserve the discipline.

"And says Willie Robbins to me, in a sharp construction of voice much unbecoming to his light hair and previous record:

"'You ought to be shot, Ben, for emitting any such sentiments. A man that won't fight for his country is worse than a horse-thief. If I was the cap, I'd put you in the guard-house for thirty days on round steak and tamales. War,' says Willie, 'is great and glorious. I didn't know you were a coward.'

"'I'm not,' says I. 'If I was, I'd knock some of the pallidness off of your marble brow. I'm lenient with you,' I says, 'just as I am with the Spaniards, because you have always reminded me of something with mushrooms on the side. Why, you little Lady of Shalott,' says I, 'you underdone leader of cotillions, you glassy fashion and moulded form, you white-pine soldier made in the Cisalpine Alps in Germany for the late New-Year trade, do you know of whom you are talking to? We've been in the same social circle,' says I, 'and I've put up with you because you seemed so meek and self-un-satisfying. I don't understand why you have so sudden taken a personal interest in chivalrousness and murder. Your nature's undergone a complete revelation. Now, how is it?'

"'Well, you wouldn't understand, Ben,' says Willie, giving one of his refined smiles and turning away.

"'Come back here!' says I, catching him by the tail of his khaki coat. 'You've made me kind of mad, in spite of the aloofness in which I have heretofore held you. You are out for making a success in this hero business, and I believe I know what for. You are doing it either because you are crazy or because you expect to catch some girl by it. Now, if it's a girl, I've got something here to show you.'

"I wouldn't have done it, but I was plumb mad. I pulled a San Augustine paper out of my hip-pocket, and showed him an item. It was a half a column about the marriage of Myra Allison and Joe Granberry.

"Willie laughed, and I saw I hadn't touched him.

"'Oh,' says he, 'everybody knew that was going to happen. I heard about that a week ago.' And then he gave me the laugh again.

"'All right,' says I. 'Then why do you so recklessly chase the bright rainbow of fame? Do you expect to be elected President, or do you belong to a suicide club?'

"And then Captain Sam interferes.

"'You gentlemen quit jawing and go back to your quarters,' says he, 'or I'll have you escorted to the guard-house. Now, scat, both of you! Before you go, which one of you has got any chewing-tobacco?'

"'We're off, Sam,' says I. 'It's supper-time, anyhow. But what do you think of what we was talking about? I've noticed you throwing out a good many grappling-hooks for this here balloon called fame—What's ambition, anyhow? What does a man risk his life day after day for? Do you know of anything he gets in the end that can pay him for the trouble? I want to go back home,' says I. 'I don't care whether Cuba sinks or swims, and I don't give a pipeful of rabbit tobacco whether Queen Sophia Christina or Charlie Culberson rules these fairy isles; and I don't want my name on any list except the list of survivors. But I've noticed you, Sam,' says I, 'seeking the bubble notoriety in the cannon's larynx a number of times. Now, what do you do it for? Is it ambition, business, or some freckle-faced Phœbe at home that you are heroing for?'

"'Well, Ben,' says Sam, kind of hefting his sword out from between his knees, 'as your superior officer I could court-martial you for attempted cowardice and desertion. But I won't. And I'll tell you why I'm trying for promotion and the usual honors of war and conquest. A major gets more pay than a captain, and I need the money.'

"'Correct for you!' says I. 'I can understand that. Your system of fame-seeking is rooted in the deepest soil of patriotism. But I can't comprehend,' says I, 'why Willie Robbins, whose folks at home are well off, and who used to be as meek and undesirous of notice as a cat with cream on his whiskers, should all at once develop into a warrior bold with the most fire-eating kind of proclivities. And the girl in his case seems to have been eliminated by marriage to another fellow. I reckon,' says I, 'it's a plain case of just common ambition. He wants his name, maybe, to go thundering down the coroners of time. It must be that.'

"Well, without itemizing his deeds, Willie sure made good as a hero. He simply spent most of his time on his knees begging our captain to send him on forlorn hopes and dangerous scouting expeditions. In every fight he was the first man to mix it at close quarters with the Don Alfonsos. He got three or four bullets planted in various parts of his autonomy. Once he went off with a detail of eight men and captured a whole company of Spanish. He kept Captain Floyd busy writing out recommendations of his bravery to send in to headquarters; and he began to accumulate medals for all kinds of things—heroism and target-shooting and valor and tactics and uninsubordination, and all the little accomplishments that look good to the third assistant secretaries of the War Department.

"Finally, Cap Floyd got promoted to be a major-general, or a knight commander of the main herd, or something like that. He pounded around on a white horse, all desecrated up with gold-leaf and hen-feathers and a Good Templar's hat, and wasn't allowed by the regulations to speak to us. And Willie Robbins was made captain of our company.

"And maybe he didn't go after the wreath of fame then! As far as I could see it was him that ended the war. He got eighteen of us boys—friends of his, too—killed in battles that he stirred up himself, and that didn't seem to me necessary at all. One night he took twelve of us and waded through a little rill about a hundred and ninety yards wide, and climbed a couple of mountains, and sneaked through a mile of neglected shrubbery and a couple of rock-quarries and into a rye-straw village, and captured a Spanish general named, as they said, Benny Veedus. Benny seemed to me hardly worth the trouble, being a blackish man without shoes or cuffs, and anxious to surrender and throw himself on the commissary of his foe.

"But that job gave Willie the big boost he wanted. The San Augustine *News* and the Galveston, St. Louis, New York, and Kansas City papers printed his picture and columns of stuff about him. Old San Augustine simply went crazy over its 'gallant son.' The *News* had an editorial tearfully begging the Government to call off the regular army and the national guard, and let Willie carry on the rest of the war single-handed. It said that a refusal to do so would be regarded as a proof that the Northern jealousy of the South was still as rampant as ever.

"If the war hadn't ended pretty soon, I don't know to what heights of gold braid and encomiums Willie would have climbed; but it did. There was a secession of hostilities just three days after he was appointed a colonel, and got in three more medals by registered mail, and shot two Spaniards while they were drinking lemonade in an ambuscade.

"Our company went back to San Augustine when the war was over. There wasn't anywhere else for it to go. And what do you think? The old town notified us in print, by wire cable, special delivery, and a private named Saul sent on a gray mule to San Antone, that they was going to give us the biggest blow-out, complimentary, alimentary, and elementary, that ever disturbed the kildees on the sand-flats outside of the immediate contiguity of the city.

"I say 'we,' but it was all meant for ex-Private, Captain *de facto*, and Colonel-elect Willie Robbins. The town was crazy about him. They notified us that the reception they were going to put up would make the Mardi Gras in New Orleans look like an afternoon tea in Bury St. Edmunds with a curate's aunt.

"Well, the San Augustine Rifles got back home on schedule time. Everybody was at the depot giving forth Roosevelt-Democrat—they used to be called Rebel—yells. There was two brass-bands, and the mayor, and schoolgirls in white frightening the street-car horses by throwing Cherokee roses in the streets, and—well, maybe you've seen a celebration by a town that was inland and out of water.

"They wanted Brevet-Colonel Willie to get into a carriage and be drawn by prominent citizens and some of the city aldermen to the armory, but he stuck to his company and marched at the head of it up Sam Houston Avenue. The buildings on both sides was covered with flags and audiences, and everybody hollered 'Robbins!' or 'Hello, Willie!' as we marched up in files of fours. I never saw a illustriouser-looking human in my life than Willie was. He had at least seven or eight medals and diplomas and decorations on the breast of his khaki coat; he was sunburnt the color of a saddle, and he certainly done himself proud.

"OH, I DON'T KNOW. MAYBE I COULD IF I TRIED!"

The Moment of Victory

Munsey's

June 1908

Original illustration by John H. Cassel (April 19, 1874 - January 24, 1960)

Austin History Center, Austin Public Library via University of North Texas Libraries, The Portal to Texas History

"They told us at the depot that the courthouse was to be illuminated at half-past seven, and there would be speeches and chili-con-carne at the Palace Hotel. Miss Delphine Thompson was to read an original poem by James Whitcomb Ryan, and Constable Hooker had promised us a salute of nine guns from Chicago that he had arrested that day.

"After we had disbanded in the armory, Willie says to me:

"'Want to walk out a piece with me?'

"'Why, yes,' says I, 'if it ain't so far that we can't hear the tumult and the shouting die away. I'm hungry myself,' says I, 'and I'm pining for some home grub, but I'll go with you.'

"Willie steered me down some side streets till we came to a little white cottage in a new lot with a twenty-by-thirty-foot lawn decorated with brickbats and old barrel-staves.

"'Halt and give the countersign,' says I to Willie. 'Don't you know this dugout? It's the bird's-nest that Joe Granberry built before he married Myra Allison. What you going there for?'

"But Willie already had the gate open. He walked up the brick walk to the steps, and I went with him. Myra was sitting in a rocking-chair on the porch, sewing. Her hair was smoothed back kind of hasty and tied in a knot. I never noticed till then that she had freckles. Joe was at one side of the porch, in his shirt-sleeves, with no collar on, and no signs of a shave, trying to scrape out a hole among the brickbats and tin cans to plant a little fruit-tree in. He looked up but never said a word, and neither did Myra.

"Willie was sure dandy-looking in his uniform, with medals strung on his breast and his new gold-handled sword. You'd never have taken him for the little white-headed snipe that the girls used to order about and make fun of. He just stood there for a minute, looking at Myra with a peculiar little smile on his face; and then he says to her, slow, and kind of holding on to his words with his teeth:

"'*Oh, I don't know! Maybe I could if I tried!*'

"That was all that was said. Willie raised his hat, and we walked away.

"And, somehow, when he said that, I remembered, all of a sudden, the night of that dance and Willie brushing his hair before the looking-glass, and Myra sticking her head in the door to guy him.

"When we got back to Sam Houston Avenue, Willie says:

"'Well, so long, Ben. I'm going down home and get off my shoes and take a rest.'

"'You?' says I. 'What's the matter with you? Ain't the court-house jammed with everybody in town waiting to honor the hero? And two brass-bands, and recitations and flags and jags and grub to follow waiting for you?'

"Willie sighs.

"'All right, Ben,' says he. 'Darned if I didn't forget all about that.'

"And that's why I say," concluded Ben Granger, "that you can't tell where ambition begins any more than you can where it is going to wind up."

Thanksgiving

Fourth Thursday in November

"The Courtship of Miles Standish"

1858 narrative poem by Henry Wadsworth Longfellow

Miles Standish courting Priscilla Mullins

Original illustration (1903) by Howard Chandler Christy
(January 10, 1872 – March 3, 1952)

Courtesy Library of Congress

Thanksgiving Remarks

A great many people who are skeptical on other subjects swallow Thanksgiving Day without questioning the validity of its title.

There are plenty of people in Houston who will sit at the table today, with their mouths so full of turkey and dressing that they will be utterly unable to answer the smallest question about the origin of this National festival.

The United States is the only country in the world that has a day of National thanksgiving in commemoration of one special event. Among the earliest settlers in this country, with the exception of cocktails, were the Pilgrim Fathers. They were a noble band of religious enthusiasts, who sailed from England to America in a ship called the *Mayflower* after a celebrated brand of soap by the same name.

By good fortune and fast sailing they managed to reach America before Thanksgiving Day. They landed at Plymouth Rock, where they were met by Hon. F. R. Lubbock and welcomed with an address. It was a very cold, and not a good day for speeches, either.

This heroic little band of refugees were called Puritans in England, which is French for abolitionists. As they stood upon the bleak inhospitable shore, shivering in the biting blast, Captain Miles Standish, who had the stoutest heart and also the most jovial temper in the party, said: "Say, you fellows, can't you stop chattering your teeth and shaking your knees? There don't any of you look like you wanted to pass resolutions against burning anything just at present. You're a jolly-looking lot of guys."

Among the distinguished members of this band were William Bradford, Edward Winslow, John Alden, John Carver and Marc. Anthony, a nephew of Susan B.

According to the habits of true Americans, they had not been on land half an hour till they went into caucus to elect a governor.

John Carver carried around the hat and collected the ballots, and consequently was elected.

"Now," said Governor Carver, "I hereby announce my proclamation that next Thursday shall be Thanksgiving Day."

"What for?" asked Captain Standish.

"Oh, it's the proper thing," said the governor. "You'll find it in all the school books and histories."

Governor Carver then appointed a committee with Captain Standish as chairman to explore the country around.

Captain Standish set forth at the head of his devoted followers through the deep snow, while the others went to work erecting what rough shelter they could out of logs and pine boughs. Presently Captain Standish and his band returned, making tracks in the snow about ten feet apart and closely pursued by a large, brick-red, passionate Indian, who was remarking, "Waugh-hoo-hoo-hoo!" at every jump. Governor Carver advanced to meet the untutored child of the forest, and said to him in simple words:

"How! Me heap white chief. Gottee big guns. You killee my soldiers, me heap shoot. Sabe?"

"I am charmed to meet you, governor," said the Indian. "My name is Massasoit. I also am a great chief. My wigwam is down there" (pointing with graceful gesture to the southwest)—"I have just come back from slaying the tribe of the Goo-Goos. You may not have heard, governor, that the cat came back."

Governor Carver grasped the hand of Massasoit, and said: "Welcome, thrice welcome to our newly discovered continent, sir. Colonel Winthrop, give Mr. Massasoit your hand."

"I'll keep mine, and deal him another if it's all the same to you," said Colonel Winthrop.

Massasoit took his place at the side of the blanket that was spread on the snow, and the pasteboards were shuffled.

Two hours later the Pilgrim Fathers had won from the Indian chief 200 buffalo robes, 100 pelts of the silver fox, 50 tanned deer hides, 300 otter skins, and 150 hides of the beaver, panther and mink.

This was the original skin game.

Later on in the game, Governor Carver called a bet of $27 worth of wampum made by Massasoit, with his daughter Priscilla, and lost on eights and treys.

Longfellow, in his beautiful poem, describes what followed:

> Then from her father's tent,
> Tripping with gentle feet,
> Priscilla, the Puritan
> Maiden, stepped. All that she
> Knew was obedience;
> Ready to sacrifice
> All for her father's word,
> Priscilla, the dutiful,
> Gentle and meek as the
> Dove. As the violet
> Modest and drooping-eyed,
> Up from his poker game
> Gazed Massasoit,

Chief of the Tammanies,
Brave as a lion. Up
Gazed Massasoit.
Then, as a roebuck springs,
Swift as an arrow, or
Leapes Couchee-Couchee, the
Panther, or Buzzy the
Rattlesnake springs from his
Coils in the sumac bush,
So Massasoit got a
Move on his chieftainlets;
Got to his Trilby's and
Fled to the wildness.
Rushing through snowdrifts, and
Breaking down saplings, till
Far in the distance he
Looked back and saw that she
Followed not far behind;
Priscilla the sprinter was
Not very far behind;
Cutting a swath through the
Snow with her number fives;
Right on his trail was she;
Right on his track with a
New-woman look on her;
Longing and hungry look,
Look of a new-born hope,
Hope for a man that might
Be her own tootsicums.
Then Massasoit, the
Chief of the Tammanies,
Gave a loud yell that woke

Wise-Kuss the owl, and woke
Kat-a-Waugh-Kew-is, the
Ring-streaked racoon, and woke
Snakes in the forest.
Then Massasoit was
Gone like an arrow that
Speeds from the hunter; he
Only touched ground on the
High elevations; he
Fled from the land of the
Pilgrims and Puritans,
Fled from Priscilla the
Puritan maiden;
Fled from Priscilla who
Wanted to tickle him
Under the chin and call
Him her sweet toodleums.
Thus Massasoit, the
Indian warrior,
Laid down four aces and
Took to the wilderness,
Bluffed by a maiden.
Laid down a jack-pot, and
Lost his percentage.
Lost it to treys and eights,
And to the forty years
Lived by Priscilla;
Priscilla, the maiden.

Freedom From Want
The Saturday Evening Post
March 6, 1943
Illustration by Norman Percevel Rockwell
(February 3, 1894 – November 8, 1978)

The third is freedom from want—which, translated into world terms, means economic understandings which will secure to every nation a healthy peacetime life for its inhabitants—everywhere in the world.

—Franklin D. Roosevelt's 1941 State of the Union address introducing the theme of the Four Freedoms

Two Thanksgiving Day Gentlemen

There is one day that is ours. There is one day when all we Americans who are not self-made go back to the old home to eat saleratus biscuits and marvel how much nearer to the porch the old pump looks than it used to. Bless the day. President Roosevelt gives it to us. We hear some talk of the Puritans, but don't just remember who they were. Bet we can lick 'em, anyhow, if they try to land again. Plymouth Rocks? Well, that sounds more familiar. Lots of us have had to come down to hens since the Turkey Trust got its work in. But somebody in Washington is leaking out advance information to 'em about these Thanksgiving proclamations.

The big city east of the cranberry bogs has made Thanksgiving Day an institution. The last Thursday in November is the only day in the year on which it recognizes the part of America lying across the ferries. It is the one day that is purely American. Yes, a day of celebration, exclusively American.

And now for the story which is to prove to you that we have traditions on this side of the ocean that are becoming older at a much rapider rate than those of England are—thanks to our git-up and enterprise.

Stuffy Pete took his seat on the third bench to the right as you enter Union Square from the east, at the walk opposite the fountain.

Every Thanksgiving Day for nine years he had taken his seat there promptly at 1 o'clock. For every time he had done so things had happened to him—Charles Dickensy things that swelled his waistcoat above his heart, and equally on the other side.

But to-day Stuffy Pete's appearance at the annual trysting place seemed to have been rather the result of habit than of the yearly hunger which, as the philanthropists seem to think, afflicts the poor at such extended intervals.

Certainly Pete was not hungry. He had just come from a feast that had left him of his powers barely those of respiration and locomotion. His eyes were like two pale gooseberries firmly imbedded in a swollen and gravy-smeared mask of putty. His breath came in short wheezes; a senatorial roll of adipose tissue denied a fashionable set to his upturned coat collar. Buttons that had been sewed upon his clothes by kind Salvation fingers a week before flew like popcorn, strewing the earth around him. Ragged he was, with a split shirt front open to the wishbone; but the November breeze, carrying fine snowflakes, brought him only a grateful coolness. For Stuffy Pete was overcharged with the caloric produced by a super-bountiful dinner, beginning with oysters and ending with plum pudding, and including (it seemed to him) all the roast turkey and baked potatoes and chicken salad and squash pie and ice cream in the world.

Wherefore he sat, gorged, and gazed upon the world with after-dinner contempt.

The meal had been an unexpected one. He was passing a red brick mansion near the beginning of Fifth avenue, in which lived two old ladies of ancient family and a reverence for traditions. They even denied the existence of New York, and believed that Thanksgiving Day was declared solely for Washington Square. One of their traditional habits was to station a servant at the postern gate with orders to admit the first hungry wayfarer that came along after the hour of noon had struck, and banquet him to a finish. Stuffy Pete happened to pass by on his way to the park, and the seneschals gathered him in and upheld the custom of the castle.

After Stuffy Pete had gazed straight before him for ten minutes he was conscious of a desire for a more varied field of vision. With a tremendous effort he moved his head slowly to the left. And then his eyes bulged out fearfully, and his breath ceased, and the rough-shod ends of his short legs wriggled and rustled on the gravel.

For the Old Gentleman was coming across Fourth avenue toward his bench.

Every Thanksgiving Day for nine years the Old Gentleman had come there and found Stuffy Pete on his bench. That was a thing that the Old Gentleman was trying to make a tradition of. Every Thanksgiving Day for nine years he had found Stuffy there, and had led him to a restaurant and watched him eat a big dinner. They do those things in England unconsciously. But this is a young country, and nine years is not so bad. The Old Gentleman was a staunch American patriot, and considered himself a pioneer in American tradition. In order to become picturesque we must keep on doing one thing for a long time without ever letting it get away from us. Something like collecting the weekly dimes in industrial insurance. Or cleaning the streets.

The Old Gentleman moved, straight and stately, toward the Institution that he was rearing. Truly, the annual feeding of Stuffy Pete was nothing national in its character, such as the Magna Charta or jam for breakfast was in England. But it was a step. It was almost feudal. It showed, at least, that a Custom was not impossible to New Y—ahem!—America.

The Old Gentleman was thin and tall and sixty. He was dressed all in black, and wore the old-fashioned kind of glasses that won't stay on your nose. His hair was whiter and thinner than it had been last year, and he seemed to make more use of his big, knobby cane with the crooked handle.

As his established benefactor came up Stuffy wheezed and shuddered like some woman's over-fat pug when a street dog bristles up at him. He would have flown, but all the skill of Santos-Dumont could not have separated him from his bench. Well had the myrmidons of the two old ladies done their work.

"Good morning," said the Old Gentleman. "I am glad to perceive that the vicissitudes of another year have spared you to move in health about the beautiful world. For that blessing alone this day of thanksgiving is well proclaimed to each of us. If you will come with me, my man, I will provide you with a dinner that should make your physical being accord with the mental."

That is what the old Gentleman said every time. Every Thanksgiving Day for nine years. The words themselves almost formed an Institution. Nothing could be compared with them except the Declaration of Independence. Always before they had been music in Stuffy's ears. But now he looked up at the Old Gentleman's face with tearful agony in his own. The fine snow almost sizzled when it fell upon his perspiring brow. But the Old Gentleman shivered a little and turned his back to the wind.

Stuffy had always wondered why the Old Gentleman spoke his speech rather sadly. He did not know that it was because he was wishing every time that he had a son to succeed him. A son who would come there after he was gone—a son who would stand proud and strong before some subsequent Stuffy, and say: "In memory of my father." Then it would be an Institution.

But the Old Gentleman had no relatives. He lived in rented rooms in one of the decayed old family brownstone mansions in one of the quiet streets east of the park. In the winter he raised fuchsias in a little conservatory the size of a steamer trunk. In the spring he walked in the Easter parade. In the summer he lived at a farmhouse in the New Jersey hills, and sat in a wicker armchair, speaking of a butterfly, the ornithoptera amphrisius, that he hoped to find some day. In the autumn he fed Stuffy a dinner. These were the Old Gentleman's occupations.

Stuffy Pete looked up at him for a half minute, stewing and helpless in his own self-pity. The Old Gentleman's eyes were bright with the giving-pleasure. His face was getting more lined each year, but his little black necktie was in as jaunty a bow as ever, and the linen was beautiful and white, and his gray mustache was curled carefully at the ends. And then Stuffy made a noise that sounded like peas bubbling in a pot. Speech was intended; and as the Old Gentleman had heard the sounds nine times before, he rightly construed them into Stuffy's old formula of acceptance.

"Thankee, sir. I'll go with ye, and much obliged. I'm very hungry, sir."

The coma of repletion had not prevented from entering Stuffy's mind the conviction that he was the basis of an Institution. His Thanksgiving appetite was not his own; it belonged by all the sacred rights of established custom, if not, by the actual Statute of Limitations, to this kind old gentleman who had preempted it. True, America is free; but in order to establish tradition some one must be a repetend—a repeating decimal. The heroes are not all heroes of steel and gold. See one here that wielded only weapons of iron, badly silvered, and tin.

The Old Gentleman led his annual protégé southward to the restaurant, and to the table where the feast had always occurred. They were recognized.

"Here comes de old guy," said a waiter, "dat blows dat same bum to a meal every Thanksgiving."

The Old Gentleman sat across the table glowing like a smoked pearl at his corner-stone of future ancient Tradition. The waiters heaped the table with holiday food—and Stuffy, with a sigh that was mistaken for hunger's expression, raised knife and fork and carved for himself a crown of imperishable bay.

No more valiant hero ever fought his way through the ranks of an enemy. Turkey, chops, soups, vegetables, pies, disappeared before him as fast as they could be served. Gorged nearly to the uttermost when he entered the restaurant, the smell of food had almost caused him to lose his honor as a gentleman, but he rallied like a true knight. He saw the look of beneficent happiness on the Old Gentleman's face—a happier look than even the fuchsias and the ornithoptera amphrisius had ever brought to it—and he had not the heart to see it wane.

In an hour Stuffy leaned back with a battle won. "Thankee kindly, sir," he puffed like a leaky steam pipe; "thankee kindly for a hearty meal." Then he arose heavily with glazed eyes and started toward the kitchen. A waiter turned him about like a top, and pointed him toward the door. The Old Gentleman carefully counted out $1.30 in silver change, leaving three nickels for the waiter.

They parted as they did each year at the door, the Old Gentleman going south, Stuffy north.

Around the first corner Stuffy turned, and stood for one minute. Then he seemed to puff out his rags as an owl puffs out his feathers, and fell to the sidewalk like a sunstricken horse.

When the ambulance came the young surgeon and the driver cursed softly at his weight. There was no smell of whiskey to justify a transfer to the patrol wagon, so Stuffy and his two dinners went to the hospital. There they stretched him on a bed and began to test him for strange diseases, with the hope of getting a chance at some problem with the bare steel.

And lo! an hour later another ambulance brought the Old Gentleman. And they laid him on another bed and spoke of appendicitis, for he looked good for the bill. But pretty soon one of the young doctors met one of the young nurses whose eyes he liked, and stopped to chat with her about the cases.

"That nice old gentleman over there, now," he said, "you wouldn't think that was a case of almost starvation. Proud old family, I guess. He told me he hadn't eaten a thing for three days."

Christmas Eve

Some Sights and Sounds Caught on Houston Streets and Elsewhere

Houston is a typical Southern town. Although a busy, growing city that is easily holding its place among the half dozen metropolitan cities of the South, it retains most of the old-time Southern customs and traditions.

The all-absorbing haste, the breathless rush, the restless scramble for gain so noticeable in Northern cities is absent here. Houston people are prosperous, and they take things easy, believing that one may gather a few roses of pleasure on the way through life and still keep up with the march of progress. In no city in the South is Christmas more merrily welcomed with social pleasures, the exchanging of friendly offerings, and general rejoicing than in Houston. The immense crowds of people that have lined our streets and stores for the past week testify to the fact.

Yesterday was probably the busiest day among the merchants that the season has witnessed; and there is no question but that it brought to the children anticipations of the brightest nature.

Stand for a few moments on the corner and view the people.

They are moving like a colony of ants, some going, some coming, threading in and out in an endless tangled maze. When the gods lean over the edge of Mount Olympus and gaze down upon this world, while the waiter is out filling their glasses with nectar, they must be highly entertained by the little comedy that is holding the boards on earth. Our world must look to them very much as a great ant bed, over which we crawl and scramble, and run this way and that, apparently without purpose or design.

That light streak across the sky, which we call the Milky Way, is nothing more nor less than the foam spilt from tankards of nectar as the gods quaff and laugh at our strange antics. But it is Christmas eve, and what do we care for their laughter? Turn up the lights; let the curtain rise, and the Christmas crowd is on!

Did you ever watch a young lady buy a Christmas present for her father?

If not, you have missed a good thing.

They all go about it the same way. In fact, young ladies who buy Christmas presents for their fathers are just as sure to perform the operation in exactly the same way, as they are to sit on one foot while reading a novel. She always has just two dollars for this purpose, which is handed her by her mother, who suggests the idea. She goes out late in the afternoon on the day before Christmas. She first goes to a jeweler's and looks at several trays of diamond studded watches, and wonders which one her father would like. Then, after examining about one hundred diamond rings, she suddenly remembers the amount of money she has, sighs and goes off to a clothing store, where she closely scrutinizes an $18 smoking jacket, and a $40 overcoat. She says she believes she will think over the matter before buying, and leaves. Next she visits a book store, three dry goods stores, two more jewelers, and a candy shop. When Christmas morning comes, her father finds himself the proud possessor of a new red pen wiper with the fifteen cent cost mark carefully erased, and there are to be observed in a certain young lady's dressing case a new pair of gloves and a box of nice chocolate bonbons.

The fat man who is taking home a red wagon is abroad in the land.

He is generally a pompous man who prides himself on being self-made, and glories in showing his democracy by carrying home his own bundles. He holds the wagon in front of him and pushes his way through the crowd with a sterling-citizen-risen-from-the-ranks air that is quite wonderful to observe.

How the girls in their cloaks with high turned-up collars laugh and chatter and gaze in the show windows with "Oh's" and "Ah's" at everything they see! If you happen to be standing near a group of them you will hear something like this:

"Oh, Mabel, look at that lovely ring—squeezed my hand and said—sealskin, indeed! I guess I know plush when—and five from Papa, so I guess I'll buy that—going to hang them up, of course; I bet they'll hold more than yours, you old slim—good gracious! Belle let me pin your—papa asked him how he wanted his eggs for breakfast, and Charlie got mad and left, and the clock hadn't struck—No, I wear these kind that—sixteen inches around the—Oh! look at that lovely—forgot to shave, and it scratched all along—I'll trade with you, Lil; Tom said—with lace all round the—come on, girls, let's—"

The noise of a passing street car drowned the rest.

The children are out in full force.

Did you ever reflect that children are the wisest philosophers in the world? They see the wonderful things in the windows for sale; and they listen gravely to the tales told them of Santa Claus;

and, without endeavoring to analyze the situation, they rejoice with exceeding joy. They never measure the chimney or calculate the size of Santa's sleigh; they never puzzle themselves by wondering how the old fellow gets his goods out of the stores, or question his stupendous feat of climbing down every chimney in the land on the same night. If grown folks would dissect and analyze less things that are mysteries to them, they would be far happier.

Two men meet on Main Street and one of them says:

"I want you to help me think. I want to get even with my wife this Christmas, and I don't exactly know how to do it. For the last five years she has been making me ostensible Christmas presents that are not of the slightest possible use to me, but are very convenient for herself. Under the pretense of buying me a present, she simply buys something she wants for herself and uses Christmas for a cloak for her nefarious schemes. Once she gave me a nice wardrobe, in which she hangs her new dresses. Again she gave me a china tea set; at another time a piano; and last Christmas she made me a present of a side-saddle, and I had to buy her a horse. Now I want to get something for her Christmas present this year that I can use, and that will be of no possible service to her."

"H'm," said the other man thoughtfully, "it's going to be a hard thing to do. Let's see. You want something she can't make use of. I have it! Have yourself a new pair of trousers made, and present them to her."

"Won't do," says the first man, shaking his head. "She'd have 'em on in ten minutes and be clamoring for a bicycle."

"Buy her a razor, then; she can't use that."

"Can't she? She has three corns."

"Say! There ain't anything you can get that you can use and she can't."

"Don't believe there is. Well, let's go take something anyhow."

The lights are beginning to burn in the show windows, and people are gathering in front of them.

To many of the lookers-on this gazing in the windows is all the Christmas pleasure they will have. Many of them are from the country and little towns along the fourteen lines of railroad that run into Houston. A country youth presses through the crowd with open mouth and wondering eyes. Holding fast to his hand, follows Araminta, bedecked in gorgeous colors, beholding with scarce-believing optics the fairy-like splendors of Main Street. When they return to Galveston they will long remember the glories of the great city they visited at Christmas.

A solemn man in a high silk hat, attired in decorous black, edges his way along the sidewalk. One would think him some city magnate making his way home, or a clergyman out studying the idiosyncrasies of human nature. He opens his mouth and yells in a high, singsong voice: "What will mamma say when Willie comes home with a mustache just like papa's—buy one right now, boys; you can curl 'em, twist 'em, pull 'em, and comb 'em just like real ones—come on boys!" He fixes below his nose a black mustache with a wonderful curl to the ends and goes his way, occasionally selling one to some smooth-faced boy, who shyly makes his purchase. On the edge of the sidewalk a little man is offering "the most wonderful mechanical toy of the century, causing more comment and excitement than any other article exhibited at the great World's Fair." The public crowds about him and buys with avidity. Not twenty steps away in a Houston toy shop the same kind of toy has been sold for years.

On a corner stand a group of—well, say young men. They wear new style high turn-down collars and chrysanthemums. Their hats tilt backward and their front hair is brushed down low. They are gazing at the ladies as they pass. How Charles Darwin would have loved to meet these young men! But, alas! he died without completing the chain. Listen at the scraps of alleged conversation that can be distinguished above their simultaneous jabber:

"Deuced fine girl, but a little too—cigarette? I'll owe you one—she's a nice girl, but—the loveliest necktie you ever— would have paid my board, but saw that elegant suit at—kicked me clear out of the parlor without—that girl has certainly got a—haven't a cent, old man, or I would—old man said I had to go to work, but—look at that blonde with the smiled right at me, and—the little one with the blue—he struck me in the eye, and I won't speak to him now—no, the brunette in the white—I was real mad, and said, confound it—link buttons, of course."

At a corner sits a woman with blue goggles, grinding an organ, on which stands a lamp chimney, in which burns a tallow candle.

Why the candle, the observer knoweth not. At her side crouches her pale little boy. A philanthropist bends toward her with a nickel between his fingers. Far away, among the wilds near Alvin, he has a little boy about the same age, and his heart is touched. The little boy springs up. He has a cigarette in his mouth, and he hurls a big fire-cracker between the philanthropist's feet. It explodes; the boy yells with delight; and the philanthropist says: "Gol darn the kid" and reserves his nickel for beer.

Gazing with far off, longing eyes into a show window that glistens with diamonds and jewelry, stands a woman.

Her black dress and veil proclaim that she is a widow. One year ago the strong arm upon which she leaned with such love and security was her pride and joy. Tonight, beneath the sod of the churchyard, it is turning back to dust. And yet, she is not altogether desolate. She has sweet memories of her loved one to sustain her; and besides that, she is holding to the arm of the man she is engaged to marry when her time of mourning is up, and she is out selecting an engagement ring.

A policeman lurks in the shadow of an awning with his club in his hand ready to strike.

Two doors away there lives an alderman who voted against his being put on the force. It will not be long before the alderman's little boy will come out on the sidewalk and shoot off a Roman candle, and then the policeman will strike; a city ordinance will be carried out, and a little boy carried in.

A man steps up to a salesman in a fancy goods store.

"I want to get something," he says, "for my wife's mother. I think—"

"James," calls the salesman, "show this gentleman the 5-cent counter." Merchants who make a study of their customers are quick to know what they want.

A man who is unmistakably a clergyman goes into a grocery store that is next door to a saloon. The salesman attends upon him. He buys 10 cents worth of minced meat for pies, and then lingers, clearing his throat.

"Anything else?" asks the salesman.

The clerical-looking man fumbles with his white cambric tie, and says:

"Tomorrow will be Christmas, you know day of holy thoughts—peace on earth, and—and—and—our hearts should carol forth praises however, we must dine—er—er—mince pie, you know; the little ones in the family enjoy it—have the meat here—thought, perhaps—something to flavor—just a drop of—"

"Here, Jimmy," yells the salesman, "go in next door and get this gent a pint of whisky."

Christmas brings pleasure to many; it brightens some lives that hardly ever know sunshine; it is abused by too many and made a season of revelry and sin; but to the little ones it is a joy forever, so let the tin horns blow and the red drums rattle, for those restless little feet and those grimy little hands come first in the making up of Heaven's kingdom.

Merry Christmas to all.

Christmas

December 25th

Merry Old Santa Claus

Thomas Nast

Artist's Proof

Appeared in Harper's Weekly

January 1, 1881

From the Collection of Macculloch Hall Historical Museum,
Morristown, NJ, U.S.A

Courtesy of Macculloch Hall Historical Museum, Morristown, NJ, U.S.A

The Gift of the Magi

One dollar and eighty-seven cents. That was all. And sixty cents of it was in pennies. Pennies saved one and two at a time by bulldozing the grocer and the vegetable man and the butcher until one's cheeks burned with the silent imputation of parsimony that such close dealing implied. Three times Della counted it. One dollar and eighty-seven cents. And the next day would be Christmas.

There was clearly nothing to do but flop down on the shabby little couch and howl. So Della did it. Which instigates the moral reflection that life is made up of sobs, sniffles, and smiles, with sniffles predominating.

While the mistress of the home is gradually subsiding from the first stage to the second, take a look at the home. A furnished flat at $8 per week. It did not exactly beggar description, but it certainly had that word on the lookout for the mendicancy squad.

In the vestibule below was a letter-box into which no letter would go, and an electric button from which no mortal finger could coax a ring. Also appertaining thereunto was a card bearing the name "Mr. James Dillingham Young."

The "Dillingham" had been flung to the breeze during a former period of prosperity when its possessor was being paid $30 per week. Now, when the income was shrunk to $20, the letters of "Dillingham" looked blurred, as though they were thinking seriously of contracting to a modest and unassuming D. But whenever Mr. James Dillingham Young came home and reached his flat above he was called "Jim" and greatly hugged by Mrs. James Dillingham Young, already introduced to you as Della. Which is all very good.

Della finished her cry and attended to her cheeks with the powder rag. She stood by the window and looked out dully at a grey cat walking a grey fence in a grey backyard. Tomorrow would be Christmas Day, and she had only $1.87 with which to buy Jim a present. She had been saving every penny she could for months, with this result. Twenty dollars a week doesn't go far. Expenses had been greater than she had calculated. They always are. Only $1.87 to buy a present for Jim. Her Jim. Many a happy hour she had spent planning for something nice for him. Something fine and rare and sterling—something just a little bit near to being worthy of the honor of being owned by Jim.

There was a pier-glass between the windows of the room. Perhaps you have seen a pier-glass in an $8 flat. A very thin and very agile person may, by observing his reflection in a rapid sequence of longitudinal strips, obtain a fairly accurate conception of his looks. Della, being slender, had mastered the art.

Suddenly she whirled from the window and stood before the glass. Her eyes were shining brilliantly, but her face had lost its colour within twenty seconds. Rapidly she pulled down her hair and let it fall to its full length.

Now, there were two possessions of the James Dillingham Youngs in which they both took a mighty pride. One was Jim's gold watch that had been his father's and his grandfather's. The other was Della's hair. Had the Queen of Sheba lived in the flat across the airshaft, Della would have let her hair hang out the window some day to dry just to depreciate Her Majesty's jewels and gifts. Had King Solomon been the janitor, with all his treasures piled up in the basement, Jim would have pulled out his watch every time he passed, just to see him pluck at his beard from envy.

So now Della's beautiful hair fell about her, rippling and shining like a cascade of brown waters. It reached below her knee and made itself almost a garment for her. And then she did it up again nervously and quickly. Once she faltered for a minute and stood still while a tear or two splashed on the worn red carpet.

On went her old brown jacket; on went her old brown hat. With a whirl of skirts and with the brilliant sparkle still in her eyes, she fluttered out the door and down the stairs to the street.

Where she stopped the sign read: "Mme. Sofronie. Hair Goods of All Kinds." One flight up Della ran, and collected herself, panting. Madame, large, too white, chilly, hardly looked the "Sofronie."

"Will you buy my hair?" asked Della.

"I buy hair," said Madame. "Take yer hat off and let's have a sight at the looks of it."

Down rippled the brown cascade.

"Twenty dollars," said Madame, lifting the mass with a practiced hand.

"Give it to me quick," said Della.

Oh, and the next two hours tripped by on rosy wings. Forget the hashed metaphor. She was ransacking the stores for Jim's present.

She found it at last. It surely had been made for Jim and no one else. There was no other like it in any of the stores, and she had turned all of them inside out. It was a platinum fob chain simple and chaste in design, properly proclaiming its value by substance alone and not by meretricious ornamentation—as all good things should do. It was even worthy of The Watch. As soon as she saw it she knew that it must be Jim's. It was like him. Quietness and value—the description applied to both. Twenty-one dollars they took from her for it, and she hurried home with the 87 cents. With that chain on his watch Jim might be properly anxious about the time in any company. Grand as the watch was, he sometimes looked at it on the sly on account of the old leather strap that he used in place of a chain.

When Della reached home her intoxication gave way a little to prudence and reason. She got out her curling irons and lighted the gas and went to work repairing the ravages made by generosity added to love. Which is always a tremendous task, dear friends—a mammoth task.

Within forty minutes her head was covered with tiny, close-lying curls that made her look wonderfully like a truant schoolboy. She looked at her reflection in the mirror long, carefully, and critically.

"If Jim doesn't kill me," she said to herself, "before he takes a second look at me, he'll say I look like a Coney Island chorus girl. But what could I do—oh! what could I do with a dollar and eighty-seven cents?"

At 7 o'clock the coffee was made and the frying-pan was on the back of the stove hot and ready to cook the chops.

Jim was never late. Della doubled the fob chain in her hand and sat on the corner of the table near the door that he always entered. Then she heard his step on the stair away down on the first flight, and she turned white for just a moment. She had a habit of saying little silent prayers about the simplest everyday things, and now she whispered: "Please God, make him think I am still pretty."

The door opened and Jim stepped in and closed it. He looked thin and very serious. Poor fellow, he was only twenty-two—and to be burdened with a family! He needed a new overcoat and he was without gloves.

Jim stopped inside the door, as immovable as a setter at the scent of quail. His eyes were fixed upon Della, and there was an expression in them that she could not read, and it terrified her. It was not anger, nor surprise, nor disapproval, nor horror, nor any of the sentiments that she had been prepared for. He simply stared at her fixedly with that peculiar expression on his face.

Della wriggled off the table and went for him.

"Jim, darling," she cried, "don't look at me that way. I had my hair cut off and sold because I couldn't have lived through Christmas without giving you a present. It'll grow out again—you won't mind, will you? I just had to do it. My hair grows awfully fast. Say 'Merry Christmas!' Jim, and let's be happy. You don't know what a nice—what a beautiful, nice gift I've got for you."

"You've cut off your hair?" asked Jim, laboriously, as if he had not arrived at that patent fact yet even after the hardest mental labor.

"Cut it off and sold it," said Della. "Don't you like me just as well, anyhow? I'm me without my hair, ain't I?"

Jim looked about the room curiously.

"You say your hair is gone?" he said, with an air almost of idiocy.

"You needn't look for it," said Della. "It's sold, I tell you—sold and gone, too. It's Christmas Eve, boy. Be good to me, for it went for you. Maybe the hairs of my head were numbered," she went on with sudden serious sweetness, "but nobody could ever count my love for you. Shall I put the chops on, Jim?"

"'You've cut off your hair?' asked Jim, laboriously, as if he had not arrived at that patent fact yet, even after the hardest mental labour."

The Gift of the Wise Men

1911 Doubleday, Page & Company

Original illustration by Charles M. Relyea (April 23, 1863 – 1932)

Out of his trance Jim seemed quickly to wake. He enfolded his Della. For ten seconds let us regard with discreet scrutiny some inconsequential object in the other direction. Eight dollars a week or a million a year—what is the difference? A mathematician or a wit would give you the wrong answer. The magi brought valuable gifts, but that was not among them. This dark assertion will be illuminated later on.

Jim drew a package from his overcoat pocket and threw it upon the table.

"Don't make any mistake, Dell," he said, "about me. I don't think there's anything in the way of a haircut or a shave or a shampoo that could make me like my girl any less. But if you'll unwrap that package you may see why you had me going a while at first."

White fingers and nimble tore at the string and paper. And then an ecstatic scream of joy; and then, alas! a quick feminine change to hysterical tears and wails, necessitating the immediate employment of all the comforting powers of the lord of the flat.

For there lay The Combs—the set of combs, side and back, that Della had worshipped long in a Broadway window. Beautiful combs, pure tortoise shell, with jeweled rims—just the shade to wear in the beautiful vanished hair. They were expensive combs, she knew, and her heart had simply craved and yearned over them without the least hope of possession. And now, they were hers, but the tresses that should have adorned the coveted adornments were gone.

But she hugged them to her bosom, and at length she was able to look up with dim eyes and a smile and say: "My hair grows so fast, Jim!"

And then Della leaped up like a little singed cat and cried, "Oh, oh!"

Jim had not yet seen his beautiful present. She held it out to him eagerly upon her open palm. The dull precious metal seemed to flash with a reflection of her bright and ardent spirit.

"Isn't it a dandy, Jim? I hunted all over town to find it. You'll have to look at the time a hundred times a day now. Give me your watch. I want to see how it looks on it."

Instead of obeying, Jim tumbled down on the couch and put his hands under the back of his head and smiled.

"Dell," said he, "let's put our Christmas presents away and keep 'em a while. They're too nice to use just at present. I sold the watch to get the money to buy your combs. And now suppose you put the chops on."

The magi, as you know, were wise men—wonderfully wise men—who brought gifts to the Babe in the manger. They invented the art of giving Christmas presents. Being wise, their gifts were no doubt wise ones, possibly bearing the privilege of exchange in case of duplication. And here I have lamely related to you the uneventful chronicle of two foolish children in a flat who most unwisely sacrificed for each other the greatest treasures of their house. But in a last word to the wise of these days let it be said that of all who give gifts these two were the wisest. Of all who give and receive gifts, such as they are wisest. Everywhere they are wisest. They are the magi.